Being

Your Happiness, Pleasure, and Contentment

Don Lucas, Ph.D.

Department of Psychology
Northwest Vista College

Library of Congress Control Number: 2009926377

Printed in the United States of America

10 9 8 7 6 5 4 3 2 1

ISBN 978-0-7380-3180-4

Hayden-McNeil Publishing
14903 Pilot Drive
Plymouth, MI 48170
www.hmpublishing.com

LucasD 3180-4 F09

For Sember and Rayen—my happiness,
my pleasure, my contentment

Table of Contents

Chapter Four
A New Look at an Old Phenomenon: Being Theory and Happiness 81

Acknowledgements

Thanks must first go to my wife, Lisa, for putting up with my many late nights of writing and for getting me past the "I'm-never-going-to-finish" days.

I want to thank those who facilitated the discovery of **Being Theory**. Thank you Carla Kaylor, for pushing me to start writing, and showing me Being Theory's clinical applications; thank you Charles Ross, for keeping me mindful, and spending a summer thinking out loud with me about Being Theory; and thank you Ignacio Magaloni, for our home-cooking talks, and helping me see "human being" as a verb.

Thanks go to my students, colleagues, friends, and family who over the past three years have given their invaluable insights about earlier versions of this book—especially Brenda Edmonds, Brendan Dunne, Anna Evans, Kristin Bauman, Stefan Lagmark, Diana Corona, Leslie Lancaster, and Velma McClelland (aka, mum).

The students, staff, administration, and faculty of Northwest Vista College deserve mention here; they make it very easy to write about happiness.

I am forever grateful to Jill Burk of Worth Publishers, and the crew at Hayden-McNeil Publishing, especially Lisa Wess and Michele Ostovar for making my first book a reality beyond my computer.

Lastly, I want to thank Wayne Hershberger, who taught me how to combine thinking and writing.

Figures

Tables

Happiness is the meaning and the purpose of life,
the whole aim, and end of human existence.

(Aristotle)

+

The search for happiness is one of the
chief sources of unhappiness.

(Eric Hoffer)

=

Houston, we've had a problem...

(James Lovell, US Apollo 13 moon flight)

CHAPTER ONE
What Are You Going to Get Out of Reading This Book?

This book is about you. It is about something you may have forgotten. It is about being happy. It is about *you* being happy. This book is about answering a question: How do you distinguish the positive emotions of happiness, pleasure, and contentment from one another? And for that matter, how do you go about defining, gaining, and maintaining these emotions? Do you know the answers? If you do, then there is no need to read any further, oh Dalai Lama of Positive Emotions. Instead, go on with your idyllic life and spread the good news.

If you do not know the answers and are interested in learning *the answers*, then read on, my friend; for you are in the right place. The answers we come up with promise to allow you happiness, pleasure, and contentment, over your *lifetime*.

This book is interactive. In addition to answers, it has lots of questions. And *you'll* be expected to come up with answers to these questions. These questions will come through philosophical, scientific, and artful inquiry; thought-experiments; demonstrations; interactive psychological instruments; and yes—even my own personal anecdotes. But don't worry, the anecdotes don't come with any summer vacation slide shows. By reading this book and answering these questions, I expect you'll become aware of and understand true happiness—or **eudaimonia** (U-DAY-MOAN-YAH), as Aristotle put it. C'mon, don't be afraid—you can pronounce it. Say... U-DAY-MOAN-YAH. True happiness is something you've likely not had since childhood. It is a natural state of happiness—it hasn't been tainted by *learning* yet. Damn learning! True happiness occurs *only* in concert with particular levels of pleasure and contentment. All of us are born with true happiness; however, over time, as we grow from childhood to adulthood, most of us lose it. Now don't get me wrong. Adults have some form of positive emotions and happiness—but they are not likely to have the authentic form they had as children. I bet, if you think about it for a moment, the happiest people you know...happen to be children.

Additionally, this book provides:

1. A review of the current scientific research literature on happiness, so you'll know exactly what *is* and *is not* associated with happiness.
2. A recipe for your own *happiness*—with recipe card to boot (see the inside front cover).

3. A personal method to distinguish among your **happiness**, **pleasure**, and **contentment** life experiences, so that you can focus on which ones matter to you the most.
4. A measure of your own happiness, pleasure, and contentment within eleven different parts of your life:

With your partner/spouse	Relative to your finances
Within your family	Within your friendships
When you are alone	Relative to your possessions
When you are at work	Relative to your leisure time
Relative to your personal health	When you are at home
When you are learning	

5. Tools to overcome **happiness confusion** and replace **happy-ignorance** with **contentment-recognition**—this replacement often leads to true happiness, an increase in *longevity* and better *health* (through facilitating contentment activities), and a decrease in sicknesses and ill health (through negating pleasure activities). Don't worry, all these concepts will be defined within this book soon enough…
6. Scientifically based personal activities that you can do to make yourself happy in a moment's notice, and a method for you to transform negative emotions of sadness, pain, and depression into positive emotions of happiness, pleasure, and contentment.

"What I really want is to be happy." "I control my happiness." "I'd be happier with more money." "I never want to become content!" Wrong, wrong, wrong, and wrong! These are four of the most common misconceptions people—change that, *adults*—have about happiness and contentment. Change that again, adults have about *life*. If *you* believe any of these, then you are likely cultivating the opposite of true happiness. And that would make you a sadness farmer! And certainly you don't want to be a sadness farmer…right?!

The questions now are: Do *you* want to stop cultivating faux-happiness (like a faux-diamond, aka, diamonelle, on a 3 a.m. infomercial) and start cultivating true happiness—be a happiness farmer, instead of a sadness farmer? And do you want to decrease negative—energy-draining, motivation-sucking, success-robbing emotions like meanness, jealousy, anger, greed, envy, and hatred (Begley, 2007)? If you are *not* interested in learning about true happiness, and ending unnecessary negative emotions, then give this book to someone else. I'm serious—do it! There are plenty of other people hungry for knowledge about *real* human behavior and positive emotions. You can get back to reading your paperback romance novels; hardbound self-help books; or *Prozac Nation* drug pamphlets. (*Not* that there is anything wrong with this reading list—just don't expect to gain long-lasting positive emotions from it.)

WHAT DO I EXPECT OF YOU?

If you *are* interested in understanding true happiness and negating the harmful effects of avoidable negative emotions, then I expect you to be doing at least three different activities *throughout* this book. Yes, reading this book is going to require your *active* involvement. First, assuming you are an adult (with the word *adult* being defined relative to the number of years that have passed since your birth, and *not* what your best friend or spouse may say about how you act), I expect you to prepare for reading this book by forgetting everything you have learned about happiness since early childhood—I told you, learning (okay, certain types at least) was bad. You read that right—I want you to forget about everything you ever learned about happiness since your childhood (except, of course, for what you've learned in this book so far). Your adult-conditioned ideas and thoughts about happiness will only get in the way of your learning about and experiencing real positive emotions.

More on this later.

Okay—have you forgotten everything you have learned about happiness since early childhood? Well... It has only been a moment or two; maybe I am expecting too much. Just continue forgetting... While you are doing that, let's talk about the second thing I expect of you. I expect you to be thinking—yes, you will be thinking throughout this book. To start this, I want you to think about what the following things have in common:

Sex	Prayer	Vacations
Drugs	Youth	Work
Rock & Roll	Learning	Divorce
Marriage	Education	Careers
Family	Diplomas	Houses
Children	Friends	Boats
Religion	Leisure	Automobiles
God	Fame	Beauty

Well—what do you think? What do all the things on this list have in common?

The answer is happiness. Well, kinda... In our *pursuit* of happiness, we spend the vast majority of our adult years trying to obtain any one or more of the things on this list. And as Amy Lowell so eloquently describes in her poem "Happiness," we are likely to give just about anything in this pursuit.

> We rarely feel it.
> I would buy it,
> beg it, steal it,
> Pay in coins of
> dripping blood
> For this one
> transcendent good.

Here's the really tough part: All of the things on the list—and probably even the "dripping blood coins"—are for naught; for the "happiness" that results from these things is temporary, and may be best described by other positive emotions; in particular: pleasure. Further, enduring, long-lasting positive emotions are likely not emotional effects or results, but instead are likely emotional causes. Specifically, enduring positive emotions lead us to have any one or more of the things on this list; the things on this list, likely, do not lead to enduring positive emotions. Sonja Lyubomirsky, Laura King, and Ed Diener (2005) describe this bi-directional relationship between happiness and the things that are associated with happiness as the happiness-success link: Being successful *may* lead to happiness; being happy *will* lead to success. For example, successful relationships lead to marriage and we know marriage is associated with happiness. However, it is not the case that marriage causes happiness; rather, happy people get married (Stutzer & Frey, 2006). Let me repeat—because if you stay with me, this is going to be of utmost importance—enduring positive emotions are much more likely to be *causes* than effects. So, if you want to be rich, guess what you need to be first?

My third and last expectation of you is to be questioning, answering, and theorizing about your *own* happiness and pleasure and contentment throughout this book. Don't just be blindly following along with what I think happiness is. With that said, let me briefly introduce you to the main theory I will be using in this book. The theory is called **Being Theory**. (**Chapter Four** is a complete explanation of the theory.) Being Theory explains the relationship among happiness, pleasure, and contentment by using our—that is, a *human's*—perception of time (which I will call **psychophysical time**) and a human's judgment of who/what is in control of situations within his/her life (which I will call **observer perspective**). Further, Being Theory shows how to wipe out unnecessary negative emotions and serves as a guide for true happiness. So what do you really want: happiness, pleasure, or contentment? Or maybe you want some combination of these emotions? Heck, maybe you want all three? But what do you already have—do you even know? Do you want to find out?

YOU'RE NOT IMPATIENT, YOU'RE EFFICIENT

For those of you who want to get a quick sense of where this book will end up—or maybe this book was assigned reading in a class you're taking, and you don't want to read the whole thing—I dedicate this next section to you.

Here are the truths (that I'll be expanding upon in this whole book) to the four misconceptions about happiness and contentment above:

Misconceptions number one and number four: ***What I really want is to be happy; I never want to be content!*** People think they want to be happy, but what they really want is to be content. People confuse happiness with contentment (Evans, Guerra, Romero, & Lucas, 2008). By reading this book, you will learn how to define and decipher between happiness and contentment; and with this distinction, find out what you *really* want in life. Simply put, happiness is associated with *short-term* positive emotions, whereas contentment is associated with *everlasting* positive emotions. Contentment is *not* associated with being idle, lazy, or giving up; instead it is associated with the opposite: contentment is the greatest motivator of our behavior; being content is being able to do *anything.* (Misconceptions number one and number four are elaborated upon in **Chapter Two**.)

Misconception number two: ***I control my happiness.*** People believe they are in complete control of their own happiness, but in reality, people are in control of only about 45% of the variance or metabolic energy associated with happiness in particular and positive emotions in general; activities done for their own sake and things outside of a person's control—such as other people—account for the remaining 55%. True happiness is not an antisocial thing—it is a social thing. Repeat: True happiness is a social phenomenon. If the people that are close to you—family, friends, colleagues—aren't happy, or they are not happy with you, then you are going to have a tough time being happy. Through Being Theory, you will learn in detail about *three* observer perspectives that guide true happiness. For now, so you'll feel that you got your money's worth in purchasing this book, I will refer to these observer perspectives with the 13-cent words **endotelic** (which means *self*), **exotelic** (which means *environment*), and **autotelic** (which means *action*); Jung, 1978. Together with time and the particular life situation, these observer perspectives control true happiness as well as other emotions. (Misconception number two is elaborated upon in **Chapter Four**.)

Misconception number three: ***I'd be happier with more money.*** Money *is* associated with happiness. Money does not *cause* happiness. Thus, money does *not* lead to happiness. The relationship that exists between money and happiness is not about money per se, but instead appears to be solely due to the basic human necessities (e.g., food, shelter, "security") that money *may* bring. Further, as mentioned above, the direction of the relationship between money and happiness is usually in this direction: happiness → money, and *not* in this direction: money → happiness. (By the by, for those of you following along at home, "e.g." is an abbreviation for the Latin term *exempli gratia*, which means *for example*; also, I will be using the abbreviation "i.e.," which stands for the Latin term *id est*, meaning *that is*. If for no other reason, I use these Latin abbreviations in an attempt to re-confirm I deserve having a Ph.D., *Philosophiae Doctor*.) (Misconception number three is elaborated upon in **Chapter Three**.)

Okay, that's the impatient—I mean, efficient—version. Do you feel better for knowing the truths behind these misconceptions? Did you get a taste of potential true happiness? If you want to see how to apply these truths to your own life, then you're going to have to read a bit more than just a few paragraphs!

What are you going to get out of reading this book?

If you haven't done so already, at some point early in your reading of this book, you'll likely ask yourself, What am I going to get out of this book? And if I heard you ask yourself this, I would likely reply: Do you need to get any*thing*? When you finish reading this book, you'll likely know then that this simple question is one of the most powerful questions associated with getting some*thing* better than happiness, and that is your own life satisfaction, your own peace—your own *contentment.*

As I said, the primary purpose of this book is to provide you with the tools that distinguish among, and define, gain, and maintain happiness, pleasure, and contentment. And with the recent advent of Positive Psychology (Peterson & Seligman, 2005), there has been a focus on studying the strengths and virtues of human behavior within psychology, and a flourish in the number of books published for the general population on the science of happiness. For example, Mihaly Csikszentmihalyi's *Flow* (1990); David Myers' *The Pursuit of Happiness* (1992); The Dalai Lama's *The Art of Happiness* (1998); David Lykken's *Happiness* (2000); Michael Argyle's *The Psychology of Happiness* (2001); Martin Seligman's *Authentic Happiness* (2002); Martin Bolt's *Pursuing Human Strengths: A Positive Psychology Guide* (2004); Alan Carr's *Positive Psychology: The Science of Happiness and Human Strengths* (2004); William Compton's *Introduction to Positive Psychology* (2004); Stefan Klein's *The Science of Happiness: How Our Brains Make Us Happy and What We Can Do to Get Happier* (2005); Daniel Nettle's *Happiness: The Science Behind Your Smile* (2005); Gregory Berns' *Satisfaction: The Science of Finding True Fulfillment* (2005); Richard Layard's *Happiness: Lessons from a New Science* (2005); Richard Haidt's *Happiness Hypothesis* (2006); Daniel Gilbert's *Stumbling on Happiness* (2006); C.R. Snyder and Shane Lopez's *Positive Psychology: The Scientific and Practical Explorations of Human Strengths* (2006); Matthieu Ricard's *Happiness: A Guide to Developing Life's Most Important Skill* (2007); Tal Ben-

Shahar's *Happier: Learn the Secrets to Daily Joy and Lasting Fulfillment* (2007); Sonja Lyubomirsky's *The How of Happiness: A Scientific Approach to Getting the Life You Want* (2008); Ed Diener and Robert Biswas-Diener's *Happiness: Unlocking the Mysteries of Psychological Wealth* (2008); and Eric Wilson's *Against Happiness: In Praise of Melancholy* (2008). Many of these books are excellent for introductions to the scientific bases of happiness. However, none of these books systematically distinguishes happiness from the associated emotions of pleasure and contentment. Further, none of these books distinguishes and measures these positive emotions relative to different parts of your life. This book does both of these things—and stands upon the shoulders of these previous books to take our understanding of happiness to a higher level.

> Three aspiring psychologists from three different colleges were attending their first graduate school class on emotional extremes.
>
> "Just to establish some parameters," said the professor to the student from the University of Illinois, "What is the opposite of happiness?"
>
> "Sadness," said the University of Illinois student.
>
> "And the opposite of depression?" he asked the young lady from the University of California.
>
> "Contentment," said she.
>
> "And you, sir," the professor said to the young man from University of Texas. "How about the opposite of woe?"
>
> The University of Texas student replied, "Sir, I believe that would be giddy-up."
>
> (Emailed to me from sources unknown)

AVOIDING THE SELF-HELP BOOK TRAP

Although there is a good chance that you purchased this book from the "self-help" section of the bookstore, I personally don't consider *this* book a self-help book because it does *not* fall into the "self-help book trap." The self-help book trap is composed of two fundamental flaws. The first flaw of most self-help books is the assumption they make about most people being *unhappy* (e.g., Dick Meyer's recently published book, *Why We Hate Us: American Discontent in the New Millennium*). However, the opposite is actually true: Most people are relatively happy and not depressed. This book is less about helping you to be *not* depressed and more about helping you to be happier and more content. Depression and happiness are *not* on the same emotional spectrum—they are qualitatively different from one another (see **Figure 1**). A person overcoming depression is not necessarily getting happier—they're more likely to be gaining anxieties; and a person who is depressed, but getting happier, is not necessarily overcoming his/her depression (Bradburn, 1969).

Which leaves me with a question for you. What would you rather be: Happier or less depressed? (Yes, you can now say "both" and make perfect sense!)

The second flaw of most self-help books is the method they use to overcome unhappiness or make people happier: Take *more* control of your life. Rhonda Byrne's overwhelmingly popular book, *The Secret,* is a prime example of this flaw. Byrne takes this flaw to such an extreme that she would have us believe that solipsism is the key to happiness. (Bishop Berkeley would be so proud.) If you're a fan of Byrne, I'm sorry to be the bearer of bad news, but I have to tell you that being egocentric is associated with being a horse's ass, it isn't associated with being happy. Further, throughout *The Secret* (which is entirely based on a book titled *The Science of Getting Rich*) money is the most recurring theme—if you want money, then you'll likely get money. Well, here's the secret, my friend, and it ain't, "ask, believe, receive," instead, the secret is that Byrne is a television producer, she wants money, and she's getting it—with 1.7 million books sold, and counting. Taking more control of your life may increase your *self-concept* (i.e., how you *think* about yourself based upon feedback from others), but it certainly is *not* going to decrease your unhappiness or make you happier. Depressed people have as strong of a self-concept as non-depressed people (Lucas, 2004).

Figure 1. Depression is on the same continuum with happiness (**1a**), and depression is on a continuum that is different from happiness (**1b**). Science now believes depression and happiness are not on opposite ends of the same pole (**1a**); depression and happiness are two different entities, existing independently of one another (**1b**).

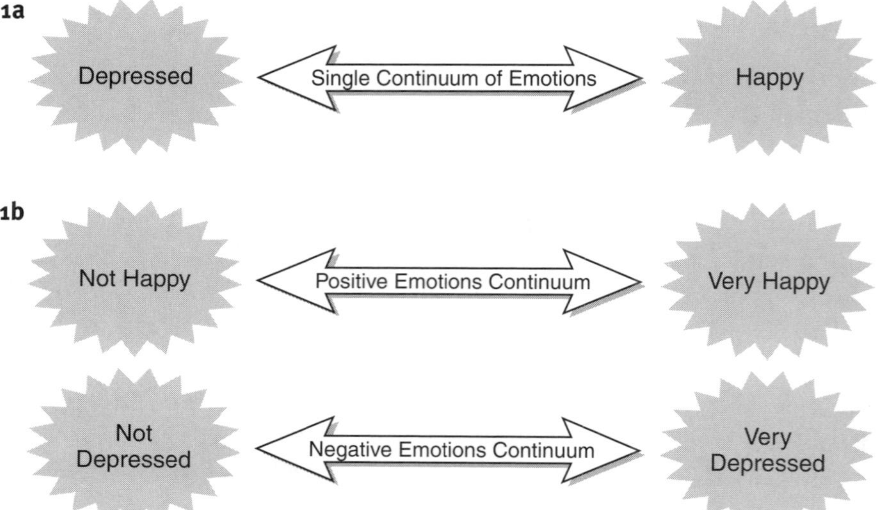

The depressed person *is* likely to have a lower self-esteem (i.e., how a person *feels* about him/herself based upon feedback from others), *not* a different self-concept. The depressed person (like the happy person) knows who he/she is (self-concept); he/she just doesn't like who that is (self-esteem). Taking more control of your life may actually lead to emotions opposite of happiness, pleasure, and contentment: depression, lethargy, anxiety, distress, sadness, dysthymia, and even pain and hatred, because you are expending more of your finite metabolic energy to be responsible for *more* persons, places, and/or things within your own life. This book will show what needs to change for you to be happier and more content; and this change has no*thing* to do with gaining more control of self; instead, it has to do with *releasing* control of self while at the same time not allowing other people, places, and things control, either.

DEFINITIONS?

It seems a book about happiness, pleasure, and contentment should actually define these terms. Don't worry—this book will. But not yet. I'm not ready to fully define happiness, pleasure, and contentment because *you* are not ready—you haven't forgotten enough of your adult-conditioned ideas about happiness yet. So please continue reading a book about happiness, pleasure, and contentment—all the while *not* knowing exactly what these terms mean.

> If you want to be happy for an hour, take a nap;
> if you want to be happy for a day, go fishing;
> if you want to be happy for a week, take a vacation;
> if you want to be happy for a month, get married;
> if you want to be happy for a year, inherit a fortune;
> if you want to be happy for the rest of your life...
>
> (Chinese Proverb)

CHAPTER TWO

The Science of Happiness: Happiness Is Objective; Happiness Is Subjective—Well, Which One Is It?

THE SCIENCE OF PSYCHOLOGY, A SCIENCE FOR HAPPINESS

Before you and I can start talking in-depth about true happiness and its relationship to the positive emotions of happiness, pleasure, and contentment, *you* must first go back to school and learn the basics of the science that studies these emotions. That's right, you're going back to school; back to Introductory Psychology—Psychology 101! If you're currently in school (maybe even in Psych 101), then congratulations, you're really in a good place to be reading this book. In any case, whether you have to go back or you're already there, you won't be alone—because I'm going to be with you. I think it is time that I introduce myself. My name is Don Lucas—or as my students call me, Dr. Don (okay, some of my students call me things *other* than Dr. Don—but that's a whole 'nother story—this book is only rated PG). I will be your professor in this *text-based classroom* that generally addresses happiness, pleasure, and contentment, and specifically addresses *your* happiness, *your* pleasure, and *your* contentment.

So without further ado:

Lesson number I, psychology is a science.

Get it?
Got it?!
Good!

Lesson number II, psychology objectively measures emotions, behaviors, thoughts, and perceptions.

Get it?
Got it?!
Good!

Lesson number III, most people do not believe **Lesson number I** or **Lesson number II.**

Based upon how *most* people learn psychology—through the media, including such things as Dr. "gift-of-gab, but-no-scientific-proof-of-his-methods-actually-working" Phil; the evening news; secondary misinterpretations of behavioral scientists like Sigmund Freud, B.F. Skinner, Carl Rogers, and Abraham Maslow; "pop-psychology"; television magazine shows; and self-*help* books and magazines—**Lesson number III** should come as no surprise. Most people believe psychology is primarily conjecture, sensationalistic, "soft," subjective, nonscientific, and unreliable—and that humans in general (and ourselves in particular) emote, act, think, and perceive in unpredictable and mysterious ways that can never be captured by science. This is what allows us to be unique, right? Well, sorry to burst your bubble (be prepared for a lot of bubble bursting), but you're really not as unique as you think you are. We humans are in fact much more psychologically alike than we are different.

The one constant about human behavior is its variability. (unknown)

Even well-educated people try to sell psychology short by saying it's not a "real" science because of its variability; they believe sciences like physics, chemistry, and biology *are* real sciences. The truth of the matter (yes—whether you like it or not, we're going to be talking truth within this book) is that human behavior is *variable*. And psychology is the science of human behavior—with behavior being defined as anything the human does that is publicly verifiable. But variability does not equate to unpredictability. In fact, all sciences have variability. The purest, most idealistic and objective science we have—math—has variability, irrational numbers, and unknowns at its core. For example, can *you* tell me how to calculate the circumference of a circle? If you're a smarty, then you'll likely share the mathematical formula $\mathbf{C} = \pi \times \mathbf{d}$, with **d** equaling the diameter of the circle, π equaling the ratio of the circumference of a circle to the diameter, and **C** equaling circumference. But there's a problem with this formula. And people rarely point out this problem: What exactly is π? You'll likely tell me, "Duh, Dr. Don, π equals 3.14159265358979323846..." [People (and computers) are spending their lives trying to figure out better representations of π.] But the truth is that neither you, nor anybody else, knows *exactly* what π is equal to. We can only approximate what π is equal to. Yet one of the most fundamental elements of our universe—a circle—is based on this enigma. Because we cannot know exactly what π is equal to, we cannot calculate the circumference of a circle, and therefore *all* circles are primarily conjecture, sensationalistic, "soft," subjective, nonscientific, and unreliable. As my mathematician friend Javi says there's no such thing as a circle, there are only "squircles." But most of us don't say things like this, because it is ridiculous to think circles aren't real. And it is just as ridiculous to think psychology isn't a real science. I am now bestowing upon you the task of bringing this enlightenment—about psychology being just as objective as any other science— to the rest of the world! I told you reading this book was going to require active engagement. The next time you hear someone say, "Psychology is a soft science" or "Psychology isn't a real science" or "Psychology is just mumbo-jumbo"—you ask that person if he/she thinks circles are mumbo-jumbo, too.

The science of psychology, like other sciences, uses controlled, agreed-upon, and objective methods. With these methods, psychology measures emotions, behaviors, thoughts, and perceptions to yield replicable and predictable results. In this book, I will be focusing on the behaviors, thoughts, and perceptions associated with the emotion that humans deem as the most important—happiness. As I am focusing on happiness, I will be recognizing (what no other book has fully recognized before) that if I am going to legitimately talk about happiness, then the emotions of pleasure and contentment *have to* be included in the discussion. This discussion can then lead to true happiness. Thus, you get a three-for-one deal with this book; not only do you get to learn about happiness and apply this learning to your life, you also get to learn about pleasure and contentment and apply *this* learning to your life.

HAPPINESS IS OBJECTIVE

Happiness is objective: all humans have it in common. When asked, "What is the one thing you want out of life"? people's most likely response is "To be happy" (Lyubomirsky, 2001). Further, in every culture throughout the world, the one behavior associated with happiness is smiling (Ekman & Oster, 1979). In **Chapter Three**, I'll introduce the **facial-feedback hypothesis** to show you what a powerful effect smiling has on happiness (and vice versa). Furthermore, throughout history, happiness is at the basis of most cultures and societies. A history of happiness is beyond the scope of this book; however, for two relatively recent and well-received reviews of the history of happiness and its effects upon culture and society, see Darrin McMahon's *Happiness: A History* (2006); and Nicholas White's *A Brief History of Happiness* (2006). It is interesting to note that to some extent, the so-called **Happiness Principle** is at the basis of most societies. The philosopher Jeremy Bentham (1843) made this utilitarian principle clear by declaring that all ethics, laws, and social rules should be based on the notion: "the greatest happiness for the greatest number."

We see the Happiness Principle within the United States of America's Declaration of Independence (1776):

> ...with certain unalienable Rights [of an American citizen], that among these are Life, Liberty and the pursuit of Happiness.

And even more important,

> ...institute new Government [by the American citizen], laying its foundation on such principles and organizing its powers in such form, as to them shall seem most likely to effect their Safety and Happiness.

Additionally, we see the Happiness Principle within France's Declaration of the Rights of Man (1789):

> ...the maintenance of the constitution [of France] and redound to the happiness of all.

The Happiness Principle is a part of not only European and American societies, but also Asian and Australian societies. Recognizing that what all people have in common is *not* the pursuit of money, but instead the pursuit of happiness, the governments of Bhutan in 1999, and Indigo Shire in 2006, adopted a Gross National Happiness index for their societies, instead of a Gross National Product index. (More on the GNP later.) The Gross National Happiness index measures the overall happiness of citizens on such factors as peace and security; cultural confidence and tolerance; world governance and political status; and nationwide environment and climate. For details about examining a society's happiness with measures other than the GNP, see the website www.happyplanetindex.org.

Although the Happiness Principle objectively supposes all humans want to be happy, it also subjectively supposes that happiness is relative. That is, relative to humans differing: (a) in their definitions of happiness (and these definitions of happiness changing over time); (b) on how they go about obtaining happiness; and (c) on how much happiness they have (if happiness can be possessed at all). I will begin to address these subjective differences relative to happiness in the following paragraphs and in-depth in **Chapter Three**, but for now, let me focus on the fact that without exception, there is at least one objective aspect of happiness, and that is: All humans want it. (If you are now saying to yourself, *but I don't want to be happy,* then you are giving an example of another behavior all humans have in common—lying—but that is a topic for another time and another book!) Not only do humans want happiness, humans are actually pretty good at being happy.

What percentage of the population do you think is happy? C'mon—make a guess...

(This is space provided solely for you to think about your answer... So—*think* about it!)

Have you made a guess yet?

Well?

Most people are surprised to find out that people are generally happy. Simply put, we think other people are not happy, when in fact 75% to 90% of the population (across cultures) rates themselves as being relatively happy (Diener & Diener, 1996; Inglehart, 1997; Lykken, 1999; Myers, 2000). For instance, a survey conducted by my laboratory posed questions to 184 individuals about their emotions on a day-to-day basis relative to a 9-point Likert scale, with 9 equaling very happy, 5 equaling neutral, and 1 equaling very unhappy (you can think of a Likert scale as being a continuum; see **Figure 2**). Seventy-nine percent of these individuals said their own day-to-day emotions are a 9, 8, 7, or 6 (with an average score of 6.6 on the 9-point Likert scale); while these same individuals said only

Figure 2. Likert scales used to measure individuals' levels of positive emotions.

Rate what *your* emotions typically are on a day-to-day basis. Circle the number that best corresponds to your rating on the following scale:

Very Unhappy				*Neutral*				*Very Happy*
1	2	3	4	5	6	7	8	9

Rate what you think *other people's* (the general population's) emotions typically are on a day-to-day basis. Circle the number that best corresponds to your rating on the following scale:

Very Unhappy				*Neutral*				*Very Happy*
1	2	3	4	5	6	7	8	9

48% of the population is happy—that is, scoring a 9, 8, 7, or 6 (with an average score of 5.6 on the 9-point Likert scale). In other words, we think we are relatively happy while others are not—why the difference?

THE SELF-SERVING BIAS, SOCIAL COMPARISON, AND OBJECTIVE HAPPINESS

The so-called, ***I'm Happy—You're Not* paradox** is a form of the self-serving bias. The self-serving bias is the inclination people have to take credit for the good things that happen to them (internal locus of control) and externalize responsibility for the bad things that happen to them (external locus of control). *I aced the test because I am smart; I failed the test because the teacher sucks.* Additionally, the self-serving bias leads people to make positive predictions about themselves much more so than about others. For example, when Kunda (1987) examined marriage, he found 80% of "married" people predicted their own marriages would *not* end in divorce, but they predicted 50% of marriages—other than their own—would. Such situations as smoking cigarettes and driving drunk have yielded similar results—*I won't die of cancer, but others will; I won't kill anybody when I'm driving drunk, but others will.* Although the *I'm Happy—You're Not* paradox is a form of the self-serving bias, it can be best explained by social comparison theory. This theory states that we have a basic need to compare our own emotions, behaviors, thoughts, and perceptions to others' emotions, behaviors, thoughts, and perceptions (Festinger, 1954). Social comparison is automatically going on with us in all social situations—we are constantly comparing our own personal **flights in life** (defined as the current perceived living circumstances of an individual) to others' flights in life.

Social comparison is another objective phenomenon associated with happiness. For example, if we compare our flight in life to somebody's flight in life who is beneath us (that is, by our own judgment, having a worse flight in life than our own), then we likely will feel better about ourselves (happier)—this is called, downward social comparing; if we compare our flight in life to somebody's flight in life who is above us (that is, by our own judgment, having a better flight in life than our own), then we likely will feel worse about ourselves (unhappier)—this is called upward social comparing. Thus, using social comparison theory to explain the *I'm Happy—You're Not* paradox is simply to say *healthy* humans automatically judge others as being beneath them (that is, downward social comparing and not as happy) when questioned about happiness in general, so as to feel better about themselves. Not only do we make social comparisons to affect our happiness in general, we also make social comparisons to affect our happiness in particular situations. For example, in situations associated with money, people tend to believe that money brings happiness (see **Misconception number**

three: ***I'd be happier with more money***). As we said, there is some relationship between money and happiness, but we will see in **Chapter Three** that this relationship is, at best, a weak one. However, social comparisons affect the strength of this relationship. For instance, let's say, for sake of argument, *you* have a household income of $125,000 per year. This is a reasonable amount of money within today's society—reasonable in that it allows you to support your family, own a home, have leisure time, and save money for your family's future. In this situation, you're satisfied with your income—no matter what the amount—as long as it represents family, home, and security. However, now let's take this income and start doing some social comparing with it (see **Table 1**).

We can begin by comparing your income to the mean (average) household income in America, which as of 2004 was $70,700 (http://www.federalreserve.gov/pubs/bulletin/2006). By being aware of this information and focusing on it, you feel good (happy) about your income—you're well above the mean. But let's continue the social comparing; let's socially compare your income to others in the U.S. with a college education—seeing that we'll assume you're college educated, it is best to compare your income to a more compatible group. In doing this comparison, you now find college-educated households in the U.S. make, on average, $117,000 (http://www.federalreserve.gov/pubs/bulletin/2006). Okay, you're still feeling pretty good about your income. But let's continue the social comparing in a realm that is most likely to happen in the real world—you find out how much your neighbors, colleagues, friends, and siblings are making: $135,000, $145,000, $155,000, and $165,000, respectively. Uh-oh! Now you're not feeling

Table 1. How do you feel about your household income?—a social comparison perspective.

Your Household Income	Compared to...	How you feel about your income...
$125,000	Average U.S. household income, $70,700	Happy!
$125,000	Average U.S. household with college or graduate degrees income, $117,000	OK.
$125,000	Your neighbors', colleagues', friends', and siblings' income, $135,000, $145,000, $155,000, and $165,000, respectively	Blah!
$125,000	NBA, MLB, NHL, and NFL players' average incomes, $4,900,000, $2,490,000, $1,790,000, and $1,260,000, respectively	Depressed.

so good (unhappy) about your salary! But let's then again continue this social comparing, staying within the "real" world: your exposure to the incomes of the individuals that you experience through the media, especially television. (And if you are wondering: watching television, in general, is associated with *un*happiness: Frey, Benesch, & Stutzer, 2007.) In watching prime-time shows, you're constantly exposed to people with possessions that make apparent they are making a lot more money than you're making—even television programming that is *real* makes you feel dismal relative to your salary. For example, let's say you watch a lot of professional sports: As of 2004, National Basketball Association (NBA) players made on average $4,900,000 per year (http://sports.espn.go.com); Major League Baseball (MLB) players made on average $2,490,000 per year (http://sports.espn.go.com); as of 2003, National Hockey League (NHL) players made on average $1,790,000 per year (http://sports.espn.go.com); and as of 2003, National Football League (NFL) players made on average $1,260,000 per year (http://sports.espn.go.com).

Argh! You now *hate* the amount of money you're making—and you feel worthless (depressed)!

Okay. Don't worry—you're *not* worthless.

Really.

Really!

Okay, this may help: the median annual income for the most populous country in the world—China, with 1.3 billion people—is below $1,800 (www.finfacts.ie, 2007). Do you feel better now?

Notice how satisfied (happy) you were with your household income when we were describing it in terms that were *not* relative to anyone but yourself. Also, recognize what happened to what you deemed as being significant relative to your income: family, home, and security become insignificant and actually disappeared when we started comparing your income to others'. What your grandma told you—at least once in your life—is true: when it comes to happiness and money, social comparing (in an upward fashion) is a no-win situation because "there will *always* be someone that will have more than you."

The only way you can *win* in terms of happiness and money using social comparison is to compare downward (Layard, 2005). For example, if we were to ask people what salary they would rather have—$150,000 per year or $300,000 per year—almost without exception, people would reply $300,000 per year. But then if we changed the scenario a bit by asking people: what salary would you rather have, $150,000 per year, while all your neighbors, colleagues, friends, and siblings are making $75,000 per year, or $300,000 per year, while all your neighbors, colleagues, friends, and siblings are making $600,000 per year? Bearing in mind social comparison, now what would people reply? Likely, downward social comparison would kick in: now there should be a significant shift in the percentage of people selecting the $150,000 per year salary. Social comparison is an important tool in combating negative emotions.

> There is more happiness in giving than there is in receiving. (Acts 20:35)

> Not he who has much is rich, but he who gives much. (Erich Fromm)

THE GOOD SIDE OF SOCIAL COMPARISON: POTENTIAL CONTENTMENT

I want to be honest with you about something. I've lied to you. I made an intentional error of omission at the end of the first chapter when I was quoting the Chinese Proverb concerning how long you will be happy doing different activities. I intentionally left out the last three words of the Proverb. It should read:

> If you want to be happy for an hour, take a nap;
> if you want to be happy for a day, go fishing;
> if you want to be happy for a week, take a vacation;
> if you want to be happy for a month, get married;
> if you want to be happy for a year, inherit a fortune;
> if you want to be happy for the rest of your life, **help other people.**
> (Chinese Proverb)

Okay, I promise not to ever lie to you again—or at least, not until after the end of this book. Sorry. So why did I intentionally leave out the last three words of this Chinese Proverb? Especially knowing that the last three words may be the most important ones, because they state what will make us happy *for the rest of our lives*? This is one of the fundamental reasons why I wrote this book: to show you what positive emotions last a long time, *and* to show you what positive emotions last a short time. I know that people want everlasting, not fleeting, positive emotions. But I also know that people have a difficult time deciphering between these two types of emotions.

I left out the last three words for two reasons: First, I was hoping that as you read the end of the Proverb, it made you curious—curious to the extent that you were wondering and maybe even coming up with your *own* answers as to what is associated with "for the rest of your life" kind of happiness. Anytime you're curious in this book, I've done my job, and you're getting your money's worth. Second, in the first chapter, we weren't ready to explain the meaning of the answer that this Proverb gives us to what is associated with lifelong happiness. But now that we have gained social comparison theory as a tool, we can explain—in terms of theory and science—the meaning of the last line of this classic allegory. And it has nothing to do with being politically correct or a bleeding heart liberal!

> ...nothing makes you happier than when you really reach out in mercy to someone who is badly hurt... (Mother Teresa)

What does it mean to *help other people*? For one thing, it means a social comparison situation. That is, if you're the one doing the helping, then from your perspective, you're in a potential downward social comparison situation: you have a better flight in life than the people who are receiving the help. It is irrelevant whether your flight in life (outside of the helping scenario) is *really* better than the flights in life of the people you are helping. What is relevant is to know the helping scenario automatically creates the *potential* for long-term happiness—or contentment—through downward social comparison. Indeed, most people who volunteer their time feel good about themselves and are happy because of it (Thoits & Hewitt, 2001). This is also why receiving a "thank you" from someone feels good—it confirms the downward social comparison. What's really neat about a thank you is that it works in both directions. Not only does receiving a thank you make you feel good, but giving a thank you makes you feel good, too. Going out of your way to thank people to whom you owe a debt of gratitude (by visiting them, calling them on the phone, writing a thank-you letter) goes a long way toward making you happier (Seligman, Rashid, & Parks, 2006).

Think about this relative to one's occupation: most people spend nearly a third of their lives working. Get ready—it's participation time again! Using only your intuition (no stereotyping!), judge how happy people are in the following occupations (who is most likely to be happy; who is least likely to be happy): accountant, mechanic, architect, gas station attendant, banker, cashier, chef, clergy, dentist, teacher, stock broker, librarian, roofer, truck driver, firefighter, housekeeper, machine operator, or electrician? What were your judgments primarily based upon? I would bet they were *not* primarily based upon the salaries associated with these occupations (if they were, then you really need to read **Chapter Three**—now); instead, your judgments were probably based upon the potential for philanthropy associated with the occupation—the higher the probability for philanthropy, the higher the likelihood for happiness. Tom Smith (2007) of the University of Chicago surveyed 50,313 people in 198 different occupations, and found the occupations with the most happy people were clergy, firefighters, and housekeepers, whereas the occupations with the least happy people were machine operators, gas station attendants, and roofers. When I describe the details of Being Theory that explain the relationship among happiness, pleasure, and contentment in **Chapter Four**, we will find that not just *any* type of helping leads to true happiness—so there are differences in helping you from the fires of Hell, a house fire, or keeping your house in order. As a precursor to the details of **Chapter Four**, I will leave you with a proverb of my own (kinda) and a couple of questions to ponder concerning different types of helping. When I teach the topic of altruism and helping behavior to my students, I use the proverbial "old lady that is in need of help crossing the street" story. Let's say *you* help the old lady cross the street (and you can assume that she really needed help crossing the street, is thankful for your help, and she enjoys being called an "old lady"). One of two situations occurs after you help her cross the street:

Situation 1: You go and tell all your friends, family, colleagues, and anybody else that will listen to you about your great deed—that, in fact, you yourself deem as being great.

Situation 2: You share this experience with nobody.

My questions to you: Do **Situation 1** and **Situation 2** represent two different types of helping? Is either situation any more likely to be associated with true happiness? Before you answer, remember: in *both* situations, the old lady did safely cross the street.

Practice Random Acts of Kindness (My second most favorite bumper sticker)

THE BAD SIDE OF SOCIAL COMPARISON: POTENTIAL MEANNESS AND HATRED

So maybe you're sitting there reading all these positive benefits about social comparison and helping, and saying to yourself: I don't want to be helping old ladies cross the street; in fact, I'm not interested in helping others at all—but I still need groups of people that are "beneath me" to make me feel happy. Can I create downward social comparison situations? The answer is yes, if you feel like being mean.

Before you answer whether or not you *feel* like being mean, I want to tell you a little story about one of the trips I took with my family to Chicago. I grew up in a suburb of Chicago (Villa Park), so I find myself in the Chicago-land area for personal and professional reasons several times a year. (I live in San Antonio.) This particular trip had me presenting at a research conference in downtown Chicago. Following the weeklong conference, my family joined me, and we took the train out to the suburbs to stay with my brother and his family for the weekend. It's about a 45-minute train ride from Chicago to Schaumburg, the suburb my brother lives in. My children love anything to do with trains. And although this was far from my children's first train ride, children will be children, and knowing the secrets of life that few adults will ever remember (unless they finish reading this book), my children were very excited about taking this train ride. We boarded the train at Union Station in Chicago along with mostly suburbanites who were getting off work on a Friday afternoon. My wife took a seat on one side of the center aisle of a train car and I took the seat immediately across the aisle from her. Soon, our car was full. Throughout the ride, my children—Sember, 5 at the time, and Rayen, 2 at the time—were either with my wife or me, or one with each of us at any one time. They were playing. They were excited. They weren't whining, loud, or obnoxious. (And I do know what whining, loud, and obnoxious is—this fact will become significant shortly!) Every time the conductor came through our car to check for new passengers and their tickets, he would smile and talk with Sember and Rayen, obviously enjoying their company. And then "it" started.

The "it" was one of the passengers in the car we were riding in. From the looks of the fellow, he worked in construction. From head to toe, he was dusty and dirty, and wore a sweat-stained bandanna around his head. He had an otherwise gruff appearance about him—unshaven and tattooed. He was maybe in his mid 30s. He was a big man. He stood over six feet tall, and he took up a good portion of the seat in which he was lounging. Shortly after the train pulled out of the station, he began talking on his cell phone—and his talking involved a lot of "F-bombs." Now even though he was near the front of the car and we were near the back of it, it was easy to hear his side of the conversation—talking well above the ambient noise within the car. (For that matter, he was talking well above the ambient noise *outside* the car—and remember, we were traveling in a speeding train, being pulled by a 2,500 horse-power, electro-diesel locomotive, for God's sake!) As he was talking, he was completely oblivious to the exchanging of stares and whispers between my wife and me, and the rest of the passengers in front of me within the car. His initial conversation was about how he wanted to kill somebody—yes, *kill* somebody. One of his phrases within the conversation went something like, "I was just hoping he was going to fucking touch me, because I told him—touch me and I'm going to fucking kill you." Now, I'm a husband and father, and my wife and pride are with me, so I was instantly in super-protection mode—as I'm *assuming* everyone else in the car was, too (and anyone else within earshot—and at his volume, that would mean anyone within 100 yards of the train). With prayerful thanks, his initial conversation ended without physical violence.

Then, his final conversation began. In this conversation, we (by we, I again mean anyone within 100 yards of the train) learn *who* he has been speaking to on the phone—his wife! This conversation is about his paycheck. Apparently, the boss's wife short-changed him in his paycheck—he was expecting $400, but received some amount less than that. And in this telephone conversation, his wife must have asked him why he didn't confront the boss's wife about short-changing him in his check. His reply was this: "Yeah, right—I'm going to fucking question my boss's wife about the amount of my check." He continued, "What do you want me to do—lose my fucking job, bitch?" This conversation then went from very bad to much worse—he started berating his wife about him possibly *ever* questioning his boss's intentions, and during this berating included the following statement: "I'm trying to respect you, bitch—now will you fucking shut up?!" By the by, all the while this emotional, domestic violence is going on, he's been drinking, and is now halfway through a six pack of Pabst Blue Ribbon.

At this point, we were 30 minutes into our *merry* little train ride from Chicago to the 'burbs. To recap, it was my family and me, with me protecting my family from drunken, emotional-domestic-violence passenger-man. The truth of the matter is that my children were completely oblivious to the situation. They were happily playing the whole time. But, suddenly *another* passenger within our train car got out of his seat from *behind* us, and stormed down the center aisle. As he was passing our seats, he grumbled aloud with acidic sarcasm, "Well-behaved fucking children!" And continued without missing a beat on his way down the aisle, *past* emotional-domestic-violence passenger-man—without saying a word to him—and exited the train car.

I sat stunned. What happened? For the past 30 minutes, I—and I certainly *assumed* everybody else in this train car—were on full red-alert, super-defensive-protection mode for ours and our loved ones' souls because of emotional-domestic-violence passenger-man, but here I come to find out that with at least *one* passenger, my assumption was completely wrong. This entire time, storming passenger-man, apparently has been focusing on—and obviously fuming about—two happy, little, giggly, playing girls and *not* the potential for destruction and harm to *all* from emotional-domestic-violence passenger-man.

Mean People Suck (My third most favorite bumper sticker)

I've often wondered why people are mean. As our grandmas might have shared with us, it's better to be nice than mean. Well, our grandmas may be wrong on this one, especially when we think about what being mean or wielding an insult does in terms of social comparison. If storming passenger-man was having such a bad day that two little kids were going to irritate him, then he should've been even *more* irritated by emotional-domestic-violence passenger-man. ***Right?*** I mean, with such an easy, obvious—even deserving—target in emotional-domestic-violence passenger-man, storming passenger-man shouldn't be taking out his wrath on some happy little kids. This doesn't make sense—mean people should be being mean to *other* mean people—right?

Or should they?

As I am writing this book, my youngest daughter, Rayen, is 5 years old. She is the happiest person I know. Constantly on the run; introducing herself to new people, who are her "friends" within minutes of meeting; smiling, laughing, and giggling; telling jokes (and laughing at them); and singing to herself—that's my Rayen. With the wealth of powerful positive behaviors Rayen possesses, she—not unlike any other child her age—can still be sad at times and cry. But guess when Rayen is most apt to cry? When she falls down and skins her knee? No. When she rolls over the go-kart? No. (Don't ask.) When people are being mean to her? Ding, ding, ding! Yes! You've just won the grand prize for being correct! Both of my daughters are smart, beautiful, and interesting—of course they are, they are *my* children! But Rayen—far more than Sember—is picked on. I used to think this was because Rayen is the young one (two and a half years Sember's junior), the little one, the irritating one... But it is not for any of these reasons. Rayen is picked on the most because Rayen is happy. Want a sad fact? Well, you are going to get it whether you want it or not: people are at their meanest usually with people who are *happy*.

To elucidate this fact, let me describe a particular personality disorder that I've discovered, but I'm sure you'll recognize—hopefully in someone other than yourself! The term **personality** refers to who you are (from an emotional, behavioral, and rational perspective) in a social situation. The term **disorder** refers to emotions, behaviors, or thoughts that are consistently maladaptive. The personality disorder that I've discovered is called: "If I'm having a bad (sad) day (week, month, year, life), then I'm going to make—for damn sure—everybody I come into contact with is going to be having a bad (sad) day (week, month, year, life) personality disorder" or for short, as my mother says, "that person has a *hateful* personality." The hateful personality (disorder) is cultivated through degrading, insulting, and "putting down" other individuals or groups. What does an insult do to a person? Figuratively and psychologically (in its effects on self-esteem) it puts "down" this person's flight in life. And now that this person is down, the person wielding the insult will feel relatively better (happy). If a person is insulted in front of a group—maybe even an audience—all the group members exposed to the insult will feel relatively better (happy), as well.

Sticks and stones may break my bones, but words will never hurt me—maybe. The person receiving an insult likely will recover quickly because a healthy self-esteem is resilient. With the recovery of the self-esteem comes a rise in the person's flight in life. As the person's flight in life returns to normal, the positive feelings gained by the person wielding the insult, will fade. This whole series of events from insult wielding to insult recovery occurs very quickly—often in a matter of moments. So guess what the person wielding the insult has to do again (in order to feel relatively good about him/herself)?: wield another insult, and another insult, and another... All of us have held both of these roles before—as the insulter and "insultee"—this is a normal part of life. What distinguishes the role of the insulter from being a normal part of life to the hatred personality disorder is its *chronicity*. This becomes a maladaptive personality for all involved, when this is the sole or primary method used by an individual to achieve his/her positive emotions. This also describes envy and jealousy in general, and the bully in particular.

The bully may be best defined in psychopathological terms as a child or adolescent with a conduct disorder (CD)—this young person more times than not is male (American Psychiatric Association, 2000). Young males diagnosed with a CD often inflict emotional and physical pain upon others. An interesting thing happens to the brains of these individuals when they *witness* pain being inflicted upon others—Decety, Michalska, Akitsuki, and Lahey (2008) found two different brain regions become strongly active: the amygdala and the striatum. The amygdala is involved in forming memories of emotional reactions; and the striatum is involved in forming feelings of being rewarded. In other words, young males diagnosed with a CD appear to take pleasure in seeing others in pain.

Do you now see why "happy people" are more likely targets for insults than unhappy people are? It's simply because a happy person is—for social comparison sake—automatically above anybody that has a low self-esteem. And certainly, one of the characteristics about the hatred personality disorder or conduct disorder is low self-esteem. This will even happen among friends. I can remember plenty of times as a teenager when I and the group of friends I hung around with would talk about "bringing down" or "giving a reality check" to one of our friends within the group who was experiencing pure bliss—usually because of a newly forming relationship (falling in love). We recognized that it was our jobs—as friends—to make sure our blissful friend was as miserable as the rest of us. Social comparison also explains vandalism. Teenagers, those in gangs or otherwise—in their search for themselves and the things that make them happy—get caught up with pleasure-inducing things (see **Vicious Cycle One** on page 35), and are responsible for the greatest proportion of vandalism. Why do teenagers (or anyone else, for that matter) vandalize? Simple: the vandalizer feels beneath whoever owns the vandalized property, and therefore needs to bring the owner down. Whether conscious of this or not, the vandalizer sees the owner's flight in life as being greater than his/her own flight in life. The owner could be the government/school (e.g., road signs or library books being destroyed and overpasses being "tagged"), a commercial entity (e.g., railroad cars being spray-painted or a business's windows being broken), or a private citizen. Unfortunately, I have personal examples as a private citizen. Every Halloween and Christmas, I decorate my house two (sometimes three!) times gaudier than the Griswold's house in the movie *Christmas Vacation*. The kids in the neighborhood love it. People in the neighborhood love it. People come from all over San Antonio just to drive by slowly for a minute or two. With all this happiness comes sadness—my Catholic roots are showing! Vandals have destroyed something almost every year that I've decorated. As part of one Halloween's decorations, I made 30 or so ghosts and put them in the front yard. Sember made sure the ghosts were female by putting eyelashes on each one of them, and Rayen made sure the ghosts were happy by putting smiles on all their faces. The night before Halloween, they were gone—stolen. Sigh. This is bad enough to experience as an empathic adult, but it goes to a whole other level of revolting experience for a child. But, as children will do, mine surprised me—especially Sember. Upon seeing the ghosts gone, she realized what had happened and said, "Robbers got them." She then turned to me and said, "Daddy, are the people who stole the ghosts sad?" To which I replied with a smile, "Yes, Sember—yes they are." Damn—I need to figure out how to get this book—as opposed to my decorations—in the hands of these people! Simply put, happy people do not vandalize, rob, or steal.

The "I'm happy when I'm putting you down" phenomenon happens on a societal scale as well. It is often said that society picks on the weakest, but society is most likely to pick on those that are the happiest. The spectrum of this phenomenon has friendly bantering on one end, to stereotyping, prejudice, discrimination, hatred, and even violence on the other end (e.g., domestic and family violence: Brewster, Nelson, Hymel, Colby, Lucas, McCanne, & Milner, 1998; Brewster, Nelson, McCanne, Lucas, & Milner, 1998; Lucas, Wezner, Milner, McCanne, Harris, Monroe-Posey, & Nelson, 2002). Measuring how happy a society or culture is by analyzing the popularity of its comedians reveals the full spectrum of this phenomenon. (As a quick measure of our own society, examine the type of comedians that currently have primetime shows on the cable channel Comedy Central.) For example, societies, cultures, or subcultures in turmoil (racial unrest, at war) or filled with sad or oppressed citizens will have as its most popular comedians those that do extreme derogatory humor, especially stereotypical and discriminatory humor. In order to feel temporarily better (relatively happy), the citizens making up these societies and cultures need these quick-fix outlets. The mass popularity of these comedians will wane as the turmoil or oppression within the society or culture decreases and its citizens become happier. There are obvious problems with this type of humor (as mentioned above: it reinforces stereotypes; increases prejudice and discrimination; and in the long-term increases physical violence), but as was also discussed above, one of the most insidious problems with this type of humor is its fleetingness—it has only short-term benefits for the person doing this type of humor. Therefore, it reinforces this person (and those who are listening to it) to do it repeatedly, which leads to potentially dangerous, sometime violent vicious cycles (see **Vicious Cycle One** on page 35).

I can read your mind. All the while we have been talking about mean people, you have been pondering, if not even outright questioning, whether this "I'm happy when I'm putting you down" phenomenon applies to—in addition to mortals—immortals. Okay, okay—I may be wrong, but you might have been pondering whether or not the "I'm happy when I'm putting you down" phenomenon appears across cultures. Well, ponder no longer, my friend, for the answer to this question is yes. According to one of the oldest cultures in the world, happiness is not only a target for mean, unhappy mortals, it is also a target for mean, unhappy immortal Emperors and Empresses.

Qi Xi (pronounced Chī-See), the seventh day of the seventh lunar month, which usually occurs in early to mid-August each year, is China's equivalent to America's and Europe's Valentine's Day. Qi Xi is based on an ancient (dating back to at least the Han Dynasty, 206 B.C. to 220 A.D.) and popular love story. The story is about Zhi Nu (pronounced Zee-New), a silk weaver—who also happens to be an immortal fairy from Heaven, and Niu Lang (pronounced Nee-Lang), a mortal cowherd from Earth. (Cowherd simply means one who herds or tends cattle.) Upon first seeing one another, Zhi Nu and Niu Lang fall madly in love with one another. In some accounts of the story, Zhi Nu is naked when they first meet—which, from a male perspective, pretty much puts the icing on the cake for marriage, let alone falling in love. I mean, an immortal fairy from Heaven is certainly dating material; but a *naked* immortal fairy from Heaven is "spend the rest of my life" (mortal or otherwise) marrying material. In **Chapter Four** (see the section titled **Classical Conditioning and Falling in Lust**), we'll get into the details of love and lust—and I'll even show you how to make anybody (yep, *anybody*) fall in love (or at least lust) with you. Now, getting back to our story...I'm sure you already guessed its next part: soon after meeting, Zhi Nu and Niu Lang marry and have children. They live a happy life on Earth with Zhi Nu weaving, Niu Lang tending cattle, and both loving and caring for their children. Their life together is so happy, that the Chinese culture holds their relationship as the example of ideal happiness.

But there are problems—not on Earth; but in Heaven. When Zhi Nu's and Niu Lang's *happiness* is discovered by the Jade Emperor—the supreme deity in Taoism and ruler of Heaven, he has Zhi Nu *immediately* returned to Heaven. The separation of Zhi Nu being taken to the immortal world and Niu Lang being left in the mortal world destroys the happiness they shared together, and thereby, predictably, from a downward social comparison perspective, makes the Emperor of Heaven happy.

The story does not end here. The sorrow Niu Lang feels about the loss of Zhi Nu is so powerful that it drives Niu Lang to make a pair of leather shoes—from his beloved, sacred cow. The shoes fly him and his children to Heaven to find Zhi Nu. But it still is not to be. For as Niu Lang is entering Heaven, the Emperor's wife pulls a hairpin out of her hair and uses it to slash Heaven in half—creating the Milky Way. The Milky Way now separates Zhi Nu and Niu Lang: Zhi Nu, represented by the star Vega in the East, weaving her silk on one side of the Milky Way and Niu Lang, represented by the star Altair in the West, taking care of their two children (the stars Gamma Aquilae and Beta Aquilae) on the opposite side of the Milky Way. The story ends with Magpies (apparently a very empathic bird) taking pity on the couple. En masse, they garner enough energy and fly to Heaven one day every year (Qi Xi) to form a bridge across the Milky Way, to allow Zhi Nu and Niu Lang to be reunited this one day of the year. If this ain't love, I don't know what is.

Fairy of the Magpie Bridge

Among the beautiful clouds,
Over the heavenly river,
Crosses the weaving maiden.
A night of rendezvous,
Across the autumn sky,
Surpasses joy on earth.
Moments of tender love and dream,
So sad to leave the magpie bridge.
Eternal love between us two,
Shall withstand the time apart.
(Qin Guan)

The hateful personality (disorder) is, in the end, ironic—and one part of a vicious cycle. The most likely characteristics of the person (or deity, for that matter) with HPD is their perspective on the world—"The world is... ignorant, dangerous, violent, unfaithful, and going to hell in a handbasket"—and to put it mildly, "the people that live within it suck." And by constantly wielding insults and pain upon *others*, the person with HPD is actually painting his/her *entire* world to be horrible—a world that ironically includes *him-/herself.* A world that he/she now perceives to be insulting and painful...

HAPPINESS AND DEPRESSION

Consistent with the *I'm Happy—You're Not* paradox are data gained from asking individuals about their own and others negative emotions—in particular, depression. A survey conducted by my laboratory asked 184 individuals about their emotions on a day-to-day basis relative to a 9-point Likert scale, with 1 equaling not depressed, 5 equaling neutral and 9 equaling very depressed (see **Figure 3**). Twelve percent of these individuals said their own day-to-day emotions are relatively depressed; that is, a score of 6, 7, 8, or 9 on the scale—and overall, the participants gave themselves an average score of 3.0; but when asked about others, these individuals said 29% of the population is depressed; that is, a score of 6, 7, 8, or 9 on the same Likert scale—and overall, the participants gave others an

Figure 3. Likert scales used to measure individuals' levels of negative emotions.

Rate what *your* emotions typically are on a day-to-day basis. Circle the number that best corresponds to your rating on the following scale:

Not Depressed				*Neutral*				*Very Depressed*
1	2	3	4	5	6	7	8	9

Rate what you think *other people's* (the general population's) emotions typically are on a day-to-day basis. Circle the number that best corresponds to your rating on the following scale:

Not Depressed				*Neutral*				*Very Depressed*
1	2	3	4	5	6	7	8	9

average score of 4.5. In other words, we generally think others are more depressed than we are. As we explained the *I'm Happy—You're Not* paradox using social comparison theory, we can do the same in explaining the ***I'm Not Depressed, but You Are* paradox**. In simple terms, although this is epidemiologically untrue, it makes us feel better (happier) to think most others are relatively more depressed than we are.

Let's talk about some of the basic epidemiological numbers associated with depression. Depression gets *a lot* more attention, research, and press than happiness, but only 5% to 10% of the population have it at any one time (Comer, 2004; Kessler, 2002). I recently performed a search on the scientific research database Medline (www.pubmed.gov; try it yourself) and found for every one published research article on topics associated with happiness, there are nearly 75 published research articles on topics associated with depression; and in just the past 58 years there have been over 220,000 published research articles on topics associated with depression. In the following chapters, we will get into the many reasons for this vast difference in psychology's focus on depression over happiness, but for now, I want you to think about how you would answer the following two sets of questions related to this difference.

First, with the knowledge that the science of human behavior (psychology) is 75 times more concerned with studying your depression than your happiness, I want to pose you the following question *again*—what would you rather be: less depressed or *more happy*?

Second, what do you think the world would look like if clinical psychologists, psychiatrists, and counselors (our mental-health practitioners) practiced not only routinely treating a person's depression (and other maladaptive psychological conditions), but also practiced routinely boosting a person's strengths, virtues, aptitudes, and propensities? Further, what would the world look like if you not only went to the mental-health practitioner when you were mentally feeling bad, but also when you were mentally feeling good and wanted to feel even better—and health insurance covered these visits?

Furthermore, in answering the former two questions, would this be a better world than the current one?

Mull over your answers for a while; we'll get back to discussing them in the following chapters. For now, let's look at the last two objective phenomena associated with happiness.

We shall not cease from exploration
And the end of all our exploring
Will be to arrive where we started
And know the place for the first time.

(Excerpt from *Little Gidding, No. 4 of Four Quartets,* T.S. Eliot)

By nature: Contentment-recognition; By nurture: Happy-ignorance

The last two objective phenomena associated with happiness are **contentment-recognition** and **happy-ignorance**. From birth, we instinctually know what makes us content (contentment-recognition), but along with most other human instincts, this instinct begins to be suppressed through early childhood (ages 3 to 5) and eventually blocked by middle childhood/early adolescence (ages 6 to 12). The suppression and blockage of contentment-recognition is happy-ignorance.

Contentment-recognition is nature-based. From birth, humans are content within *autotelic* experiences. At this point, you're most likely saying, Don't include me within this statement—I have no idea what an autotelic experience is! By the time you're old enough to be buying and reading this book, you likely do not even recognize most of the (potential) autotelic experiences you're having every day. Don't worry—by the time you are through reading this book, you will.

Ready for me to prove to you that happy-ignorance has taken you over? Prove me wrong by answering correctly a simple question: According to Santa Claus, why should children be good? I can already hear your answers, "So the children will get toys." "So Santa will come visit their home on Christmas Eve." "So they don't end up on the naughty list." "Because Santa is watching them." Wrong, wrong, wrong, and wrong. C'mon, think! Why should children be good according to the man who takes the Santa Claus Oath—an oath that maybe more than just Santa Claus(es) should take?

I will seek knowledge to be well versed in the mysteries of bringing Christmas cheer and good will to all the people that I encounter in my journeys and travels.

I shall be dedicated to hearing the secret dreams of both children and adults.

I understand that the true and only gift I can give, as Santa, is myself.

I acknowledge that some of the requests I will hear will be difficult and sad. I know in these difficulties there lies an opportunity to bring a spirit of warmth, understanding, and compassion.

I know the "real reason for the season" and know that I am blessed to be able to be a part of it.

I realize that I belong to a brotherhood and will be supportive, honest, and show fellowship to my peers.

I promise to use "my" powers to create happiness, spread love, and make fantasies come to life in the true and sincere tradition of the Santa Claus Legend.

I pledge myself to these principles as a descendant of Saint Nicholas the gift giver of Myra.

(*Santa Claus Oath*, Phillip L. Wenz)

You don't have any more guesses—do you? Well? How does it feel to be happy-ignorant? Santa, by the way, is *not* happy-ignorant.

You better watch out,
You better not cry,
Better not pout,
I'm telling you why.
Santa Claus is coming to town.

He's making a list,
And checking it twice;
Gonna find out who's naughty and nice.
Santa Claus is coming to town.

He sees you when you're sleeping
He knows when you're awake
He knows if you've been bad or good
So be good for goodness sake!

O! You better watch out!
You better not cry.
Better not pout, I'm telling you why.
Santa Claus is coming to town.
Santa Claus is coming...

(*Santa Claus Is Coming to Town*, J. Fred Coots and Haven Gillespie)

So, what is autotelic? Simply defined, autotelic means doing something for its own sake—being good, "for goodness sake." This word is more associated with true happiness than any other word I've used in this book so far! Although it is hard to define and recognize for us adults, a child easily recognizes autotelic experiences. By six months of age, children demonstrably show this knowledge every day of their young lives—through playing (learning, loving, liking, talking, questioning...) for its own sake. Most adults—and parents in particular, wonder how young children have so much energy. The answer is a simple one—contentment. I remember my wife asking me, "why does Rayen (2 years old at the time) play so much?" And me simply replying, "Because she's content."

Let's take learning as an example of the autotelic experience. Any normal child loves learning. However, what exactly do children love about learning? The answer to this question is "nothing." With the exception of our friend Calvin, there's nothing or no thing in particular about learning that children love; instead, children love learning itself. They love learning for its own sake, being curious—it doesn't matter *what* children are learning or *what* reward may come from learning, as long as they are *doing* it. For her night time story, I used to sometimes read from the owner's manual of my 1967 Pontiac Firebird to Sember, and she loved learning about my car—as much as "what she was supposed" to love learning about: Raggedy Ann, Winnie-the-Pooh, Olivia, Dr. Seuss, and so on.

> ...the purpose of playing, whose end, both at the first and now, was and is, to hold, as 'twere, the mirror up to nature...
>
> (excerpt from *Hamlet, Prince of Denmark*, William Shakespeare)

Playing is a prime example of the child's autotelic experience. Why do children play? The most accurate answer is to play. As every parent that has ever bought an expensive gift that came in a large box knows, it doesn't matter to the child "what" he/she is playing with (expensive gift or large box). The only thing that matters is that he/she is playing. Although unscientific (so shoot me!), a personal example of contentment-recognition and play comes from a game Sember and I made up. We started playing this game when she was about 2½ years old. Surprise, surprise, we called the game *Making People Happy.* Following our visits to the grocery store, we usually had coin change (pennies, nickels, dimes) from our purchases. We would take these coins in our hands with us to the parking lot. As we strolled to our car we would begin yelling (and sometimes screaming) "We're making people happy! We're making people happy!" and throwing our coins high up into the air. This made for great "fun" for all involved: onlookers, those taking the money, Sember, and myself. Now, you may already be thinking, Why are you doing this—you are throwing away money!? This is not money's *intended* purpose! Why are you randomly throwing money away? Well, guess what's "making" you say these things—happy-ignorance. If you want to overcome this ignorance and just "be happy," then read on; we'll be addressing the adult problem of happy-ignorance in just a moment.

Sember never needed a reason for *why* she was throwing money up in the air. She was giving—and enjoying it—for its own sake; she recognized contentment and went with it. Guess whether she wanted to do it again? "Again Daddy! Again Daddy!" Also, guess whether she ever adapted to doing it repeatedly (and again)—the nth time we played it together was as fun, exciting, and delightful as the first time we played it together—the purest definition of motivation and contentment.

Meanwhile, her dear old dad enjoyed it as well—but of course, my adult (happy-ignorant) mind had me analyzing *why* we were doing it. What does a person do when he/she finds a penny or a quarter or some change on the ground? He/she is usually happy about finding money—or at the least bit, feels lucky. But guess who else is smiling and laughing? Those people who are giving. The key to this story about our little game is to recognize to whom my daughter and I were giving the money and why we were giving it. Respectively, the answers are *anyone* and *for its own sake.* If only temporarily, my daughter allowed me into her contentment-recognition world. Hmm...this may be one reason why adults have children.

> At one time most of my friends could hear the bell, but as years passed, it fell silent for all of them.
>
> (excerpt taken from *The Polar Express*, Chris Van Allsburg)

Contentment-recognition begins being suppressed during early childhood (starting from about 3 to 5 years of age) and is eventually blocked by middle childhood/early adolescence (anywhere from 6 to 12 years of age)—the developmental phenomenon of happy-ignorance. Happy-ignorance is based on children being taught and reinforced by adults: parents, family, and teachers about *endotelic* and *exotelic* experiences that appear (to a person with happy-ignorance) to be connected to contentment. For example, endotelic and exotelic experiences have parents doing *for*, instead of doing *with* (autotelic), their children. Endotelic and exotelic experiences are not associated with contentment. Repeat: Neither of these types of experiences is associated with contentment. Simply defined, endotelic experiences, or experiences about your *self*, are those experiences done for *intentional* sake, whereas exotelic experiences, or experiences about your *environment*, are those experiences done because they are *required*. Although easy to define and recognize for the adult, the child finds these experiences unnatural and difficult to understand. By the time Sember reached kindergarten (at 5 years old), her learning was no longer autotelically based—that is, based upon learning itself; instead, it was based upon time (how long it took her to read and write) and standardized tests!

Let's take learning as an example again, but this time relative to happy-ignorance. Adults eventually start to define and compartmentalize learning relative to themselves (endotelic, selfish), and the people, places, and things surrounding themselves (exotelic, environmental). Selfish-based learning yields comments like, "I only learn what *I* find significant and important, or what I am good at or what my favorite subject is." Environmental-based learning comes from things like *grades* or *timing* (not *did you solve the problem*, but *did you solve it within a set period*) or some form of *payment* or a *promotion*. Even though a person may be happy with selfish-based learning and often gains pleasure from environmental-based learning, both of these emotional outcomes, in the end, will become fleeting and not satisfying. Additionally, people who spend their adult years primarily using these two types of learning are more apt to get Alzheimer's disease. Of interest to note: during this same age range (6 to 12 years) is when stereotypical (environmental) differences in mathematical and verbal scores between boys and girls first appear (Hyde & Linn, 1988; Tapia & Marsh, 2004).

Happy-ignorance often leads to situations with undo expectations. For example, people repeatedly expect when some person, place, or thing brings them pleasure or makes them happy one day, then this person, place, or thing will continue to bring them pleasure or make them happy the following day, week, month, or year. But what people often find is disappointment because the person, place, or thing over subsequent days, weeks, months, or years actually does not bring them pleasure or make them happy in the same way (if even at all). This disappointment may lead people to question whether or not they had pleasure or were happy in the first place. Alternatively, it may lead to happiness' opposite: sadness or possibly even dysthymia (chronic sadness). Or most likely, it will lead people to search for some *other* person, place, or thing to start the process all over again. This quickly can turn into vicious cycles within different situations (at home or work; within friendships, marriages, or other romantic relationships; with money or possessions) of people's lives. The vicious cycle is based on the premise that the one thing people are searching for (happiness) is the one thing people cannot obtain.

> Happiness is a butterfly, which when pursued, is always just beyond your grasp...
>
> (Nathaniel Hawthorne)

These vicious cycles within different life situations are most likely to come in one of two forms:

Vicious Cycle One. People doing what are generally viewed as being pleasure-inducing activities (for example, sexual trysts, using alcohol or drugs, gambling, overeating, etc.) that they mistakenly believe will bring them happiness—and then being disappointed when happiness is not obtained. As a specific example, **Vicious Cycle One** is probably the number-one reason for the epidemic proportions of alcoholism, obesity, and pornography in America today. So if you want to stop drinking, lose weight, and stop surfing for porn on the Internet, read on, my friend, read on.

Vicious Cycle Two. People doing what are generally viewed as being happiness-inducing activities (for example, following a religion, getting married, forming a friendship, working for money, etc.) that they mistakenly believe will bring them contentment—and then being disappointed when contentment is not reached (Evans, Guerra, Romero, & Lucas, 2008). As a specific example, **Vicious Cycle Two** is probably the number-one reason for the epidemic proportions of divorce in America today. So if you want to stay married, read on, my friend, read on.

Vicious Cycle Three. There is a third, but more uncommon form of the vicious cycle: People may be doing what are generally viewed as contentment-inducing activities (for example, helping, teaching, mediating, volunteering, mentoring, loving, etc.) that they mistakenly believe will bring them pleasure or happiness—and then are disappointed when pleasure, happiness, or "fun" is not obtained. As a specific example, **Vicious Cycle Three** is probably the number-one reason for (perceived) job dissatisfaction. So if you want to be happy working, read on, my friend, read on.

Of course, all of these vicious cycles bring on an uncertainty (of emotion and time) that stands directly in the way of people actually becoming qualitatively happier or content for any extended period. In **Chapter Four**, I will show you how to protect yourself from these vicious cycles by knowing exactly what happiness, pleasure, and contentment is.

A HAPPINESS SET POINT?

Happy-ignorance is the primary reason for the so-called happiness set point. A review of the scientific research literature reveals the happiness set point has three fundamental features: it is determined at conception, it is stable over time, and it is not affected by your day-to-day experiences. (So why are you reading this book?!) For example, studies of identical twins (Lykken & Tellegen, 1996) empirically support these fundamental features by finding that across the adult lifespan, people's baseline levels of happiness remain relatively (about 80%) stable. There are certainly emotional highs and lows in life, relative to celebrations (e.g., winning the lottery, getting married, witnessing the birth of a child), and tragedies (e.g., experiencing the death of a loved one, going through a divorce, losing a good job), but in the end, emotional levels return to about the same set level or point.

With all this said and done, there is a *but*—there always is one, isn't there? This research comes with a stipulation—and few scientists recognize this stipulation—the stability in baseline levels of happiness *only* occurs throughout the *adult* years. It does *not* occur throughout the entire lifespan. It may be the case that happy adults generally remain happy throughout their adulthood, and unhappy adults generally remain unhappy throughout their adulthood. And it may further be the case that happy children *may* grow into happy adults, and unhappy children *may* grow into unhappy adults. But it is also the case that happy children *may* grow into unhappy adults, and unhappy children *may* grow into happy adults. Thus, the happiness set point is more accurately described as *not* being determined at conception at all—instead, it appears to begin during the childhood transition from contentment-recognition to happy-ignorance; it is stable only over adulthood—and it may in fact be significantly affected by day-to-day experiences. Throughout this book, I will show you how positive emotions in general, and the happiness set point in particular, are by nurture more than they are by nature. Additionally, I will show you how they can be changed (**Chapter Six**)—and, in fact, elevated, at *any* time during your lifespan—even at the age you're at right now while reading this book!

HAPPINESS IS SUBJECTIVE

Although there is this great objectivity to being happy (everybody wants it, societies are based upon it, most people are relatively good at obtaining it, young children have contentment-recognition, and adults have happy-ignorance)—happiness begins to break down subjectively and becomes more or less idiosyncratic when it is examined relative to what people are actually doing to obtain it. As I said in the opening passages of this book, people literally are doing thousands of different things to obtain and keep happiness: trying to get more money, creating families, practicing religions, building careers, making houses, establishing friendships, dissolving friendships, vying for awards, getting married, getting divorced, having sex, not having sex, believing in God, not believing in God, drinking alcohol, shopping, celebrating (others') birthdays, ignoring (their own) birthdays, doing things for themselves, doing things for others, and vacationing—all in the name of happiness. We've already said that none of these things are likely to lead to happiness, but which of these things are, at least, *associated* with happiness?

CALVIN AND HOBBES © 2010 Watterson. Dist. By UNIVERSAL PRESS SYNDICATE. Reprinted with permission.

In the cartoon above, Calvin (Watterson, 1989)—a "philosopher" we will continue to refer throughout this book—has an idea about which of these things is associated with happiness...but is he correct? Is Calvin's idea consistent with what scientists have found?

What's associated with happiness—and pleasure—and contentment?

Based upon empirical studies, we'll be examining and naming the things that are and *are not* associated with happiness. We'll do this examination relative to the emotions of pleasure and contentment. The differences amongst these emotions will cause a person to *obtain* (or obstruct) true happiness. People *identify* these emotions as being different from one another. For example, when asked to name the first three things that come to mind when hearing the words "happiness," "pleasure," and "contentment," people name substantially different things. For happiness, the top three responses are: family, friends, and significant other (spouse, partner, boyfriend/girlfriend); for pleasure, the top three responses are: sex, food, and leisure; and for contentment, the top three responses are: work, school (learning), and success (Ancira & Lucas, 2007). Although people *rationally* identify these emotions as being different from one another, the more important question is: do people recognize and act upon these differences when they are actually *experiencing* these emotions? A recent study in our laboratory found evidence that people do *not* act upon these differences, and instead confuse pleasure and happiness actions for contentment (Evans, Guerra, Romero, & Lucas, 2008)—we've aptly named this **happiness confusion**.

Happiness confusion

Happiness confusion—an emotional-cognitive barrier to true happiness—is developmentally constructed through childhood from misconceptions about happiness and contentment. By standing in the way of you emoting and knowing yourself, happiness confusion inhibits your self-esteem, veils your self-concept, and decreases your ability to be satisfied with self. Happiness confusion is something you most likely have right now as an adult; that is, *again* assuming that *you* are an adult—but let's not get into that metaphysical discussion again. Happiness confusion pretends to be true happiness, when in reality it is most likely just some signs of pleasure. By becoming aware of and understanding happiness confusion, you'll be able to overcome *any* barriers in the way of achieving your optimum levels of positive emotions.

> Whoever wrote "...and they lived happily ever after..." should have been clear to inform the reader that this is the *beginning* of the story, not the end of it.
>
> (Me)

Happiness confusion has two parts:

The first part. Most people have the illusory belief that *other* people, places, and things, such as money, families, religions, careers, houses, friendships, awards, marriage, sex, God, alcohol, education, and vacations lead to positive emotions like happiness. The first part of happiness confusion is related to the paradox of hedonism as discussed by Henry Sidgwick in his book *The Methods of Ethics* (1874/1907). Sidgwick contends positive emotions in general—and pleasure in particular, cannot be gained by direct pursuits (people, places, and things)—instead, positive emotions can only be gained by indirect pursuits. However, as mentioned above, short-term positive emotions may work in this fashion, but long-term positive emotions do not. Enduring positive emotions are *not* effects; they are causes. Enduring positive emotions commonly *lead* to such things as riches, relationships, etc., whereas such things as riches, relationships, etc. uncommonly lead to enduring positive emotions. So if you want to be wealthy, you'll want to be happy first (or marry into a rich family). If you want a good marriage, you'll want to be happy—first. If you want a good job, you'll want to be happy—first. If you want... Your most likely bet for getting any of the things is not to focus your attention on any of these things in particular, but instead to focus your attention on your own happiness and contentment in general. Rarely do those mountaineers who focus on the top of Mount Everest succeed in climbing the mountain;

often those mountaineers who focus on the next step while climbing succeed in climbing Mount Everest. This book will show you how to focus on your own happiness and contentment in general. However, we will see that exactly *what* you're focusing your attention on has a significant condition—and this condition is the second part of happiness confusion.

The second part. Most people think they want happiness, when in reality—and unknown to them—they really want *contentment.* What people do not realize is that happiness is relatively temporary, and contentment is everlasting. If people knew this, then they would want contentment over happiness. But people do not know this. For instance, how many people have you ever heard say, "I want to be content" versus the number of people you've heard say, "I want to be happy"? What is causing this confusion between happiness and contentment is pleasure. As pain gets in the way of happiness, so too does pleasure get in the way of contentment. Pleasure makes you believe you want happiness, when all you really want is contentment.

We will be solving happiness confusion in **Chapter Four**. But before we do this, I want to share a recipe with you—a recipe for happiness, called Happiness and You. And I'm sure this recipe is unlike any other you've followed before—because scientists, instead of chefs, developed it. Let's see if Calvin is right.

Chapter Three

Happiness and You: A Ten-ingredient Recipe for Happiness, Prepared by Scientists, Not Chefs

You've likely gotten this far into reading this book because you want to find ways to facilitate your own *happiness.* (Or maybe it's required reading for a class you're taking?!) Let's be honest with one another, I know what you're *also* likely saying at this point in your reading: To Hell with what this so-called "Dr. Don" is saying about *contentment* and *true happiness*—I just want to be *happy*! Very well then, this chapter is for you. Let's do some pretending.

Ready?

I'm a frog and you're a princess...

Whoops—wrong part of my imagination. Let's try that again; you're *not* reading a book on happiness—instead, you're reading a cookbook, and you're looking up a recipe for happiness—a recipe specifically called Happiness and You.

Look no further, my friend, for here it is.

The fodder leading up to the recipe

I didn't discover the ingredients that compose the recipe Happiness and You. Nor is this recipe an old family secret, developed by my grandmother. I made it up. However, dozens of *other* behavioral and social scientists, including Ed Diener, David Lykken, Sonja Lyubomirsky, Martin Seligman, Mihaly Csikszentmihalyi, David Myers, Michael Argyle, Martin Bolt, Alan Carr, William Compton, Stefan Klein, Richard Layard, Richard Haidt, Daniel Gilbert, and C.R. Snyder, to name a few, empirically discovered the ten ingredients that compose Happiness and You. Happiness is correlated (associated) with each of the ingredients—but none of the ingredients necessarily *causes* happiness. The ultimate goal of these scientists *is* to discover what actually causes happiness. However, if you remember, the first part of **happiness confusion** stands these scientists' ultimate goal on its head. Specifically, if one were to believe the first part of happiness confusion, then one would argue the search for this ultimate goal is likely to be fruitless. Because, as the first part of happiness confusion states, true happiness—over the long-term—is itself a cause; faux-happiness or positive emotions over the short-term, may be effects. In addition to—and really, in combination with—sharing the Happiness and You recipe in this chapter, I'll begin addressing this fundamental difference between the current book's hypothesis (positive emotions are causes and effects) and traditional hypotheses (positive emotions are *only* effects) about happiness.

POSITIVE PSYCHOLOGY

Although people have been talking and philosophizing about happiness since people have been talking and philosophizing (McMahon, 2006; White, 2006), good, scientific research on happiness is a relatively recent phenomenon. This recent scientific research on happiness has been remarkable in both quantity and quality, and is much owed to Martin Seligman's challenge in 1998 to the 150,000+ members of the American Psychological Association to begin scientifically investigating and focusing on the strengths, virtues, and positive aspects of human behavior, instead of on the negative, dysfunctional, and abnormal ones (Seligman, 1999). This challenge has developed into the **Positive Psychology** movement within psychology, a movement that takes a scientific look at human behavior from an intentionally positive perspective instead of a negative one. The times, they are a-changing... At a growing number of colleges and universities [over 100], not only can a student enroll in an Abnormal Psychology course, he/she can also enroll in a Positive Psychology course; and not only can we objectively differentiate between and diagnose abnormal behaviors, thoughts, and emotions, using the *Diagnostic and Statistical Manual of Mental Disorders* (American Psychiatric Association, 2000), we can also objectively describe and facilitate positive behaviors, thoughts, and emotions, using *Character Strengths and Virtues: A Handbook and Classification* (Peterson & Seligman, 2005). Positive Psychology investigates questions about a human's strengths and virtues. For example, instead of being curious about the human's inclination towards depression, Positive Psychology is curious about what makes the human happy. And, as we found out in **Chapter One**, what makes a person happy is not necessarily opposite to what makes a person depressed. A Positive Psychologist or Positive Psychotherapist might treat a person's depression by not only attempting to negate it (as we do now), but by building a person's personal strengths that would compete against the depression and never allow it to come back again (Seligman, Rashid, & Parks, 2006; Seligman, Steen, Park, & Peterson, 2005). Additionally, Positive Psychology investigates such topics as friendships, self-control, empathy, love, altruism, optimism, relationships, commitment, self-respect, hope, athleticism, and wisdom. Happiness stands as the primary (superordinate) Positive Psychology topic—people seek all other Positive Psychology topics in the name of gaining or wanting (more) happiness. Further, happiness is the only Positive Psychology topic associated with every other Positive Psychology topic.

Finally, the ingredients!

Without further ado, here are the ingredients for Happiness and You, listed in order of importance, with the ingredient listed first, *Friendship*, being the most important within the recipe, and the ingredient listed tenth, *Money*, being the least important within the recipe:

1. Friendship
2. Acquaintances and other General Social Relationships
3. Extraversion
4. Optimism
5. Marriage
6. Employment
7. Religious Spirituality
8. Subjective Physical Health
9. Democratic Freedom
10. Money

Wait! Before you go running out to your local store to buy these ingredients (Hell, I wouldn't doubt if a Super Wal-Mart actually sold some of them), let me briefly describe how these ingredients were originally gathered and exactly what characteristics you should be looking for in each one of these ingredients—so you know what you're looking for (at your local Super Wal-Mart or otherwise). After all, keeping with our recipe theme, you wouldn't want to buy just any old lemons to make your grandmother's famous lemonade recipe—now would you? (And if you would, then you need to talk to me after class.)

How do you measure happiness?

With these ten ingredients in mind, you may be wondering *how exactly scientists came up with these items—and for that matter—how scientists measure happiness.* There are several different methods that can be used to scientifically measure happiness. Before we get into the characteristics of the individual ingredients within Happiness and You, let me briefly describe five of these methods. When you're reading the descriptions of the scientific methods to measure happiness, you'll probably find similarities between them and your own intuitive methods. Although each of the following methods has its own merit concerning validity (truth) and reliability (consistency), each method also has its own idiosyncratic shortcomings and problems. Thus, the best way to measure happiness (or anything, for that matter)—whether you're doing it scientifically or intuitively—is to use a combination of worthy methods.

Self-awareness tests. Self-Awareness Tests (SATs) of happiness assume people are aware of their own happiness. SATs simply ask a person his/her opinion about how happy he or she is. A person may take an SAT via answering questions given by a computer, or with just a paper and pencil test. Ed Diener's Satisfaction With Life Scale (SWLS; Diener, Emmons, Larson, & Griffin, 1985) is the most popular SAT found in the scientific research literature (see **Figure 4a**). The SWLS is a 5-item SAT with answers on a 7-point Likert scale. The SWLS operationally defines happiness as being positively associated with a person's total SWLS score. Thus, the higher the SWLS score, the higher the probability the person taking the test is happy (to take this test, and view your results relative to others', go to http://www.authentichappiness.sas.upenn.edu/). **Figures 4b** (Oxford Happiness Questionnaire), **4c** (Subjective Happiness Scale), and **4d** (Positive Affect Negative Affect Schedule, PANAS) are three other popular SATs. **Figure 4e** shows just how simple an SAT can be—it can be a single question. To see where you rate on happiness according to these tests, simply read the instructions for taking and scoring the tests in the figures themselves.

Figure 4a. Ed Diener's Satisfaction With Life Scale (SWLS; Diener, Emmons, Larson, & Griffin, 1985).

Below are five statements that you may agree or disagree with. Using the 1–7 scale below, indicate your agreement with each item by placing the appropriate number on the line preceding that item. Please be open and honest in your responding.

7 Strongly agree
6 Agree
5 Slightly agree
4 Neither agree nor disagree
3 Slightly disagree
2 Disagree
1 Strongly disagree

_____ In most ways my life is close to my ideal.

_____ The conditions of my life are excellent.

_____ I am satisfied with my life.

_____ So far I have gotten the important things I want in life.

_____ If I could live my life over, I would change almost nothing.

Scoring instructions: Total your answers; this is your measure of life satisfaction. The higher your score, the more satisfied you are with your life. The maximum score you can have with life satisfaction is 35.

From Deiner, E., Emmons, R., Larsen, R. & Griffin, S. (1985). The satisfaction with life scale. *Journal of Personality Assessment. 49*(1), 71–75, Table 1. Reprinted with permission via RightsLink.

Figure 4b. Oxford Happiness Questionnaire (Hills & Argyle, 2002)

Instructions: Use the following 5-point Likert scale, from 1 (Less True) to 5 (More True), to answer the following 29 questions.

1	2	3	4	5
Less True				More True

1. I am incredibly happy
2. I feel that the future is overflowing with hope and promise
3. I am completely satisfied about everything in my life
4. I feel that I am in total control of all aspects of my life
5. I feel that life is overflowing with rewards
6. I am delighted with the way I am
7. I always have a good influence on events
8. I love life
9. I am intensely interested in other people
10. I can make decisions very easily
11. I feel able to take anything on
12. I always wake up feeling rested
13. I feel I have boundless energy
14. The whole world looks beautiful to me
15. I feel fully mentally alert
16. I feel on top of the world
17. I love everybody
18. All past events seem extremely happy
19. I am constantly in a state of joy and elation
20. I have done everything I ever wanted
21. I can fit in everything I want to do
22. I always have fun with other people
23. I always have a cheerful effect on others
24. My life is totally meaningful and purposive
25. I am always committed and involved
26. I think the world is an excellent place
27. I am always laughing
28. I think I look extremely attractive
29. I am amused by everything

Scoring instructions:

- **Total your answers for items 3, 5, 6, 8, 9, 14, 17, 24:** This is your measure of life satisfaction. The higher your score, the more satisfied you are with your life. The maximum score you can have with life satisfaction is 40.
- **Total your answers for items 1, 2, 19, 21, 22, 23, 26, 29:** This is your measure of joy. The higher your score, the more joy you have in your life. The maximum score you can have with joy is 40.
- **Total your answers for items 7, 13, 16, 25, 28:** This is your measure of self-esteem or how you feel about yourself. The higher your score, the greater your self-esteem. The maximum score you can have with self-esteem is 25.
- **Total your answers for items 12, 15, 18:** This is your measure of calmness. The higher your score, the more calm you have in your life. The maximum score you can have with calmness is 15.
- **Total your answers for items 4, 10, 11, 27:** This is your measure of control. The higher your score, the more control you have in your life. The maximum score you can have with control is 20.
- **Total your answer for item 20:** This is your measure of efficacy or your belief in your ability to succeed. The higher your score, the more efficacy you have in your life. The maximum score you can have with efficacy is 5.

Figure 4c. Subjective Happiness Scale (Lyubomirsky & Lepper, 1999)

For each of the following statements or questions, please circle the number that you feel is most appropriate in describing you:

1. In general I consider myself:

   1 2 3 4 5 6 7

   not a very happy person … a very happy person

2. Compared to most peers, I consider myself:

   1 2 3 4 5 6 7

   less happy … more happy

3. Some people are generally very happy. They enjoy life regardless of what is going on, getting the most out of everything. To what extent does this characterization describe you?

   1 2 3 4 5 6 7

   not at all … a great deal

4. Some people are generally not very happy. Although they are not depressed, they never seem as happy as they might be. To what extent does this characterization describe you?

   1 2 3 4 5 6 7

   not at all … a great deal

Scoring instructions: Begin by reversing the number you circled on question 4. So if you circled a 1, then make this a 7; if you circled a 5, then make it a 3, etc. A single composite score for "global subjective happiness" can now be computed by averaging your responses to the four questions (with the fourth question's response reversed). Thus, the range of possible scores on the Subjective Happiness Scale is from 1.0 to 7.0 with higher scores reflecting greater happiness.

How'd you do?

Figure 4d. Positive and Negative Affect Schedule, PANAS (Watson, Clark, & Tellegen, 1988).

This scale consists of a number of words that describe different feelings and emotions. Read each item and then circle the appropriate answer (1, 2, 3, 4, or 5) next to that word. Indicate to what extent you have felt this way *in general*.

		Very little or not at all	A little	Moderately	Quite a bit	Extremely
1.	Interested	1	2	3	4	5
2.	Distressed	1	2	3	4	5
3.	Excited	1	2	3	4	5
4.	Upset	1	2	3	4	5
5.	Strong	1	2	3	4	5
6.	Guilty	1	2	3	4	5
7.	Scared	1	2	3	4	5
8.	Hostile	1	2	3	4	5
9.	Enthusiastic	1	2	3	4	5
10.	Proud	1	2	3	4	5
11.	Irritable	1	2	3	4	5
12.	Alert	1	2	3	4	5
13.	Ashamed	1	2	3	4	5
14.	Inspired	1	2	3	4	5
15.	Nervous	1	2	3	4	5
16.	Determined	1	2	3	4	5
17.	Attentive	1	2	3	4	5
18.	Jittery	1	2	3	4	5
19.	Active	1	2	3	4	5
20.	Afraid	1	2	3	4	5

Scoring instructions:

- **Total your answers for items 2, 4, 6, 7, 8, 11, 13, 15, 18, and 20:** This is your "negative affect score." A negative affect score is associated with negative emotions—and decreases the probability of you having positive emotions. The higher your negative affect score, the more negative emotions you have within your life. The minimum negative affect score is 10; the maximum negative affect score is 50. People who score a 29 or higher have substantially more negative affects than the general population; people who score a 10 have substantially fewer negative affects than the general population.
- **Total your answers for items 1, 3, 5, 9, 10, 12, 14, 16, 17, and 19:** This is your "positive affect score." A positive affect score is associated with positive emotions—and decreases the probability of you having negative emotions. The higher your positive affect score, the more positive emotions you have within your life. The minimum positive affect score is 10; the maximum positive affect score is 50. People who score a 44 or higher have substantially more positive affects than the general population; people who score a 21 or less have substantially fewer positive affects than the general population.

Figure 4e. A single-item scale for measuring happiness (Abdel-Khalek, 2006).

Instructions: Imagine your global estimation and general feelings—not your present feelings—to answer the following question:

Do you feel happy in general?

Answer this question on the following scale with 0 being the minimum and 10 being the maximum.

0 1 2 3 4 5 6 7 8 9 10

Scoring: Most people using this scale have scores between 3 and 9. This scale yields averages ranging between 5.89 and 7.36.

Memory tests. Quick! Recall a memory—the first memory that comes to your mind. Write it down.

Well, did you do it? Remember, I said active participation is required in reading this book—or else I'll stop writing.

So—did you do it or not?

Sigh.

Well? Are you going to do it? Okay, I'm stopping…

Really—I am. I'm not going to write anything else until you participate…

…and take an active role in the reading of this book…

I'm still waiting…

…until you do it.

Well?

Did you do it?

Okay—good! Now, do it again. Recall any other memory of your life—the first thing that comes to mind now, and write it down. Repeat this eight more times, so you have ten unique memories that you've recalled. Now rate each of these memories as either a generally good (happy) memory or a generally bad (unhappy) memory. One way to define a person's life (in general) is by his/her memories. Your self-esteem, self-concept, and morals are all dependent upon your memories. Remembering these things allows for the existence of self. If you ever have the chance to see the movie *Memento*, take it—it is a fascinating portrayal of what happens to a person who is unable to take on new memories (anterograde amnesia). People with anterograde amnesia are capable of doing anything—and I do mean *anything*. Not to give away the movie's ending, but let's just say, memory in general and happiness in particular keeps our morals in check. One way to define a person's happiness is to calculate the ratio of his/her happy (numerator) memories to unhappy (denominator) memories—the higher the ratio (that has a range between 0 to 1), the happier the person is.

$$\frac{\text{Number of Happy Memories}}{\text{Total Number of Memories}} = \text{Happiness}$$

What is your ratio?

Speaking of memories, are you continuing to forget everything you've ever learned about happiness since your childhood? It is hard to forget, isn't it? I cannot completely explain Being Theory until you've done this.

Okay. Let's get back to it.

Significant others report. If you ever want to read good fiction, then read an autobiography—anybody's autobiography. One school of thought about knowing thyself and finding out who you *really* are is to ask the person who knows you best—that person being *you*; whereas another school of thought about finding out who you really are (the one that is actually true!) is to ask the person who knows you best—and that person is *not* you. Instead, this school of thought argues the people who know you best are some combination of your friend(s), family, colleague(s), and significant other(s). The Significant Others Report (SOR) works much the same way as the SAT, with the exception of who is taking the test. SORs do not ask a person his/her own opinion about how happy he or she is; instead, SORs ask the friend(s), family, colleague(s), and significant other(s) of the person whose happiness is being measured.

So... What would your friends, family, and acquaintances have to say about your happiness?

Smiling. I have a question for you: What behavior (any overt action or reaction of an organism) is most associated with being happy?

The obvious answer is a smile. Did you get it? But just as obvious, you may be saying, is the fact that people smile for reasons that are not *associated* with happiness. Okay, that's fair; but I have another question for you: Do you think it is possible to distinguish between smiles associated with happiness from smiles that are not associated with happiness? For example, in **Photograph 1**, can you discern which of my student's smiles, **a** or **b** is associated with him being happy?

If you cannot tell, don't worry, because I will show you *how* to discern the happy smile from the not-happy smile by answering yet another question; a question that makes anyone posing it, relative to a psychological phenomenon, seem reasonably intelligent: Is the phenomenon by nurture or nature? This is *the* fundamental question for all psychological phenomena. Did *I* sound intelligent posing that question—or at least reasonably intelligent? Well, try this one on for size: When people are happy, do they learn (by nurture) to smile, or is this emotional (happiness)-behavioral (smiling) connection an instinct (by nature)?

Photograph 1. Dr. Don's student smiling **(a)** and Dr. Don's student smiling **(b)**.

(a)

(b)

Wow! Did that question make me sound intelligent or what?! For an answer to this nature-nurture question, we need to start acting like babies—for it appears we instinctively have this emotional-behavioral connection from (just about) day one.

Duchenne versus Pan Am smiling: I'm so happy, I could kill myself. It wasn't too long ago when the scientific community thought neonates (babies less than two weeks of age) had *no* intentional behaviors—that is, they had no behaviors done under their own will and volition. We (I'll put myself in error too) thought babies' behaviors were merely reflexive actions to their environment. We now know that babies have many intentional behaviors—and, one of the ontogenetically (a fancy word meaning development *within* the species) first intentional behaviors occurring within the human species is the ability to smile (Kawakami, Takai-Kawakami, Tomonaga, Suzuki, Kusaka, & Okai, 2006). By about two weeks of age, babies are able to intentionally smile—that is, control, in a coordinated fashion, their zygomaticus major muscles and orbicularis oculi muscles when they *want* to—not just when they have gas or they're poopin' (see **Photograph 2** and **Figure 5**)! When activated, these muscles make a smile, called a Duchenne smile (after its Italian discoverer, the physiologist, Guillaume Duchenne [Doo-Shen]) that *is* associated with people feeling happy and (subjectively) reporting to be happy (Ekman, Davidson, Richard, & Friesen, 1990). In the present case for this book, we may also call this type of smile a contentment-recognition or a true-happiness smile.

The Duchenne smile is different from a fake smile (a smile not associated with happiness). The fake smile usually results from certain "demanding" situations—like having gas or meeting your new in-laws, or some combination thereof. It's the type of smile that is plastered on your face during visits with the aunt or uncle, on the broken branches of your family tree (we all have at least one within our family) who always buy you orange and grey knee-high socks for your birthday (likely purchased at a garage sale), and treat you like you're everlastingly five years old. The fake smile results from the activation of the zygomaticus major muscles *without* the activation of the orbicularis oculi muscles (see **Figure 5**).

The scientific name for the fake smile is a Pan American or Pan Am smile (or in the present case for this book, a happy-ignorance smile), named after the defunct airline, Pan American. The smile derives its name from what flight attendants—in any airline, for that matter—do. For example, when boarding, the Pan Am smile on the flight attendant's face is usually accompanied by him/her saying, "Welcome aboard, we hope you'll enjoy your flight," which *really* means, "Shut up, take your damn seat, and don't cause any trouble, like ordering a soft drink or bag of peanuts; else I'll have the Federal Air Marshal aboard this plane rough you up and arrest you for being a radical." When exiting, the Pan Am smile on the flight attendant's face is usually accompanied by him/her saying, "Bye-bye, we hope you enjoyed your flight," which really means, "*Leave!*" I pick on flight attendants because of the fake smile's scientific name derivation, but I actually could pick on any number of professions, especially those within the service industry that demand "happy" employee-customer interactions—*Have a Disney day!*

Photograph 2. Smiling baby. Is she giving us a Duchenne or a Pan Am smile?

Figure 5. The right orbicularis oculi muscle and right zygomaticus major muscle.

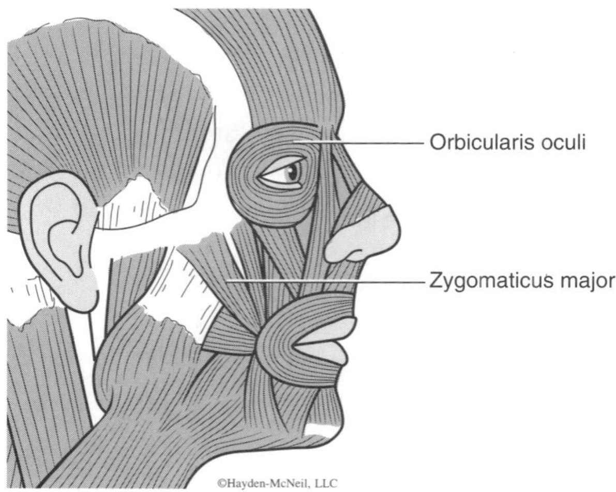

Many professions within the service industry require its employees to be "happy." The professions that are training its employees to be happy are most likely training its employees to Pan Am smile, instead. Remember, the Pan Am smile is *not* associated with happiness; it *is* associated with demanding social or professional situations and with emotions other than happiness, including anxiousness, nervousness, fear, sarcasm, deceit, and the emotions associated with meeting new people. Jack Nicholson may have done the ultimate Pan Am smile in the movie *The Shining* (the scariest movie of all time!), when he is chasing his wife with an axe; and upon breaking through a door that she's locked behind, he announces his arrival with a Pan Am smile and the statement, "Here's Johnny!" The potential long-term (as well as short-term) effects of Pan Am smiling may be best illustrated by the words of the immortal philosopher, Ren, from *The Ren & Stimpy Show* (episode: "Stimpy's Invention") who, upon being forced to wear a Stimpy-invented "happy helmet," is compelled by the helmet to be happy. Ren's response, after Pan Am smiling ear-to-ear while dancing to the "Happy Happy Joy Joy" song: "I've never been this *angry* in my entire life!" (Watch and listen to Ren and Stimpy philosophize, dance, and sing it out loud at: http://www.youtube.com/watch?v=SNqrNIdcPMA).

Hello boys and girls, this is your old pal, Stinky Wizzleteats
This is a song about a whale, NO this is a song about being happy
That's right!
It's the happy happy, joy joy song!
Happy happy, joy joy
Happy happy, joy joy
Happy happy, joy joy
Happy happy, joy joy
Happy happy, joy joy
Happy happy, joy joy
Happy happy, joy joy joy
I don't think you're happy enough, that's right!
I'll teach you to be happy!
I'll teach your grandmother to suck eggs!
Now boys and girls, let's try it again...
Happy happy, joy joy
Happy happy, joy joy
Happy happy, joy joy
Happy happy, joy joy
Happy happy, joy joy
Happy happy, joy joy
Happy happy, joy joy joy!
Iffen you ain't the granddaddy of all liars!
The little critters of nature...they don't know that they're ugly.
That's very funny! A fly marrying a bumblebee!
I told you I'd shoot, but you didn't believe me!
WHY didn't you believe me?

Happy happy, joy joy
Happy happy, joy joy
Happy happy, joy joy
Happy happy, joy joy
Happy happy, joy joy
Happy happy, joy joy
Happy happy happy happy happy happy happy happy happy happy, joy joy joyyyy!
("Happy Happy Joy Joy," "Stimpy's Invention," *The Ren & Stimpy Show*)

One touch is worth a thousand smiles. But I digress—let's get back to our babies. By two weeks of age, most babies have coordinated, muscular control over two distinct smiles: Duchenne smiles for when they're happy, and Pan Am smiles for when they have gas or for when they are involved in demanding social situations that may or may not also involve bodily functions. For babies—and sometimes too for adults (the smart ones, at least), smiling is a means to an end, with *touch* being the end. (If you ever want a certain someone to initiate touching you, then simply start the proverbial ball rolling by making eye contact with this person while smiling at him/her. You'll be surprised how far a smile *really* can get you [Givens, 2005].)

Why touch? Touch given to a baby is positively associated with at the least, that baby's future social aptitude as an adult; and at the most, his/her very survival (Field, 1998; Harlow, 1959; Harlow, Harlow, & Suomi, 1971; Harrison et al., 1996; Spitz, 1945, 1946). Happiness and smiling is at the very core of a human's survival and existence. In other words, having the ability to smile allows a baby control over not only its immediate survival (thriving), but its future survival (social aptitude) as well—but this survival is dependent upon you!

To demonstrate, let's go on a little smile trip (no drugs necessary): what do *you* do when someone smiles at you? Either you smile back at the person (smiles demand reciprocity) or—if you have your own baggage—you question what evil thing this person is up to that he/she *has* to be smiling at you. Let's take this question away from an adult smiling at you—with possible malfeasance behind the smile and give it to a two-week-old baby smiling at you. Now what do you do? There is a very high probability that you'll reciprocally smile back at the baby (unless you have a *whole lotta* baggage). This baby is smiling for a reason! If you stay within close proximity of the baby and the baby continues smiling at you, then what else might you do with the baby—the baby that is making you smile and making you feel so good about yourself. It doesn't matter if you're a man, a woman, or somebody that likes to trip three-legged dogs—you'll likely want to touch the baby; maybe even pick up the baby. Now the baby is being touched—possibly even caressed, held, and hugged—it is getting what it wanted; what it needs to survive and thrive.

Touch is one of the most important things necessary for normal human infant physical and psychological development. (Nutrition is the *other* most important thing necessary for normal infant development; however, even if we properly fed an infant, but didn't touch it, this infant would likely have significant, sometimes even life-threatening problems.) In one of the classic experiments within the science of psychology, Harry Harlow (Harlow, 1959; Harlow, Harlow, & Suomi, 1971) demonstrated that monkeys (specifically, rhesus macaque monkeys that have a 93% to 98% match in DNA to us humans) raised in isolation and without touch from their mothers during their first year of life, but otherwise raised with a normal environment of food, toys, and medical care, when compared to monkeys who were raised by their mothers were more likely to:

1. Have smaller statures
2. Weigh less
3. Be physically unhealthy (having colds and infections)
4. Be less curious
5. Be socially inept
6. Have shorter life spans

Harlow was the first to empirically demonstrate love; with the empirically based operational definition of love (at this age) being physical bonding specifically, soft, yielding, warm, communicative touches—hugs and caresses. Harlow named these types of touches contact-comfort touches.

This is what the obstetrician is referring to—when he/she advises parents leaving the hospital with their new baby to "just love your baby." Human babies without contact-comfort touches during the critical period of development from birth to about two years of age—a phenomenon referred to as infantile neglect—are most likely to have severe psychological conditions. For example, infantile neglect may lead to reactive attachment disorder. A toddler or child diagnosed with reactive attachment disorder doesn't have the ability to bond with other human beings for the rest of his/her life, including his/her mother and father. Reactive attachment disorder is diagnosed based upon an infant or child having behaviors such as rage, sensitivity to touch/cuddling, poor eye contact, no reciprocal smiling, inability to give and receive affection, and unsuccessful peer relationships (Zeanah & Fox, 2004).

The facial-feedback hypothesis. We now know smiling is objectively associated with happiness. However, we also now have another potential cause-effect, chicken-or-the-egg conundrum: Does happiness lead to smiling or does smiling lead to happiness? It seems intuitive to think that emotions lead to behaviors—you've made me happy (emotion), so I smile (behavior); you've made me angry (emotion), so I grimace (behavior); you've made me sad (emotion), so I frown (behavior). But let's stand our intuition on its head, and examine the question of whether behaviors lead to emotions. When little Lisa, from *The Simpsons*, doesn't "feel like smiling," might her mother's advice be correct?

> Well, it doesn't matter how you feel inside, you know. It's what shows up on the surface that counts. That's what my mother taught me. Take all your bad feelings and push them down. All the way down, past your knees, until you're almost walking on them. And then you'll fit in, and you'll be invited to parties and boys will like you, and happiness will follow.
>
> ("Moaning Lisa," February 11, 1990, *The Simpsons*)

Hmm, I don't know if I'm going to recommend people to be "walking on" their bad feelings, but the question remains: If I'm smiling (for no apparent reason), will this make me happy? If I'm grimacing (for no apparent reason), will this make me angry? If I'm frowning (for no apparent reason), will this make me sad? It appears that not only do emotions lead to behaviors; behaviors lead to emotions, too!

Let's do a little experiment to demonstrate. I invite you and nine of your friends to participate in an experiment I'm conducting on humor. When the ten of you show up to my laboratory, I randomly assign you and your friends to one of two conditions. The experiment requires you to participate as individuals. Once you enter my laboratory, I say aloud the experimental instructions:

> I'm interested in your judgments about how funny a series of cartoons are. I'm going to give you ten cartoons to read. Your job is to rate each of these cartoons, with pen and paper, on a five-point Likert scale, with one equaling not funny and five equaling very funny. Upon reading and rating all the cartoons, the experiment will be over. When you're reading the cartoons, I will not be in the same room as you, but I will be videotaping you—to ensure you're actually reading the cartoons. Because I do *not* have a high-fidelity video camera to best see your face and confirm you're actually reading, I'm going to ask you to be doing *this* with your face, the entire time you're reading and rating the cartoons.

With this last statement, I make a big smile and confirm you mimic my exact facial expression—I never mention the word "smile," I just ask you to make the same facial expression as I'm making. I end by saying, "Do you understand your task?" If you understand the task, the experiment commences, and usually only lasts about 15 minutes. Four of your friends participate in this exact same experiment. Each of your other five friends participates in the exact same experiment, with one exception—instead of making a big smile and confirming they mimic it, I make a big *frown* and confirm they mimic my exact facial expression.

The question is, are there any differences between the judgments in the two experimental conditions? Will you and your four friends who were smiling while reading the cartoons rate these cartoons as being any funnier than your five friends who were frowning while reading the cartoons? What do you think—want to take a guess?

Based upon the results of dozens of other experiments performed in the same fashion as the one just described (for the seminal study, see Buck, 1980), we most likely would find you and your four friends' judgments of the cartoons to be higher (funnier) than the judgments of your five friends in the other condition. Why? Do you and your four friends have a better sense of humor than your other five friends do? No. Participation in the experimental conditions was randomly determined—the odds against the five people (out of ten) with the best senses of humor separated from the five people with the worse senses of humor are astronomical. (For the math and betting enthusiasts, the odds are 1024 to 1.) The **facial-feedback hypothesis (FFH)** best explains these results. The FFH states that not only do emotions lead to behaviors, but behaviors also lead to emotions. Thus, having a "pseudo-happy" face (behavior; Pan Am and Duchenne smiles were not monitored in these experiments—need a dissertation topic?) caused a greater sense of humor (emotion) and judgments of the cartoons to be funnier as compared to the "pseudo-sad" face, which caused a lesser sense of humor and judgments of the cartoons to be less funny. The FFH demonstrates that happiness (and sadness, for that matter) is as much an objective behavior as it is a subjective emotion. (J.B. Watson would be so proud!) Further, the FFH demonstrates that a person cannot separate his/her behaviors associated with happiness from his/her emotions associated with happiness—in fancy terminology, behaviors and emotions are psychophysically connected. **Figure 6** shows how a canonical loop (**6c**—a fancy way to describe behavior in a non-linear fashion) can be used to

Figure 6. Serial and canonical loop models of the facial-feedback hypothesis.

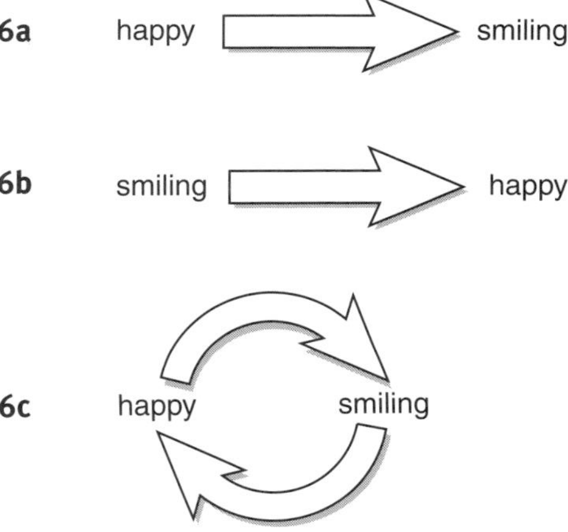

model behavior (the facial-feedback hypothesis) as opposed to serial models of behavior (**6a** and **6b**—a fancy way to describe behavior in a linear, cause-effect fashion), I'll distinguish between these two basic ways of modeling behavior in greater detail in **Chapter Four** when I explain Being Theory. (By the by, for your curiosity, the advice of Marge, Lisa's mother, is best modeled by **Figure 6b**.)

Left frontal lobe activity, oxytocin, and prolactin. Just as there are ways to measure psychophysiological stress (for example, hypertension and various stress hormones like cortisol), there are ways to measure psychophysiological positive emotions (for example, left frontal lobe activity, and the production of the hormones oxytocin and prolactin). Klein (2005); Lane, Reiman, Bradley, Lang, Ahern, Davidson, & Schwartz (1997); Tomarken, Davidson, Wheeler, & Doss (1992); and Pelletier, Bouthillier, Levesque, Carrier, Breault, Paquette, Mensour, Leroux, Beaudoin, Bourgouin, & Beauregard (2003), as well as other neuroscientists, have demonstrated when people are having happy thoughts, specific areas of the brain become more active, including the left temporal, left pre-frontal, and left frontal lobes (see **Figure** 7). However, the problem with this type of method to measure happiness is that it does not fully discriminate between emotions *other than* happiness that may be causing these areas of the brain to become more active. Specifically, the left frontal lobe is associated with *most* higher-order forms of behavior. (For example, most of a person's personality characteristics are driven by the frontal lobe in general and the left frontal lobe in particular.) A more discriminant psychophysiological method to measure positive emotions is monitoring relative levels of the hormones oxytocin and prolactin. A gentle stroke (a contact-comfort touch) of a human child, adolescent, adult, or elder will stimulate their body to release the hormones oxytocin and prolactin. (Eating a dark chocolate bar may bring on some oxytocin, too; Johnson, 2003.) Oxytocin release is associated with physical growth, the relief of stress and pain, and subjective reports of love, pleasure, happiness, and calmness (Stern, 1986; Uvnas-Moberg, 1998); whereas prolactin is associated with sexual satisfaction and relaxation (Brody & Krüger, 2006).

Heavy sigh

Figure 7. Drawing of the brain showing the left hemisphere and some of its underlying structures, including the prefrontal lobe. Note the relative locations of the left frontal and temporal cortices in the midsagittal and lateral views of the brain at the bottom of the figure.

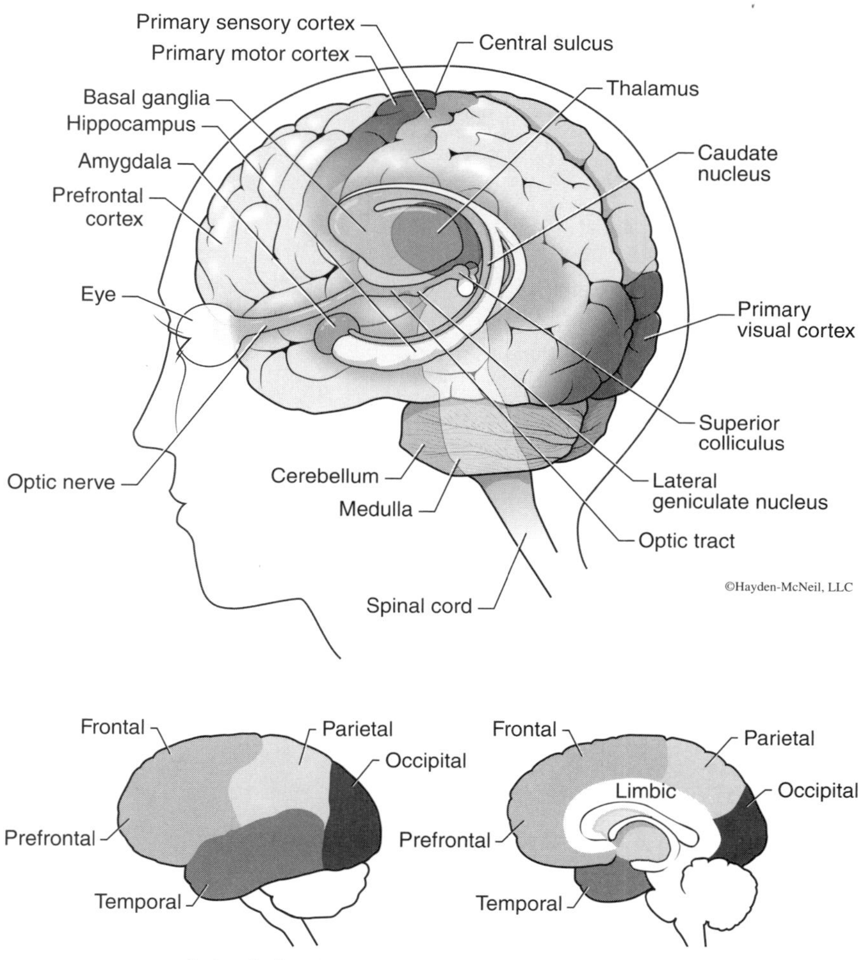

Let's test to see if you've learned anything (good) yet—ready for a quiz? Ready or not—here it is...

Quiz

1. **Which of the following is a good definition of psychology?**
   a. Something Dr. Phil kinda talks about.
   b. The science that studies affects, behaviors, and cognitions.
   c. A word that is very difficult to pronounce when the p isn't silent.

2. **Who is Martin Seligman?**
   a. The neighbor's real name in the popular 1990s sitcom, *Home Improvement.*
   b. The psychologist who coined the term Positive Psychology.
   c. Er, is this the name of the person who wrote the book I'm reading?

3. **Positive Psychology focuses its studies on:**
   a. Abnormal behavior, like depression, anxiety, and learning disabilities.
   b. Confectionery.
   c. Human character strengths and virtues, like friendships, helping behavior, love, and happiness.

4. **What percentage of Americans rates themselves as being happy?**
   a. about 10%
   b. about 50%
   c. greater than 75%

5. **What percentage of Americans is clinically depressed?**
   a. about 5% to 7%
   b. about 50%
   c. about 70%

See **Appendix Four** for answers.

Well? How did you do? If you didn't score a perfect 5—you cannot go on. Return this book to the store, or else give it to someone that has a bigger memory capacity than a goldfish. I'm kidding! All you have to do is go back and re-read the first 59 pages again...

FINALLY, THE CHARACTERISTICS OF THE INGREDIENTS!

> True happiness consists not in the multitude of friends, but in their worth and choice.
>
> (Samuel Johnson)

Friendship. The first and relatively most important ingredient in our recipe should come as no surprise to you—it is friendship. The classic film *It's a Wonderful Life* is a must see if you haven't seen it before—and *if* you haven't seen it before, as a psychologist, and your friend, please tell me about the mole hole you've been living in, because I need to fill it up. *It's a Wonderful Life* brilliantly illustrates the reward of friendship in its climactic scene. This scene has George Bailey, the film's protagonist, who has been searching for his own "success" throughout the film, surrounded by dozens of his friends toasting him as "the richest man in town." The toast confuses George for a moment until an angel from afar reveals, "...no man is a failure who has friends." *It's a Wonderful Life* portrays *significant* friendships. Significant friendships are the most popular variables in the research literature associated with happy people. *Quality* defines significant friendships, not quantity. Most people have less than five quality friendships over their lifetime! Quality friendships are *communal* and *empathic.*

The relationship within a communal friendship has an identity of its own. The relationship is a gestalt; it is different and independent from the individuals that compose the relationship. Further, there are no explicit (or expected) rewards for the individuals involved within a communal friendship (Clark & Mills, 1993). Let's contrast a communal friendship to a reciprocal friendship. At least one of the individuals involved within a reciprocal friendship is continuously monitoring (and expecting) the giving and taking going on within the relationship. The differences between a communal and reciprocal friendship are easy to recognize in public—especially at a restaurant. ☺

Let's say friends X and Y (within a reciprocal friendship) go out to dinner at a restaurant with one another. When the check comes for the meal, the payment process is highly scrutinized—if friend X picks up the check and says he/she will pay for it, then friend Y will feel immediately in debt, and will know that he/she will have to do something relatively soon (to alleviate the in-debt stress) to repay friend X. If friend X and Y decide to split the check, then this process is highly monitored as well, in that each individual attempts to put in the exact amount he/she owes—if one person puts in too much, then the other will again feel in debt and feel that he/she has to quickly repay this debt. Sometimes there is a difference in the implicit definition of a friendship within the friendship itself—one person is monitoring the giving and taking, while the other is not. Most of us have had this type of a friend before—every time you go out to eat with this person, when the check comes you feel almost obligated to pay for *all* of it, because your friend consistently does not have any cash on him/her, or just before the check comes, your friend seems to always be in the bathroom—for 15 minutes! These relationships are still reciprocal—for it only takes a single person within a relationship to define a reciprocal friendship. If you're monitoring all the times the weasel—I mean, your friend—has not paid the check, then you're implicitly defining the relationship as being reciprocal. As a side note, this is often the same type of "friend" that, if he/she decides to split the check with you, he/she does it in a fashion where he/she will say, "let's just split it 50/50," *after* he/she orders steak and lobster with five alcoholic drinks and dessert while you ordered a small dinner salad with a glass of tap water.

Taking our restaurant example again, let's now say communal friends *j* and *k* go out to dinner with one another, and the check comes—now the check is paid based upon whoever has money, with no strings attached. Here, *friends* owe money for their meal—not individual friend *j* or individual friend *k*—because communal friendships are gestalts; the individuals that compose the friendship, *j* and *k*, no longer exist as separate entities. If friends *j* and *k both* have money, then likely the waiter makes out! Both friends may throw their money down for the check to be paid and neither friend will be monitoring how much change he/she "should" get back. And no, this isn't about being rich or a spendthrift, this *is* about friendship. Because there is no monitoring going on, the extra money is the tip—server, friend *j*, and friend *k* are happy. Marriages—change that, *good* marriages—are often communal friendships: Plural pronouns rule the relationship; there are a lot of "ours" and "we" and few "yours" and "mines." Want a marriage that will likely end in divorce? Then be sure to get a pre-nuptial agreement and two separate checking accounts! More on this later, as I specifically discuss the characteristics of the ingredient marriage.

Proximity is *the* litmus test for communal friendships. Physical distance negatively affects—and often dissolves—reciprocal friendships; it does not affect communal friendships. For example, what happened to the friends you had in high school or in a former work place? Likely, you had "best-of-friends" friends within these two different situations, but you also likely don't keep up with these friends anymore, if not for an occasional holiday or birthday card. These friendships were reciprocal. What you and your friends could (and did) give to one another was relative to being physically close to one another. Reciprocal friendships often bring pleasure in the guise of happiness (see **Vicious Cycle One** on page 35).

In addition to being communal, a quality friendship is empathic. Empathy is a learned emotion that allows a person to take on other people's emotions—these emotions may be positive, negative, or some combination. Empathy is different from sympathy. Sympathy is a learned cognition (higher-order thought process) that allows a person to recognize other people's emotions; there is no "taking on" or "feeling" these emotions within sympathy. If I'm sympathizing with you, I'm aware of what you're going through and what you're feeling, but this is not going to *affect* me. When I'm empathizing with you, I'm not only aware of what you're going through and feeling—it also affects me: if you're happy, then I'm smiling; if you're sad, then I'm frowning. When good things happen to one friend, then in turn, the good things happen to the other (empathic) friend, too. Conversely, when bad things happen to one friend, then in turn, bad things happen to the other (empathic) friend, too. This leads to helping behavior. Friends help friends through crises. Strangely, but often, when going through a crisis, one friend will withdraw, and say or think something along the lines of, "I don't want to burden my friend with my troubles." This statement cannot be further from the truth about significant, quality friendships.

I often tell my students, empathy is the most powerful of all human emotions because it allows your own emotions to be multiplicatively experienced. For example, let's say you're having a good day and feeling happy about it. As the day continues, you meet up with one of your friends who also happens to be having a good day and feeling happy about it—with empathy, you will feel *twice* as happy as you did when you were by yourself. If you meet up with two of your friends who are both having a good day and feeling happy about it, then you'll feel *three* times as happy. If you meet up with three friends…

You get the idea. This is where life truly *can* become a celebration—any time one of your friends has something good happen to him/her, then something good is happening to you, too! Of course, as I said, true empathy does not discriminate: it allows one to take on positive as well as negative emotions. The word empathy has as its roots within the definition "to suffer together." Not all of our friends are always having good days—they are likely having bad ones, too. Because the quality friendship is communal—and therefore, not dependent upon the giving and taking being about good or bad experiences—sharing bad experiences will not have any negative impact on the friendship. In fact, this is what allows for helping behavior between friends to go to the extent of sometimes being altruistic.

> Acquaintance: A person whom we know well enough to borrow from, but not well enough to lend to.
>
> (Ambrose Bierce)

Acquaintances and other general social relationships. The second most important ingredient within our recipe is acquaintances and other social relationships. Social relationships may be qualitative friendships (as just discussed) and spouses (we will be covering this ingredient separately), but are more well defined by relationships in the forms of reciprocal friendships, family, business partners, colleagues and associates at work, acquaintances, neighbors, fellow church/synagogue/mosque worshipers, classmates, fellow sports fans, etc. None of these forms of social relationships is more important than any other form. Instead, the significance of this ingredient, as described in the research literature on happiness, is its total number (quantity). Happy people have *more* opportunities for social interactions than unhappy people do. This is going to be a "duh" statement—but sometimes we need duh statements. As humans, we are social beings before we are anything else, and the *more* social we are, the happier we are.

Why is social interaction associated with being happy? Primarily, two reasons: first, social interaction facilitates physical activity; and second, it allows people to vent. Researchers have known for years that there is an inverse correlation between physical activity and depression; that is, the more physically active people are, the less likely they are to be depressed (Camacho, Roberts, Lazarus, Kaplan, & Cohen, 1991). Treatments (like jogging, walking, swimming, aerobics, etc.) for depression, based upon these data, have varying levels of success. The fundamental problem with these treatments is getting disinterested, inactive, and lethargic people *motivated* to be involved within these physical activities. Social interaction solves this problem. The indirect effect of having opportunities for social interactions is physical activity—*having* to get to the actual places where the social interactions are occurring (home, the work place, the place of worship, the volunteer organization, the ball park, the gym, the school, the restaurant, etc.) requires physical activity. Thus, social relationships are positively associated with happiness not only because of the actual people involved during the social interaction itself, but also because of the energy and physical activity it requires to travel from one social interaction to the next.

For human beings, anxiety and stress are a normal part of living. Ignoring this anxiety and stress, however, is *not* normal, and can be quite maladaptive to mental (lethargy, depression, violence) as well as physical health (high blood pressure, heart disease, stroke, and even death). Most of us have our own idiosyncratic ways to alleviate stress. Some of these ways may be more adaptive than other ways—for example, one might argue that relieving stress by drinking alcohol may not be as adaptive as working on a crossword puzzle. Whatever the manner of stress relief may be, one thing is for sure: stress is best relieved within a social setting. You're likely to relieve much more stress drinking alcohol *with your buddies* and working on a crossword puzzle *with a friend* than you are drinking and working alone.

Interestingly, the social setting does not require your active participation. It can be something as simple as you going for a jog by yourself—in a public place—say, a park; or you going to eat by yourself—at a restaurant; or you shopping by yourself—at a mall; or you reading by yourself—at a coffee shop. If you actually talk with others within the social setting, your own stress levels are likely to decrease even more. For instance, let's say, on your drive to work one morning, a car cuts you off at your exit, which in turn makes you have to suffer through an extra hour of driving through heavy traffic. By the time you do get to work, you're distressed and angry. Frankly, you're pissed off! However, after talking with your office colleagues about what happened to you in the morning traffic, you're laughing and making light of the situation. How does the saying go? Most things are "better" with (at least) one partner. A true statement—when we replace the word "better" with the word "happier."

> Personality is born out of pain. It is the fire shut up in the flint. (J. B. Yeats)

Extraversion. The third most important ingredient and first personality trait within our recipe is extraversion. This should come as no surprise to you as an ingredient after the first two ingredients: extraversion is a person's ability and, in some ways, his/her energy to put him/herself into a social setting. Happy people have higher levels of extraversion within their personalities than unhappy people do. If you have quality friendships and many social relationships, then you're likely to be an extrovert—duh! How this ingredient differs from the first two ingredients is that it is *intrinsic*. Extraversion is a part of a person's *character*, whereas quality friendships and social relationships are a part of a person's *environment*.

> The greatest predictor of success is failure. (Me)

Optimism. The fourth most important ingredient and second personality trait within our recipe is optimism. Optimism is a person's ability to put a positive light onto ambiguous and negative life situations. Happy people have higher levels of optimism within their personalities than unhappy people do. The prototypical example of optimism—the optimist answering "half full" to the question, "Is the glass half empty or half full?"—only tells a part of the story about how optimism is associated with happiness. The true measure of optimism and its association with happiness comes when situations are not ambiguous, but negative. This is when the optimist's attitude serves as a motivator for him/her to keep moving forward towards his/her goal.

One of the most famous optimists, and greatest American inventors, of all time was Thomas Edison—Edison gained over 1,000 patents for his inventions. One of the more famous stories about him captures an example of Edison's optimism. He had failed more than 10,000 times in his storage battery experiments before coming up with a solution, but this is not how Edison described it. "Why, I have not failed. I have just found 10,000 ways that won't work." For Edison, for true optimists, "failure" and other negative situations in life are opportunities for learning and success. Edison was obviously a brilliant man, but his success was less about brilliance—the intelligent man surely would have stopped after the first 100 or 200 experiments! Instead, Edison's success was more about his optimism, which led to his persistence in spite of failure. Success is 99% perspiration and only 1% inspiration—to the optimist, failure is a prediction about getting closer to success, whereas to the pessimist and realist, failure is an end. Optimism allows people to get *past* failure. And for most people, happiness lies *beyond* failures (see **Figure 8**).

Figure 8. Are you a realist, a pessimist, or an optimist? Realism and pessimism reinforce failure to be a stopping point, whereas optimism reinforces failure to be a step closer to success.

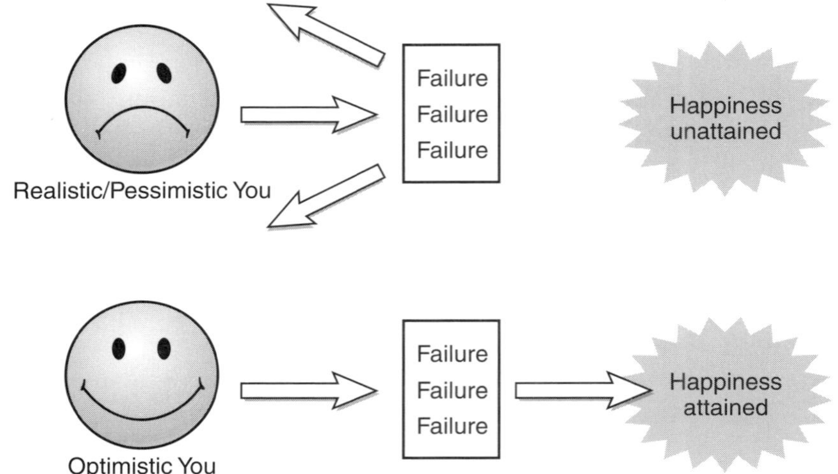

> Marriage has no guarantees. If that's what you're looking for, go live with a car battery.
>
> (Erma Bombeck)

Marriage. The fifth ingredient in our recipe is marriage. We've already discussed the reasons why friendships and social relationships are associated with people reporting to be happy in the research literature. Married people are happy for all the same reasons associated with friendships and social relationships, and more: marriage is also associated with having a long-term confidant—someone you can completely trust. Although trust is significant in most quality friendships and social relationships, it is greatest within marriage. Here's something you never heard before—trust is the basis of a good marriage. Duh!

Okay, let's try that again. Here's something you *really* never heard before—trust is the basis of a happy, healthy, long-term marriage; and marriage is the basis of *life's* longevity. Married people, when compared to unmarried people, are less likely to get sick; and when they do get sick, are more likely to recover from the sickness and recover at a faster rate—in fact, laboratory tests confirm married people have stronger immune systems than unmarried people do (Waite & Gallagher, 2000). Insofar as life-risk factors are concerned, being *un*married is one of the greatest; being unmarried decreases one's life expectancy by about 10 years, whereas a heart disease (the number-one killer of human beings in the Western hemisphere) only decreases one's life expectancy by about six years (Cohen & Lee, 1979). Ninety percent of *married* men alive at age 48 will live to age 65—only about 60% of *un*married men at 48 will be around at their retirement parties; ninety percent of *married* women alive at age 48 will live to be 65—only about 80% of *un*married women will live to see their 65th birthday (Waite & Gallagher, 2000). Since longevity and that search for eternal youth (not necessarily achieving it) is associated with being happy, marriage is associated with being happy. (In **Chapter Six**, we will comprehensively explore the link between happiness and longevity.)

> The more I want to get something done, the less I call it work. (Richard Bach)

Employment. The sixth ingredient within our recipe is employment (outside of the home). This ingredient probably comes as a surprise to you. You're probably thinking this is one of the *last* things associated with happiness, not one of the *first* six things associated with it. Employment and work *not* being associated with happiness is the second greatest myth about happiness. (Don't worry—I'll be sharing the number-one myth about happiness with you shortly.) However, some simple thoughts about what work is about can easily break this myth. Work is about social relationships, friendships, goal setting, personal achievement, and money. Work as an adult is analogous to play as a child. Play for a child is blissful and as we discussed in **Chapter Two**, play for a child is autotelic—contentment-inducing. Unfortunately, the development of Happy-Ignorance cognitively restructures play into work. And with this restructuring comes the false impression most people have about work. (In **Chapters Four** and **Five**, we will comprehensively explore the relationship between work and happiness.)

> Without philosophy, man cannot know what he makes; without religion, he cannot know why.
>
> (Eric Gill)

Religious spirituality. The seventh ingredient within our recipe is having religious spirituality. Consistent with what I described about marriage, having religious spirituality is also about trust and faith. The main difference between the faiths associated with religious spirituality and marriage is that religious spirituality's faith is in something *beyond* what is corporeal, whereas marriage's faith is in the people composing the marriage. *Meaning* is significant when it comes to happiness. One of the greatest sources of distress and anxiety is ambiguity. When this ambiguity is at the highest level—within the meaning of life—depression is likely to result. Victor Frankl, a survivor of a Nazi concentration camp, wrote one of the greatest books on this topic: *Man's Search for Meaning.* No matter who you are, this book is a must read. Religions typically provide us this life's meaning. No one religion is any better at providing happiness than any other religion, as long as the religion provides trust and faith, goals, direction, and meaning in life.

> For he who has health has hope; and he who has hope, has everything.
>
> (Owen Arthur)

Subjective physical health. The eighth ingredient within our recipe is a person's perception of his/her own physical health. This ingredient, behind extraversion and optimism, is in some ways, the third personality trait associated with happiness. This ingredient is *not* objective physical health. Physically healthy people are not *necessarily* happier than physically unhealthy people are. For example, a person who is at the worst end of the spectrum for physical health, confined to bed or a wheelchair for life, is not likely to be unhappier than a perfectly healthy person is (Veenhoven, 2006). This ingredient is one's *interpretation* of one's physical health. Social comparison is at the basis of this ingredient. For example, we cannot predict, based upon physical health, that Maria, diagnosed with skin cancer following her physical, is any less happy than Susana, who just got a clean bill of health from her doctor after her physical. Instead, we'd have to inquire how Maria and Susana view their health. This inquiry may reveal that Maria is feeling relatively positive—yes, positive. Her first response after the diagnosis was, "Thank God I do not have breast cancer!" (Breast cancer is a much more difficult form of cancer to treat.) Further, her thoughts after the diagnosis were for people diagnosed with untreatable forms of cancer. Maria is obviously downward social comparing her way out of the depression that may have accompanied the diagnosis—she may even be happy, and is certainly hopeful, about it! Meanwhile, our inquiry with Susana finds her comparing her current physical health and fitness to her sister's—who happens to be an Olympic-caliber marathon runner. Susana is obviously upward social comparing. With these inquiries in mind, now let's ask the question again—who is happier about their health, Maria, who has cancer, or Susana who has a clean bill of health? And the answer is: Maria.

> Freedom means the opportunity to be what we never thought we would be.
>
> (Daniel J. Boorstin)

Democratic freedom. The ninth ingredient within our recipe is the democratic freedom one has within the country he/she lives. The research literature on happiness shows that happiness differs among cultures relative to how the country of which the culture is a part governs its citizens. The more oppressive the government is in ruling its citizens, the lower the overall levels of happiness will be; the more democratic the government is in ruling its citizens, the higher the overall levels of happiness will be.

There are extensive studies comparing levels of happiness among countries, cultures, and societies (e.g., Inglehart, 1997; Myers, 2000). This research has two clear conclusions: First (as I shared with you in the first chapter), no matter where you go, the number-one thing people report to be interested in having in their lives is happiness. Second, happiness *does* differ among countries, not only based on their level of democratic freedom, but also on their median income and social relationships. High levels of democratic freedom, high income levels, and lots of quality friendships, kin, and other social relationships is associated with a happy culture, whereas low levels of democratic freedom, low income levels, and few quality friendships, kin, and social relationships is associated with an unhappy culture (see **Figure 9**). Respectively, Iceland, the Netherlands, Sweden, Denmark (it doesn't hurt that the Danes consume the most candy [36 pounds] per person

Figure 9. Ratings of happiness across cultures.

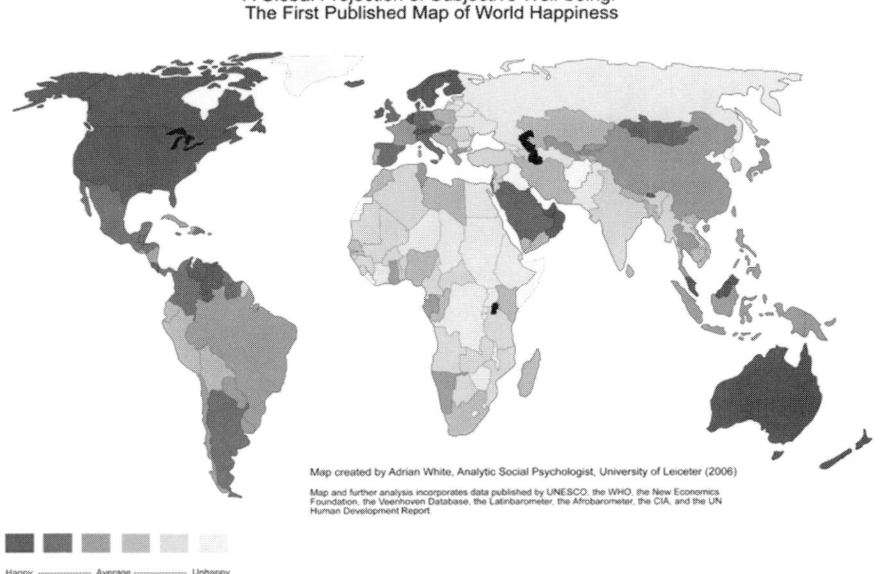

A Global Projection of Subjective Well-being:
The First Published Map of World Happiness
Map created by Adrian White, Analytic Social Psychologist, University of Leiceter (2006)
Map and further analysis incorporates data published by UNESCO, the WHO, the New Economics Foundation, the Veenhoven Database, the Latinbarometer, the Afrobarometer, the CIA, and the UN Human Development Report
Happy Average Unhappy
Cartographic Unit • University of Leicester

"A Global Projection of Subjective Well-being: The First Published Map of World Happiness." Reprinted by permission of Professor Adrian White, University of Leicester.

per year of any country in the world [National Confectioners Association]), Norway, and the United States are often found at the top of this list, whereas Bulgaria, Ukraine, Moldova, Belarus, and Russia are often at the bottom (Myers, 2000).

> They who are of the opinion that Money will do everything, may very well be suspected to do everything for Money.
>
> (George Savile, *Complete Works*, 1912)

Money. The last ingredient in our recipe is the amount of money a person possesses. Although it is the last ingredient in our recipe, it is still difficult, for me, to include this ingredient at all, because there is so much more written about money and happiness that is just plain false (propagated by the Western media) than there is written about money and happiness that is true. The media presents so much false information about money that I specifically included money (and its predictive validity to happiness) as one of the primary misconceptions (Misconception number three) people have about happiness. Let me start by saying, money does not—I repeat, money does *not*—buy happiness (although it might hire out pleasure for an hour or two [caution, the previous statement is rated NC-17]). Buying happiness is the *biggest* myth associated with happiness. Two simple, little thought experiments will show how this *is* a myth.

Ready?

Imagine someone could grant you fame and fortune *or* happiness. You could have the world's respect and own everything you could dream of, but without happiness. Or you could live each day joyfully, having only your basic needs met.

Which one would you pick?

Ready for one more?

Okay, here's $100,000. Really, I'm giving you $100,000. Would this make you happy? Certainly, I'd at least put a (Pan Am or otherwise) smile on your face.

Okay, let me up the ante. Here's one million dollars. Would this make you happy? The heck with smiling, you should be doing somersaults! Well, are you happy?

Hmm...

Within one year of winning the lottery, most lottery winners are no happier than they were before winning. In fact, many lottery winners have higher levels of *dissatisfaction* in their lives than they did before winning the lottery—no longer being able to enjoy the routine activities they once did (Brickman, Coates, & Janoff-Bulman, 1978). Texas, where I live, participates in the Powerball multistate lottery. This lottery often has jackpots in the hundreds of millions of dollars.

When a jackpot reaches a level like this, people come out of the woodwork to play the lottery, and all the corner stores with lottery machines will have lines out their doors, with people wanting to buy lottery tickets on the day of the drawing. Not too long ago, I was in one of these lines (waiting to purchase a couple of gallons of milk for my kiddos—ain't I righteous?). I noticed that the clerk selling the tickets was asking each customer what they would do with the money if they actually won the lottery. By the time there were only two people in front of me, I could clearly hear the conversations going on between the clerk and the customer. An elderly man who was buying his tickets replied to the clerk's question with the following, "I'm going to give it (the lottery winnings) to my grandchildren." To which, without pause, the person immediately in front of me in line questioned the elderly gentleman, "Don't you like your grandchildren?"

Some people get it—they understand that money buys more stress, anxiety, responsibility, disenchantment, and sorrow than happiness. However, most people do not get it—and are instead enthralled with the idea that money leads to happiness—enthralled with the "American Dream," and unaware of the fact that some dreams are nightmares. The question is, why do most people *not* get it?

Can you say—the media? Television is the worst of all the media outlets in propagating this myth—with commercials like that for Lexus stating, "Whoever said money can't buy happiness isn't spending it right," and programs like The Learning Channel's (*Learning?* Are they serious?), *Jackpot! Overnight Millionaires* that present such a narrow and subjective perspective (in time and scope) on money that it is completely ridiculous—but it *is* sensational.

As a side, but related note, I have to mention one of E channel's most popular television programs, *Dr. 90210* (which does the same thing—propagating a myth, but on a much more dangerous level) propogates the idea that changing one's body (specifically breast augmentation surgery) will increase one's self esteem and happiness over the long term. No! Although you can find "research" that will say this relationship exists—published by the manufacturers of breast implants and breast augmentation surgeons within their own journals (e.g., Cash, Duel, & Perkins, 2002)—the consensus within the psychological research literature on this topic is that this relationship does *not* exist. In fact, the relationship appears to be as opposite to improving one's self-esteem as it can get. At the time of surgery, women receiving breast implants merely for cosmetic reasons are as physically healthy as women not receiving breast implants; however, following surgery, women receiving breast implants have a significantly higher mortality rate than women not receiving implants—and are significantly more likely to commit suicide (Brinton, Lubin, Cay Burich, Colton, & Hoover, 2001, 2006). Breast implants often lead to greater body dissatisfaction because after the surgery, women start to focus on *other* parts of their body that are not *symmetrical* like their man-made (yes, I do mean to say *man*-made!) breasts, or like some near-impossible-to-achieve cultural standard (Goldenberg, McCoy, Greenberg, Pyszczynski, & Solomon, 2000). But I digress—again. Sorry!

Need more evidence of the myth of money buying happiness? Since World War II, there has been a steady increase in economic growth and personal income in America. Americans today, on average, make nearly three times as much personal income as they did in 1957. The myth would predict if we all have more money, then we all should be happier… We are not. America today, controlling for inflation, has statistically the same percentage of people rating themselves as very happy and very unhappy as it did in 1957 (Myers, 2004, see **Figure 10**).

Figure 10. Wealth and happiness levels post WWII (Myers, 2004).

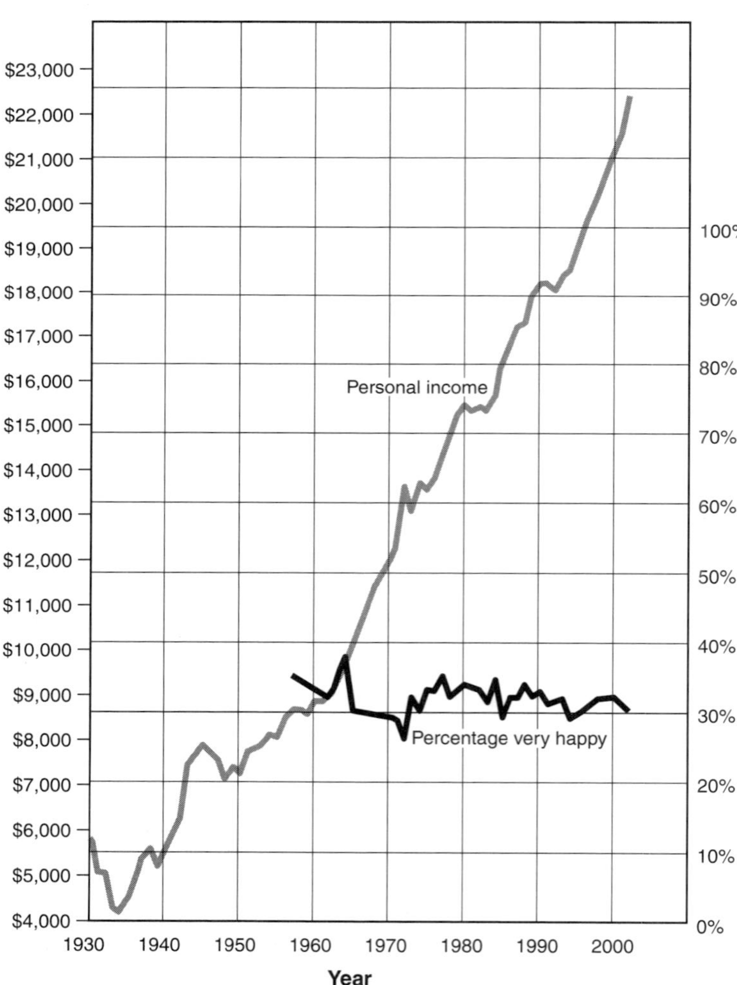

From *Psychology*, 8e by David G. Myers. © 2007 Worth Publishers. Used with permission.

So why do I include money in the recipe? Because it is important *below* and *at* the poverty line—if one's income level threatens having the basic human necessities (water, food, shelter), then having money (to overcome this threat) is predictive of happiness. Once above the poverty line (as of 2008, about $22,200 for a family of four in the U.S.), the relationship between money and happiness is negligible (Inglehart, 1990). A family of four in America making $30,000 per year *is* likely happier than a family making $10,000 per year. However, a family of four in America making three million dollars per year is likely *no* happier than the family making $30,000 per year. (Note: Money is unnecessary for any of the other nine ingredients within the recipe, Happiness and You.)

Money is insidious when it comes to happiness. When asked directly, "Do you think money brings happiness?" only 35% of people say yes (Lucas & Ancira, 2007); and 89% of people say "our society is too materialistic" (Wuthnow, 1998). However, the vast majority (74% to 80%) of people's primary reasons for their own higher education and career is money—well ahead of such reasons as developing a meaningful philosophy of life, helping others, becoming an authority (in their field), and raising a family (Sax, Lindholm, Astin, Korn, & Mahoney, 2001); and 84% of people wish they had more money (Wuthnow, 1998). When propagated outside of one's awareness, myths are at their most dangerous; when tied to happiness, money is most dangerous.

BRIEFLY, WHAT'S NOT IN THE RECIPE

I want you to recognize ingredients that many people *think* are associated with happiness, but are, in fact, not. Scientific research has *not* consistently found any of the following seven items to be associated with happiness: age (however, see David Blanchflower and Andrew Oswald's [2008] argument for happiness following a "U-shaped" pattern over the lifespan, with the youngest and oldest being happiest and the middle-aged, 40- to 50-year-olds, being the least happiest), gender (even though females are twice as likely to be diagnosed with clinical depression and males are four times as likely to commit suicide), ethnicity, intelligence, beauty/physical attractiveness, leisure, and family. Thus, generally speaking, the young are no happier than the old are. Men and women are not different when it comes to measuring happiness. No ethnic group is happier than any other is. The very intelligent are no happier than those with average intelligence are. Although the Halo Effect often causes physically attractive people to get away with and gain more from their environment (Nisbett & Wilson, 1977), they are no happier than physically average and unattractive people are. People at leisure and on vacation are relatively discontent when compared to people at work (Csikszentmihalyi & LeFevre, 1989). Parents are no happier than non-parents.

Correlation versus causation: Is this recipe going to work on me or not?

We already know the most significant—in proportion—of these ingredients is friendship, followed by acquaintances and general social relationships, extraversion, optimism, marriage, employment, religious spirituality, subjective physical health, democratic freedom, and money. So, if I just gave you these ingredients, weighted by their relative proportions, would you be happy? Well, let's go back to our cookbook analogy. If I gave you some flour, water, and yeast, would this guarantee that you'd be eating some good bread—or any bread at all, for that matter? By analogy, giving you each of the ingredients within the Happiness and You recipe would actually *not* guarantee happiness. As with making good bread—or bread at all—making happiness (as it relates to its recipe) is based upon *how* you use and combine the ingredients.

As I mentioned at the beginning of this chapter, the ingredients in Happiness and You are *correlated* (associated) with happy people—they do not necessarily *cause* happiness. In fact, there have been no major scientific *experiments* demonstrating any causative effect for these ingredients leading to happiness. Instead, *studies* seeking what factors are associated with happy people yielded these ingredients. Okay, you're probably asking at this point, "if the ingredients are only correlational, then why in the Hell did you include them at all?!"

Calm down… I included these ingredients for three reasons: First, I wanted to get you frustrated about the damn recipe even working! Did I succeed?

I'm kidding!

I actually made up this recipe for *only* two reasons: First, this *is* the current state of the scientific research on happiness—there isn't any more advanced research than what I've presented to you. Currently, correlational studies are where it is.

Second, happiness—certainly pleasure, and even contentment—are within these ingredients; however, the secret to finding these positive emotions is *not* only in the ingredients themselves—but instead, is in *how* these ingredients are combined and used. If traditional perspectives on positive emotions—which state these emotions are effects and not causes—guide the use and combination of the ingredients, then the recipe will result in nothing more than pleasure; or, at best, short-term happiness, and certainly not contentment. However, if a novel perspective on positive emotions, called Being Theory—which recognizes positive emotions can be causes *and* effects—guides the use and combination of the ingredients, then I predict the recipe will result in happiness, pleasure, and contentment.

How are you doing on forgetting what you learned about happiness in adulthood? Keep on forgetting…

ARE YOU READY FOR A REVOLUTION?

If you *are not* ready to go beyond the traditional and current perspectives on positive emotions and stand happiness on its proverbial head, and you do not feel like reading my drivel any longer, then good luck to you. As I stated near the beginning of this chapter, I'm sure your local Super Wal-Mart sells many of the ingredients within this recipe; buy them all, and use and combine them by your own judgment! A word of caution, though: as with acids and bases, all the ingredients within Happiness and You do *not* necessarily mix. Mixing these ingredients the "wrong" way will yield calamitous emotional consequences—sadness instead of happiness, pain instead of pleasure, depression instead of contentment....

If you *are* ready for a revolution—a revolution the scientific community may not even be *quite* ready for—then cut out the following recipe card and keep it near you, because we're going to be using it throughout the remaining parts of this book. In addition, fill out and score the SEA-weighting Instrument in **Figure 11**. The SEA-weighting Instrument will show you how many of these ingredients you already have in your own life. Instructions for filling out and scoring the instrument are included in the figure. We'll soon begin interpreting your score on the SEA-weighting Instrument. We'll also be discussing the SEA-weighting Instrument relative to happiness, pleasure, contentment, and true happiness, as we introduce Being Theory in more detail in the next chapter.

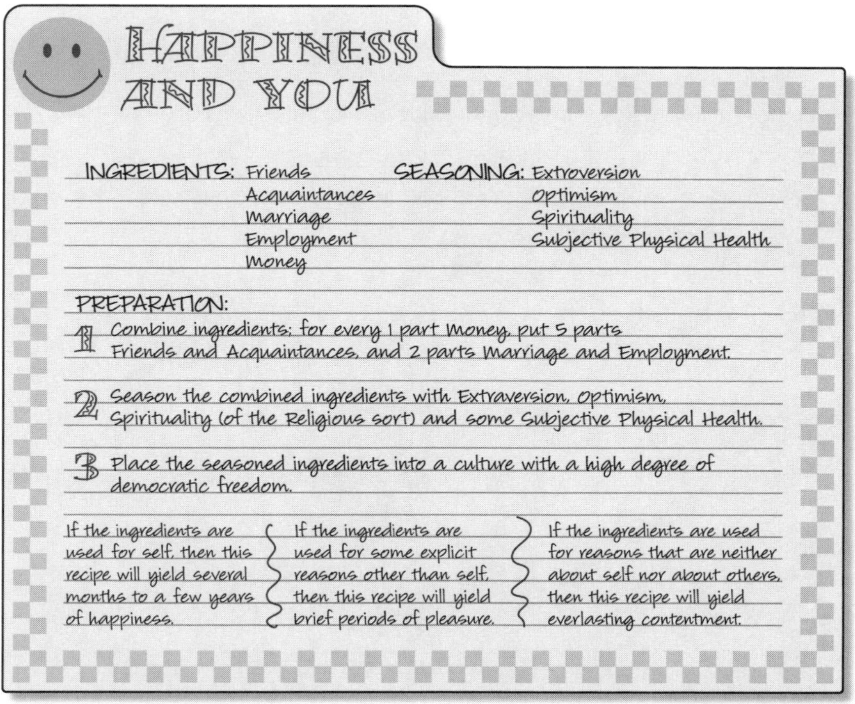

Figure 11. SEA-weighting Instrument.

Instructions: Answer the following 11 questions. Questions 3, 8, and 9 require additional instruments, found on the following pages.

1. On average, how many hours of sleep do you get per night? _____
2. On average, how many hours of exercise do you do per week? _____

3a. What is your overall score on the Empathy scale (see page 78)?

- a. Less than 5
- b. Between 5 and 8
- c. Between 9 and 12
- d. Greater than 12

3b. Do you have at least one good friend? Yes or No
If question 3b is "No," then skip to question 4a.

3c. If question 3b is "Yes," then how many good friends do you have? _____

4a. During your waking hours, during **weekdays**, what percentage of your time, on average, is spent with other people? _____ %

4b. During your waking hours, during **weekends**, what percentage of your time, on average, is spent with other people? _____ %

5. Are you happily married? Yes or No

6a. Are you employed? Yes or No
If question 6a is "No," then skip to question 7a.

6b. If question 6a is "Yes," then does your employment require you to work outside of your home? Yes or No

6c. If question 6a is "Yes," then do you enjoy being employed? Yes or No

7a. How many people, including yourself, live at your household? _____

7b. How much money (after taxes) does your household earn per year?

- a. Less than $20,650
- b. Between $20,650 and $100,000
- c. More than $100,000

8. What is your score on the Extraversion scale (see page 79)?
    a. Less than 17
    b. Between 17 and 24
    c. Between 25 and 32
    d. Greater than 32

9. What is your score on the Optimism scale (see page 80)?
    a. Less than 13
    b. Between 13 and 17
    c. Greater than 17

10a. Do you have faith in something greater than human existence, knowledge, and power? Yes or No

10b. What percentage of your time is devoted to helping others; for example, volunteerism?
    a. Less than 10%
    b. Between 10% and 30%
    c. Greater than 30%

10c. Do you attend church, synagogue, or mosque on at least a weekly basis? Yes or No

11. Using the following scale, how do you rate your general physical health? _____
    1. Very unhealthy
    2. A little unhealthy
    3. Neutral
    4. A little healthy
    5. Very healthy

Scoring instructions: Go to **Appendix Three** to score the SEA-weighting Instrument.

Empathy scale

For each item, indicate the degree to which the statement is self-descriptive using the following scale:

0	1	2	3	4
Does not describe me well				Describes me very well

____ 1. Before criticizing somebody, I try to imagine how I would feel if I were in their place.

____ 2. I sometimes find it difficult to see things from the "other guy's" point of view.

____ 3. When I see someone being treated unfairly, I sometimes don't feel very much pity for him or her.

____ 4. I am often quite touched by things that I see happen.

Scoring

- In scoring your responses, first reverse the numbers before statements 2 and 3 (i.e., 0 = 4, 1 = 3, 2 = 2, 3 = 1, 4 = 0). Then add the numbers in front of all four items to obtain a total score. The lowest total score is 0; the highest total score is 16. Higher scores indicate a greater capacity for perspective taking and empathetic concern (Bolt, 2004).

This scale is from Davis (1980).

Adapted from Davis, M.H. (1980). A multidimensional approach to individual differences in empathy," *JSAS: Catalog of Selected Documents in Psychology, 10,* 85–104. Reprinted by permission from the BMDS Literature Collection, PO Box 110287, Pittsburgh, PA 15232-0787.

Extraversion scale

Please write a number next to each statement to indicate the extent to which you agree or disagree with that statement.

1 = Disagree strongly   **2** = Disagree a little   **3** = Neither agree nor disagree

4 = Agree a little   **5** = Agree strongly

I see myself as someone who...

_____ 1. Is talkative.

_____ 2. Is reserved.

_____ 3. Is full of energy.

_____ 4. Generates a lot of enthusiasm.

_____ 5. Tends to be quiet.

_____ 6. Has an assertive personality.

_____ 7. Is sometimes shy, inhibited.

_____ 8. Is outgoing, sociable.

Scoring: Reverse your scores for questions 2, 5, and 7. Then simply add all the scores together.

Scoring Range: 8–40. Higher scores indicate more extraversion.

This scale is from John & Srivastava (1999).

Optimism scale

Respond to each statement using the following scale:

0 = strongly disagree **1** = disagree **2** = neutral **3** = agree **4** = strongly agree

____ 1. In uncertain times, I usually expect the best.

____ 2. If something can go wrong for me, it will.

____ 3. I'm always optimistic about my future.

____ 4. I hardly ever expect things to go my way.

____ 5. I rarely count on good things happening to me.

____ 6. Overall, I expect more good things to happen to me than bad.

To score yourself, first reverse the numbers you placed in answer to statements 2, 4, and 5. That is, for each of these items, change 0 to 4, 1 to 3, 3 to 1, and 4 to 0 (a 2 remains a 2). Leave the numbers in front of the rest of the statements unchanged. Then add up the numbers in front of all items to obtain a final score. Scores range from 0 to 24, with higher scores reflecting greater optimism. The average (mean) score is between 14 and 15 (Bolt, 2004).

This scale is from Scheier, Carver, & Bridges (1994).

Chapter Four

A New Look at an Old Phenomenon: Being Theory and Happiness

Happiness is fickle?

Before discussing how to use and combine the ingredients within the recipe Happiness and You, I have to get something off my chest because it has been bothering me for a long time—so please bear with me. Whenever my mother reads an article on happiness in a popular magazine or newspaper, she sends it to me. Since I've been studying happiness, she has sent me dozens of articles, and it is *frustrating*. No—my mother does not frustrate me. I love my mother, my mother loves me, and Freud has nothing to do with the wonderful relationship we have! What is frustrating is how fickle the articles she sends me are—fickle in as far as one article reporting *factor X causing happiness*, and then a different article, published the next week or month, reporting that same *factor X **not** causing happiness*, and then yet another article published the next week or month after that, reporting that same *factor X causing happiness*...

I imagine I'm not the only one frustrated by this fickleness. And this certainly happens with things other than happiness reported to the public. For instance, how many times have you read that multivitamins are good for you/bad for you; that milk is good for you/bad for you; that eggs are good for you/bad for you; that calcium for postmenopausal women is good for them/bad for them; that a glass of wine a day or antioxidants prevent cancer/don't prevent cancer; that jogging for your health is good for you/bad for you—the list goes on and on. What is most troubling to me, though, as a happiness scientist-practitioner, is that the reporters writing the articles are *not* the ones providing the content. If the reporters were providing the content, then I could easily ignore the fickleness for being intentionally sensationalistic to attract an audience and sell magazines or newspapers—I would be able to sleep at night. But, I cannot sleep at night. Most of the articles my mum sends me are interviews with the *actual* scientists doing the work in the field! To be fair, due to editing, interviews aren't often perfectly accurate. And the science of Positive Psychology is relatively new, and with any new science, there are bound to be controversies with its early development. However, this certainly should not include making empirically based predictions that are literally *opposite* to one another.

Right?

One example of this "opposite" fickleness is the relationship between money and happiness. The *Los Angeles Times* ran a story that said, "...recent research into happiness—or subjective well-being, as social scientists call it—reveals that beyond the surprisingly low level of about $15,000 a year, the link between economic growth and happiness evaporates. Americans are three times wealthier than we were half a century ago, but we are no happier" (November 13, 2006: *A Bigger Economy Doesn't Always Buy Happiness*). Only two weeks later, the *New York Times* ran a story on happiness that stated, "'There is overwhelming evidence that money buys happiness,' said Andrew Oswald, an economist with the University of Warwick" (November 27, 2006: *If You've Got the Money, Honey, You May Be a Little Bit Happier*). It is contrasting stories like these that lead my mother to email me and ask, "Well, Donnie, should I retire now and be (happy) depressed, or keep on working for the money to be happy (depressed)"?

Blame you—or should I blame "it"?

Who is to blame for such radical differences in the information presented to the public about happiness? Should we blame the newspaper reporters, its editors, or even its recipients, for buying the newspapers, and accepting this type of divergent reporting? Probably not, because the sad thing is, I find this fickleness in the *scientific* research literature, too. I have not dozens, but *hundreds*, of articles published in peer-reviewed research journals with data finding happiness related to age, gender, ethnicity, culture, marriage, family, religion, money, personality traits, etc.; and *not* related to age, gender, ethnicity, culture, marriage, family, religion, money, personality traits, etc.

So what does this mean? First off, this means you need to thank me. I did you a great service by weeding through the dense scientific research literature on positive emotions and finding the "real" factors related to happiness, the ingredients within the Happiness and You recipe.

Well? Are you going to thank me or not?

...

You're welcome.

Second, this means that maybe we should blame the scientists for this fickleness. Hell, blame me! To continue the example of the fickle relationship between money and happiness, maybe it can be simply explained by psychologist-scientists *not* having much money. (Take it from me—we don't!) So psychologists are certainly not going to design experiments that will yield results demonstrating that money is predictive of happiness, else they'd be showing themselves not to be happy. However, economist-scientists will design these experiments. Economists have money. And they love to make money worth more than it really

is—including being associated with happiness. For example, economists love to say, or at least try and make us believe, a country's Gross National Product or Gross Domestic Product (GDP) (the total goods and services a nation produces over a given period) is positively associated with happiness. Okay, it may be *associated,* but it certainly is not a causal factor—remember, everything that goes into the GDP includes such things as court costs associated with divorce, murder, and rape; war funds; and monies associated with hurricanes, tornadoes, floods, and other natural disasters—and guess what—whether you are Hitler or not, these things are *not* associated with happiness (Cobb, Glickman, & Cheslog, 2000).

You think I'm kidding about my supposition of blaming the natural biases of the scientists, don't you? Well, let's take a gander at what two prominent economists have to say about happiness. David Blanchflower of Dartmouth College and Andrew Oswald of the University of Warwick theorize happiness to be a bank—yes, a *bank.* Everything you do is relative to putting money in or taking money out of your happiness bank. For example, if you have a lasting marriage, Blanchflower and Oswald argue that is worth 100,000 happiness dollars per year in your happiness bank; if you have sex once or more a week, that is worth 50,000 happiness dollars per year in your bank. Blanchflower and Oswald never say whether or not you *have* to be having sex with your spouse to be earning these 50,000 happiness dollars; however, they do say divorce is worth 66,000 happiness dollars being taken *out* of your bank (Blanchflower & Oswald, 2004). So the fickle data in the research literature for the relationship between money and happiness may be simply explained by psychologist-designed studies *not* finding the relationship does exist; and economist-designed studies finding the relationship *does* exist. Blaming the scientists and their biases associated with being psychologists, economists, sociologists, biologists, etc., seems like a worthy explanation for such fickle data, if for not one problem: money isn't the only fickle factor associated with happiness. As I mentioned above, there are many fickle factors, and a scientist's natural biases cannot account for them all.

Maybe the root of the problem is not a "who," but an "it." Maybe the blame should go on the main theory driving the research studies. Most scientific studies on happiness today have the underlying assumptions that:

1. Happiness is an effect—that is, a result of you getting something or doing something, and
2. Happiness is not different from the positive emotions of pleasure and contentment.

So, the theories behind most studies on happiness surmise positive emotions, in general, result from some *thing* (money, age, ethnicity, friends, etc.). You know the routine. See Jimmie be an emotionless tabula rasa (blank slate). Give Jimmie some money (a thing or some other ingredient from Happiness and You). Now see Jimmie be *happy* (the *effect* or result of this thing). These theories predict I can "make" Jimmie happy by replacing money with any one of a variety of other things—for instance, the ingredients in our Happiness and You recipe. But how about these traditional theories about happiness are wrong? (Get ready to stand on your head.) How about happiness is actually a cause, not an effect? Thus, see Jimmie be happy—because Jimmie is happy, Jimmie gets money, and married, and friends, and faith, and employment, and optimism... How about money doesn't make Jimmie happy at all, but it instead brings him only pleasure or contentment? But can science really be this wrong about something as basic and important as our own happiness? If history tells us anything, the answer to this question is a resounding yes.

Classical Conditioning and Falling in Lust

Okay, start dreamscape sequence with *Twilight Zone* music; let's take a brief look back at arguably one of the most important scientific discoveries within the past 100 or so years of psychological research—and how initially fickle in result it was. It took nearly 50 years *after* Nobel Prize winning scientist Ivan Pavlov discovered classical conditioning (Pavlov, 1927) for other scientists (Harris, 1941) to figure out the conditional stimulus (CS, what is to be learned) must be presented *before* (see **Figure 12**, Classical Conditioning), *not after* (see **Figure 13**, Backward Conditioning) the unconditional stimulus (UCS, what is already learned) in order for *any* associative learning to result from classical conditioning. How important is associative learning? Most of what you've learned in this

Figure 12. Classical conditioning.

Classical Conditioning

Classical conditioning, occurring by nature or in the laboratory, can be broken down into three steps.

Step 1: Conditional Stimulus (CS; Quarter) → Conditional Response (CR; No Response)

The first step of classical conditioning demonstrates the CS to be neutral. The CS is anything within your environment that, when presented to you, will have no natural effect on your nervous system. In the laboratory, an experimenter will initially present the CS alone to a subject. This initial presentation of the CS will result in a CR of no reaction. For example, let's pretend I give you a quarter—and this is the first time you've ever seen money before. Your response—"Eh, what's this?"

Step 2: CS (Quarter) + Unconditional Stimulus (US; Hug) → Conditional/ Unconditional Response (C/UR; Good Feelings)

The second step of classical conditioning allows acquisition to occur. In the laboratory, the experimenter pairs the CS with a US. The US is anything within your environment that has an automatic effect on your nervous system. In the laboratory, the experimenter presents the CS to the subject first, and then after a short delay, presents the US to the subject. The pairing of the CS + US results in a C/UR of what the US naturally causes when presented by itself to the subject. Dependent upon what the CS and US are, the experimenter may present the CS + US pairing to the subject anywhere from only once to several hundred times. To continue our example from Step 1, let's say that every time I give you a quarter, I *follow* that with giving you a hug—and hugs unconditionally feel good to you.

Step 3: CS (Quarter) → C/UR (Good Feelings)

The third step of classical conditioning demonstrates learning has taken place and that the CS is no longer neutral. In the laboratory, the experimenter presents the CS alone to the subject. This presentation of the CS will result in a C/UR like that which occurred during acquisition. To finish our example from Step 1 and Step 2, I now give you only a quarter. Your response—"Hmm, I like money..."

Figure 13. Backward conditioning.

BACKWARD CONDITIONING

Backward conditioning, occurring by nature or in the laboratory, can be broken down into three steps.

STEP 1: Conditional Stimulus (CS; Quarter) → Conditional Response (CR; No Response)

The first step of backward conditioning demonstrates the CS to be neutral. The CS is anything within your environment that, when presented to you, will have no natural effect on your nervous system. In the laboratory, an experimenter will initially present the CS alone to a subject. This initial presentation of the CS will result in a CR of no reaction. For example, let's pretend I give you a quarter—and this is the first time you've ever seen money before. Your response—"Eh, what's this?"

STEP 2: Unconditional Stimulus (US; Hug) + CS (Quarter) → Conditional/Unconditional Response (C/UR; Good Feelings)

The second step of backward conditioning attempts to allow acquisition to occur. In the laboratory, the experimenter pairs a US with the CS. The US is anything within your environment that has an automatic effect on your nervous system. In the laboratory, the experimenter presents the US to the subject first, and then after a short delay, presents the CS to the subject. The pairing of the US + CS results in a C/UR of what the US naturally causes when presented by itself to the subject. Dependent upon what the US and CS are, the experimenter may present the US + CS pairing to the subject anywhere from only once to several hundred times. To continue our example from Step 1, let's say I give you a hug *before* every time I give you a quarter—and hugs unconditionally feel good to you.

STEP 3: CS (Quarter) → CR (No Response)

The third step of backward conditioning demonstrates no learning takes place and that the CS is still neutral. In the laboratory, the experimenter presents the CS alone to the subject. This presentation of the CS will result in a CR like that occurred during Step 1—no response. To finish our example from Step 1 and Step 2, I now give you only a quarter. Your response—"Eh, what's this?"

book—and in fact, your *life*, was through associative learning. It is why you eat at McDonalds (even though it certainly isn't good for you and you really don't like it), drink Coca-Cola (carbonated sugar water for a buck a can), and wear Nike *tennis* shoes (even though you haven't played *tennis* since you were six). In the simplest sense, just about everything you learn is based—at least in part—on things you already know.

Are you still not impressed with how important classical conditioning is? Well, how about this: Classical conditioning initiates most romantic relationships.

And it fools you into thinking you're in love with pleasure. If I may be so bold, let me ask you: What are you initially attracted to in a romantic partner? Before you answer, I'll tell you! (Am I being presumptuous or what?) Genetics mostly determine your gender and sexual orientation; however, genetics have very little control over the emotional, cognitive, and physical attributes you find appealing in romantic partners. You are attracted to certain scents, facial features, body types, and personalities because at sometime during your life experiences, these attributes were associated with things that unconditionally brought you pleasure. Today, you say, "Hubba-hubba" to a petite, thin, blonde woman or a tall, muscular, broad-shouldered man (or to both), because petite, thin, and blonde; and tall, muscular, and broad-shouldered were unconditionally associated with lust, sex, beauty, or love in your past. By manipulating these unconditional associations, I can show you how to make anyone fall in love with you. Yes, you heard me right—*make* any one fall in love with you.

Before I show you how you can do this, let's take a look at *exactly* what love is, and for that matter, what lust is, too.

Biologically speaking, lust is our basic, physiological reaction to some other person. We generally don't lust after people we've known for a long time; we direct lust towards someone new in our lives. This physiological reaction is directly associated with physical attraction, and may include an arousal in heart rate, blood pressure, sweat gland activity, and respiration rate. This is the so-called "butterfly-pitter-patter-firework effect," when you have "butterflies" in your stomach, your heart goes "pitter-patter," and you see "fireworks" whenever you are around that special someone. The autonomic nervous system—specifically, its sympathetic branch—drives this physiological arousal. The autonomic nervous system is a part of the peripheral nervous system, and as its name alludes to, its workings are mostly outside of our awareness and control. You really don't have to think about, nor are you aware of digesting food, blood flow to your periphery, breathing, your heart beating, your kidneys functioning, or your body cooling or heating itself. Under stressful conditions, the sympathetic branch of the autonomic nervous system is active; under non-stressful conditions, the parasympathetic branch of the autonomic nervous system is active (see **Figure 14**). So far, so good—but now it gets weird. Although there are only four possible categories of events—called the "4 Fs" (Feeding, Fighting, Flighting, and Sex)—that arouse the autonomic nervous system, the autonomic nervous system *cannot* determine what is arousing it. Because the autonomic nervous system doesn't have higher-order "thinking" brain centers, its physiological reaction is the same for a Whopper with cheese being fed to it, a boxer punching it, a lion chasing after it, or a lover embracing it. It never knows which "F" was the culprit. It takes the central nervous system's involvement, specifically the cerebral cortex, to determine if the cause of

Figure 14a. Sympathetic branch of the autonomic nervous system.

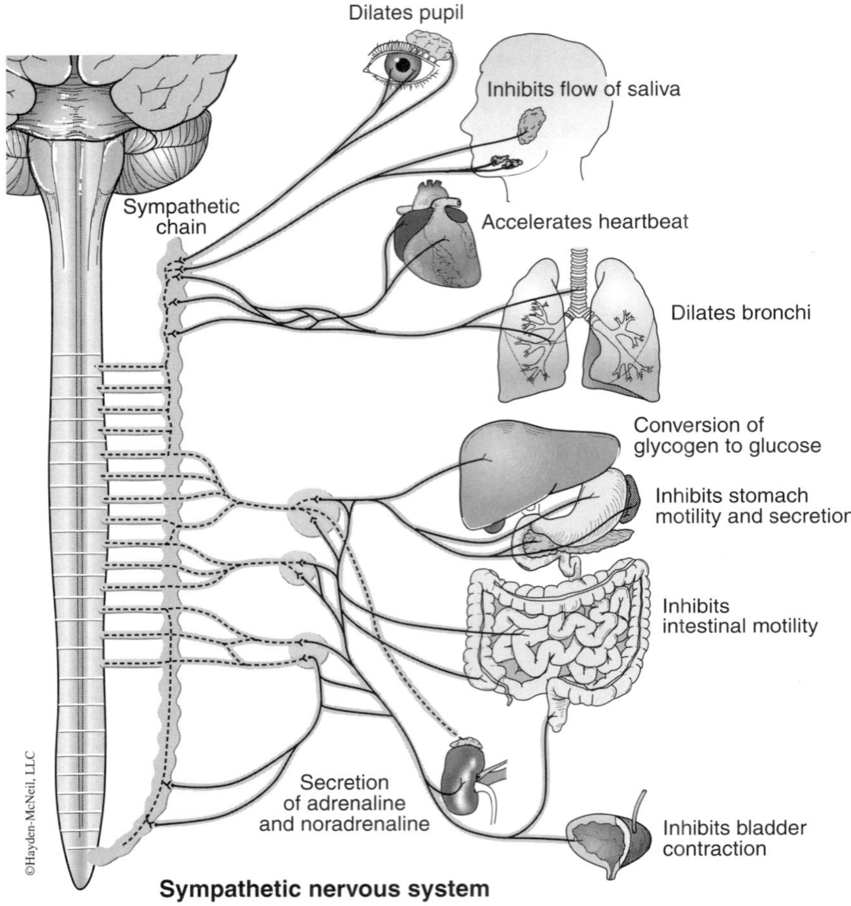

this arousal was feeding ("Mmm, broiled instead of fried"), fighting ("Ouch!"), flighting ("Run away!"), or sex ("I love you").

So let's make someone fall in love with you—let's make this someone a blind date. You go to pick up your date at his/her home. When he/she opens the front door, he/she looks you over and smirks. You quickly surmise that this was not a smirk of attraction, but instead, one of "oh-hum." You, on the other hand, are attracted to this person. The key to making this person fall in love with you is determining exactly *what* you're going to be doing on this date—and what you're going to be doing on this date needs to be increasing your "victim-of-love's" heart rate, blood pressure, sweat gland activity, and respiration rate. For instance, you may begin your date with a drive in your convertible—or better yet, on your motorcycle—to an amusement park, where you together ride a Ferris

Figure 14b. Parasympathetic branch of the autonomic nervous system.

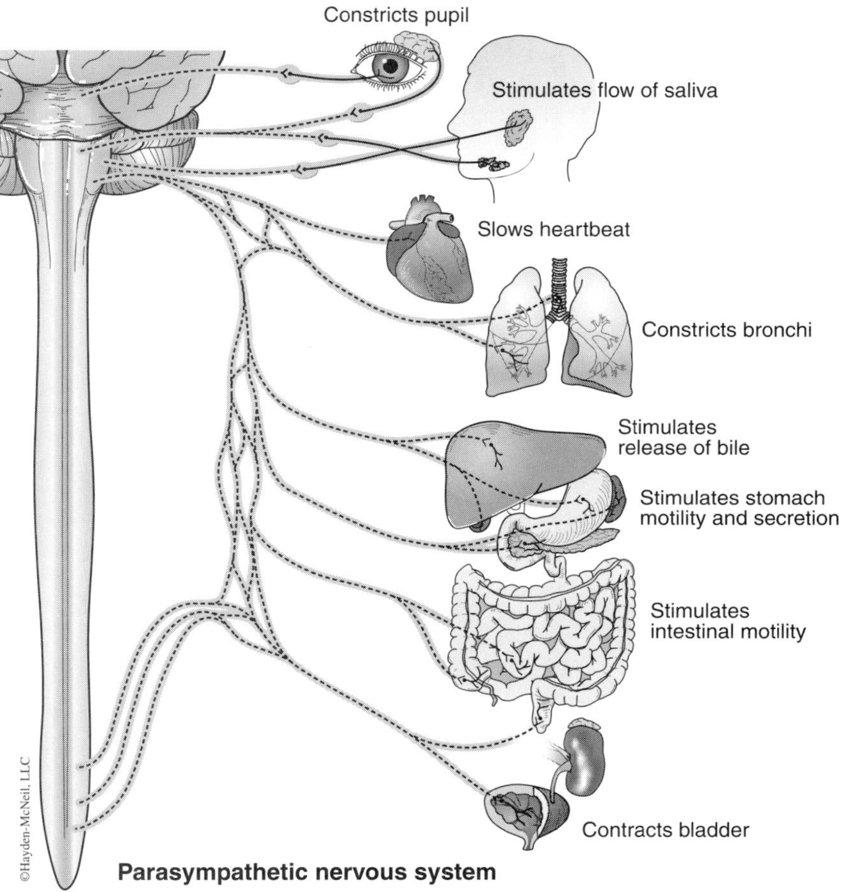

wheel, several roller coasters, and lots of bumper cars. Next, you drive to a movie theater and watch a horror film, then you drive to the nearest big city for a late-night bite to eat at a restaurant atop the tallest building in the city. Every big city has a restaurant like this; for instance, Atlanta has the Sun Dial rotating atop the 73-story Westin Peachtree Plaza building, Chicago has the Signature Room at the 95th perched near the top of the John Hancock building, San Antonio has the Tower of Americas Restaurant rotating atop the 750-foot Tower of Americas, and Seattle has Sky City rotating atop the 605-foot Space Needle. Before ending your date, you take a nice, quiet, leisurely stroll through a peaceful park. Remember, part of the key to making your victim-of-love fall in love with you is doing each of these things within close visual proximity. By the end of the date, your victim-of-love will be doing anything but smirking at you. I promise.

Now, using what we know about classical conditioning and the physiology of lust and love, let me explain what is happening to your victim-of-love. First, you are the conditional stimulus within the classical conditioning paradigm. How's it feel to be a conditional stimulus? When you first meet your victim-of-love, he/she didn't automatically react to you in a positive or negative fashion. He/She merely smirked. So consider your interaction with your victim-of-love at his/her door to be **step 1** in the classical conditioning paradigm (see **Figure 15**). Next, you selected what you would be doing and where you would be going on your date, based solely on increasing your victim-of love's physiological arousal. Driving in a convertible, riding on a motorcycle, going on a Ferris wheel, riding roller coasters, riding bumper cars, being frightened by a movie, and eating at "high altitude" are all unconditional stimuli within the classical conditioning paradigm. So consider the activities you did with your victim-of-love to be **step 2** in the classical conditioning paradigm (see **Figure 15**). Last, you systematically selected how to end the date—in a nice, quiet place, where *you* are the most prominent and obvious part of your victim-of-love's environment. So consider this quiet time with only you and your victim-of-love to be **step 3** in the classical conditioning paradigm (see **Figure 15**). In **step 3**, you, instead of the unconditional stimuli from **step 2**, will be causing the sympathetic branch of your victim-of-love's autonomic nervous system to become aroused. The facts of the matter have the two of you walking together, your victim-of-love being aroused, and he/she knowing *you* are causing this arousal. Your victim-of-love may interpret this arousal from you in three different fashions:

Victim-of-love's interpretation one: "This arousal is a residual from the earlier events of the date; it doesn't have anything to do with the person I'm with right now."

Victim-of-love's interpretation two: "This arousal is negative; the person I'm with right now is causing me pain, like that associated with being hungry (Food) or frightened (Flight or Fight); I can't wait till this person gets away from me."

Victim-of-love's interpretation three: "This arousal is positive; the person I'm with right now is causing me to be attracted to him/her (Sexual); I'm falling in love with the person I'm with right now."

The Excitation Transfer Theory and thirty-seven years of research showing evidence for it (e.g., Meston & Frohlich, 2003; Zillman, 1971), tells us what interpretation your victim-of-love is most likely to take—interpretation three, "I feel tingly and oogly all over—I want him/her." Thus, the Excitation Transfer Theory posits that classical conditioning makes people fall in lust (pleasure), but also leaves them—unknowingly—with the false impression that lust is the basis of love (happiness); see **Vicious Cycle One** on page 35. On average, *lust, infatuation, and falling in love* last about 6 to 9 months (pleasure); *being in love*

Figure 15. Classical conditioning and the Excitation Transfer Theory: Let's go out on a blind date.

Step 1

Conditional Stimulus (CS; You) → Conditional Response (CR; Smirk)

Step 2

CS (You) + Unconditional Stimulus (US; Drive in a Convertible) → Conditional/Unconditional Response (C/UR; Feelings of Exhilaration)

CS (You) + US (Drive on a Motorcycle) → C/UR (Feelings of Exhilaration)

CS (You) + US (Ride on a Ferris Wheel) → C/UR (Feelings of Exhilaration)

CS (You) + US (Rides on Roller Coasters) → C/UR (Feelings of Exhilaration)

CS (You) + US (Rides on Bumper Cars) → C/UR (Feelings of Exhilaration)

CS (You) + US (Eating at Altitude) → C/UR (Feelings of Exhilaration)

Step 3

CS (You)→ C/UR (Feelings of Exhilaration—Love)

lasts about 5 to 9 years (happiness). As a note of interest, the average length of a marriage before divorce in the United States is 8.2 years; and *loving* lasts forever (contentment). We will get back to this discussion of lust and love later in this chapter when we explicitly define pleasure.

Thus, for about 50 years, findings on classical conditioning and associative learning were fickle—with some reports replicating Pavlov's initial results and others showing *no* conditioning to occur by his method. Might Positive Psychology in general, and happiness in particular, have the same type of fickle roots as classical conditioning theory? If this were true, it would affect studies examining happiness by making seemingly objective causes of happiness fickle—like the results currently found within the popular and scientific literature.

SCIENCE IS AT ITS BEST WHEN IT PROVES OUR INTUITION WRONG

Because of its inadequate theories about happiness, the scientific research literature on happiness may be caught in vicious cycles, like those we often get caught in when searching for our own positive emotions. As described in **Chapter Two**, Vicious Cycle One describes people doing pleasure-inducing activities and mistakenly believing these activities will bring them happiness. Vicious Cycle Two describes people doing happiness-inducing activities and mistakenly believing these activities will bring them contentment. And Vicious Cycle Three describes people doing contentment-inducing activities and mistakenly believing these activities will bring them pleasure or happiness. Contemporary theories about happiness cannot recognize these vicious cycles, because contemporary theories about positive emotions infer happiness, pleasure, and contentment are a single, amorphous positive emotion called subjective well-being or "happiness."

Our own language reinforces this error. How many times have you had conversations with friends, family, colleagues, etc., about what brings you *happiness*—I'm going to assume a lot. But now let me ask you this—how many times have you had conversations with others about what brings you *pleasure* or *contentment*? I'm going to assume few—at least, far fewer than the number of conversations you've had about happiness. In fact, if we were to examine English speakers and their frequency of using these three terms, we would find the terms *happiness* and *happy* are used 5.26 more times than the term pleasure; and 7.32 more times than the terms content and contentment (Carroll, Davies, & Richman, 1971). For those of you who are curious about how negative emotions stack up to happiness: the terms happiness and happy are used 2.63 more times than the terms sadness and sad; 4.84 more times than the term pain; and 25.38 more times than terms depression and depressed (Carroll, Davies, & Richman, 1971).

I propose that we are really not talking about happiness that many more times than pleasure and contentment—but instead confusing contentment and pleasure for happiness. Let's talk about sex for a moment, shall we? Sex is actually a good analogy of this fundamental problem of confusing one positive emotion for another. Let me be clear: we certainly talk a lot about sex—usually in indirect and comical fashions—but we rarely talk about sex as it relates to our own contentment or pleasure. Instead, if at all, we associate it with happiness. Think for a moment about the number of conversations that you had about "happiness," but were really about pleasure or contentment. For example, you may ask a friend about her new boyfriend: "Is he making you happy?" When you really mean to say, "…with all the sex you two are having, how's the pleasure?" Indeed, our own vernacular concerning "happiness" may be actually about pleasure or contentment, thereby causing such fickle results.

Studies of happiness may be doing this same type of thing—confusing one concept of positive emotion for another (Haybron, 2007; Veenhoven, 2001). As an example, let's pretend **Study A** reports factor Y causes happiness (relative to its operational definition of happiness); however, **Study B** reports the same factor Y does *not* cause happiness (relative to its different operational definition of happiness). Fickle results again—Argh! But wait, we now have a worthy explanation for these fickle data. It could simply be because **Study A** actually is measuring happiness (relative to its operational definition of happiness), whereas **Study B** is really measuring pleasure (relative to its *different* operational definition of happiness) or vice versa.

With our new explanation for the fickle happiness results in mind, let's revisit money's relationship with happiness. If I designed a study to measure the relationship "happiness" has with money by operationally defining the relationship as "how *you* spend *your* money for sex, alcohol, and food," I would likely find *no relationship* to exist between money and your happiness because this operational definition of happiness (basic needs and wants) is more about your *pleasure* than your *happiness*—confusing pleasure for happiness is analogous to Vicious Cycle One, described in **Chapter Two**. If I designed a study to measure the relationship "happiness" has with money by operationally defining the relationship as "how you spend your money on acquaintances, friends, and spouses," I would likely *find* a relationship to exist between money and happiness, because this operational definition (social networks) is associated with your happiness. Lastly, if I designed a study to measure the relationship "happiness" has with money by operationally defining the relationship as "how you randomly give your money away;" I would likely find *no relationship* to exist between money and happiness, because this operational definition of happiness (giving) is more about your *contentment* than your happiness—confusing contentment for happiness is analogous to Vicious Cycle Three, described in **Chapter Two**.

These three hypothesized studies of the relationship between "happiness" and money, fickle in result, make clear that a *legitimate* theory of happiness—whether it be your own or science's:

1. Must *not* define happiness as only an effect; instead, it must allow happiness, as well as other positive emotions, to be effects *or* causes,
2. Needs to objectively distinguish happiness from other types of positive emotions; specifically, pleasure and contentment.

In order to meet these needs, we have to find some "thing" that objectively differs among happiness, pleasure, and contentment. There are plenty of subjective things—things that differ from one individual to the next. But are there any objective things—things that are exactly the same for one individual to the next? One answer comes in the form of time. Time is objective. And people's perceptions of time differ relative to experiencing each of these emotions. When experiencing pleasure, people overestimate time; when experiencing contentment, people underestimate time; and when experiencing happiness, people are relatively accurate in their estimates of time. For a similar time distinction, see Philip Zimbardo's **time perspective theory**, which suggests all of a person's experiences are filtered through that person's perspective of his/her future, present, or past (Gonzalez & Zimbardo, 1985). I argue, controlling time controls whether a person is experiencing happiness, pleasure, or contentment.

I know, I know what you're saying: "Uh, control time Dr. Don? That sounds easy—not! Egad!" Don't worry; I have a method to do this. Being Theory models this method. The goal of the remaining parts of this chapter is to teach you about time and then show you how Being Theory uses time to objectively decipher among happiness, pleasure, and contentment. I promise, by the end of this chapter you'll have the ability to control time and your positive emotions; and you'll know exactly how to apply the Happiness and You recipe.

CALVIN AND HOBBES © 2010 Watterson. Dist. By UNIVERSAL PRESS SYNDICATE. Reprinted with permission.

Time and space

Let's talk about Einstein, so we can sound smart. Seriously, Einstein's theories have led to our current definitions of time. So let's begin our discussions about time by using Einstein's definition and description of the physical world as an analogy to a definition and description of the *psychophysical* world. The physical world is anything that is corporeal and the psychophysical world is composed of emotions, behaviors, thoughts, and perceptions; and is anything psychical within *corporeal* space. The definition of the psychophysical world—or psychophysics—should sound familiar, because psychophysics—the science that measures the relationship between things that are psychical (mind) and things that are physical (body)—is the root science of psychology. The physical world has both time and space, according to Einstein. In one of his most famous papers, *On the Electrodynamics of Moving Bodies*, published in 1905, he supposed that neither time nor space is absolute. Instead, time is relative to space, and space is relative to time. There is interdependency and intertwining of time and space: without time there is no space, and without space there is no time—when time changes, so does space, and when space changes, so does time. Thus, anything that you can describe or think of that changes relative to time (let's say, you aging) will have some change relative to space (you wrinkling, losing your hair, and your bones decreasing in density).

The psychophysics of space: Voice within language

Let's take Einstein's idea of time being relative to space into the psychophysical world, and suppose our *perception* of time is relative to our *perception* of space. While stuff like baryonic matter, dark matter, and dark energy—that I'm sure you're familiar with—inhabit space within the world of *physics* (Turner, 1990), language—spoken, written, or otherwise—occupies space within the world of *psychophysics*. Nouns and verbs make up language, with nouns defined as people, places, and things, and verbs defined as the actions associated with people, places, and things. Do you feel like you're in first grade again? Don't worry, whether you like it or not, I'll be getting you to graduate school and beyond in just a few paragraphs, so stay with me! Nouns are *corporeal* objects; verbs are *not*. Are you starting to see the analogy? Nouns represent things; verbs represent no *thing*. "I am writing," "I am talking," "I am typing," "I am thinking," "I am confusing"; each of these statements is about me—a person—and each of these statements reveals something about me—but you only know something about me, that it is me at all, from the (pro)noun, "I." The verbs "writing," "talking," "typing," "thinking," "confusing," reveal nothing about me; you do not know what or why or how I'm writing, talking, etc. Verbs are in fact nothing, they do not represent any *corporeal* objects: not people, not places, not things, but they do exist; they exist as action, and action by itself does not exist corporeally within psychophysical space.

Grammatically, we use nouns and verbs within language through voice. Voice refers to whether a sentence's subject is performing (i.e., active voice) or receiving (i.e., passive voice) the action taken by its verb (Hacker, 2006). If a sentence's subject (i.e., people, places, and things) is performing the action taken by its verb, then one's focus is likely on the verb (i.e., action) and not on the subject. Conversely, if a sentence's subject is receiving the action of the verb, then one's focus is likely on the subject. For example, "Dr. Don had written a book," is a sentence written in active voice. When reading this sentence, you primarily focus on or attend to the verb "written." Whereas "A book was written by Dr. Don" is a sentence written in passive voice. When reading this sentence, you primarily attend to the proper noun "Dr. Don." Thus, passive voice composes more psychophysical space than active voice, because passive voice puts more attention on nouns (the subject) than verbs. Following Einstein's lead again (when space changes, time changes), we can suppose that when voice changes (from passive to active and then back again or vice versa), so should our perception of time.

Are you still with me? Let's take a breather with a little experiment to show evidence for (or against) our supposition of voice's effect upon the perception of time. In the experiment, we have two groups of individuals read a story. One group reads a story that is written with somewhat of a passive-voice slant (51%

of the story's sentences are written in passive voice; 49% of the story's sentences are written in active voice), whereas the other group reads the same story context-wise (shift in voice need not alter the context of a sentence, Haegeman & Gueron, 2000), but written mostly with an active-voice slant (10% of the story's sentences are written in passive voice; 90% of the story's sentences are written in active voice).[1] After reading their respective stories, measures of the differences between how long an individual perceived it took to read the story and how long it actually took to read the story are taken. Following Einstein's general supposition that any changes in space will thereby cause changes in time, and more specifically his supposition of time dilation—as speed increases, time decreases[2]—we should expect the time perceptions of those individuals reading the active-voice story to be significantly less than: (a) the actual amount of time it took for them to read the story, and (b) the time perceptions of those individuals reading the passive-voice story.

If our hypotheses are true, the results of this experiment would objectively quantify the influence voice has on our perception of time—as voice becomes "more active," then our perception of time slows. Of course, our perception of time is likely never to slow to the extent of stopping by using active voice within language, because language is never purely active. This fact, however, does not take away from our comparison between Einstein's suppositions about time and space and our current hypothesis about our own perceptions of time and voice; if anything, it makes the comparison between the two that much more robust, for neither perfect active voice nor perfect motion (i.e., perfect speed, achieving the speed of light) can be achieved. Because of the infinite amount of mass that would be created by achieving the speed of light, it stands as a theoretical impossibility. See **Figure 16**, which shows function of voice (passive to active) relative to perception of time (slow to fast).

---

1 Ideally, there should be the same percentage of active-voice sentences within the active-voice-story condition as the percentage of passive-voice sentences within the passive-voice-story condition. However, realistically, upon developing a passive-voice-story condition it is very difficult to have any more passive-voice sentences than the actual number mentioned (51%) without losing the story's meaning. This is not to say the context of the story would have changed by increasing the percentage of passive-voice sentences; this is to say the actual sense and meaningfulness of the text would have been lost.

2 Einstein supposed the closer a person gets to traveling at the speed of light (186,000 miles per second), the slower time becomes for this person *relative* to some other person, place, or thing not traveling at this speed—time slowing due to motion is called time dilation. (For empirical evidence supporting this supposition see Allie, 1975.) With greater speed comes the compression of space; and as space is compressed, so too is time slowed. The analogy of this space compression within the psychophysical world is language becoming more active in voice—less about context (passive voice) and more about action (active voice).

Figure 16. The effect active and passive voice has on perception of time.

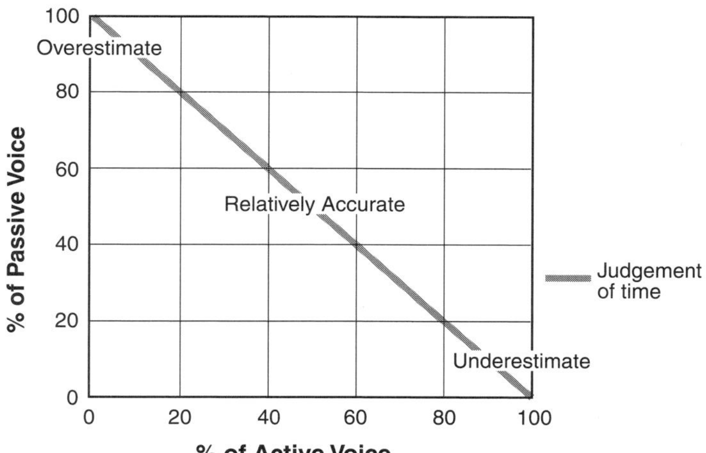

> Jacob was in love with Rachel and said, "I'll work for you seven years in return for your younger daughter Rachel." Laban said, "It's better that I give her to you than to some other man. Stay here with me." So Jacob served seven years to get Rachel, but they seemed like only a few days to him because of his love for her.
>
> (Genesis 29:18–20)

TIME FLIES WHEN YOU'RE HAVING FUN

So what does this "psychophysical time dilation" have to do with happiness, pleasure, and contentment? I completed a version of the above-described experiment (Lucas, Lloyd, & Magaloni, 2005). The experiment my colleagues and I completed was like the one just described, with one exception: instead of measuring individuals' perceptions of time, we measured participants' affective satisfaction levels (i.e., "...how do you feel after reading the story?"). We found both groups (passive voice and active voice) affectively satisfied following their readings—reading, in general, is associated with being satisfied or content (writing is, too—more on this later), but one group was significantly more content than the other was. Care to guess which group was the most content? The group that read the story with the active-voice slant was the most content—this group was significantly more content than the group that read the story with the passive-voice slant. But how did reading have an effect on these individuals' levels of contentment? Voice has an impact on individuals' perceived changes of time and their positive emotions because of *observer perspective*. As mentioned in **Chapter One**, there are three possible observer perspectives: endotelic—relative to Self; exotelic—relative to Environment; and autotelic—relative to Action. Passive voice varies relative to Selfish and Environmental perspectives, and active voice varies relative to the Action perspective. Pay attention, my friend; this is one of the most important parts of this whole dang book—the details about observer perspective!

Ready?

Observer perspective is your conscious (or unconscious) perception of who/what is in control of your life circumstances. You take one or more (of a possible three) observer perspectives in every life circumstance.

THE THREE OBSERVER PERSPECTIVES

1. Endotelic. Endotelic is the fancy way to describe this observer perspective, but let's not be fancy anymore. Let's use the less fancy but more descriptive word to describe this perspective—**Selfish**. This observer perspective is relative to and controlled by *you*. You *want* selfish experiences—you *like* selfish experiences. For example, "I want to get a raise at work" is a selfish observer perspective on working and money, because the person perceives the control (the desire) in his/herself. Contrast this with the statement, "I need to get a raise at work," which is an exotelic/Environmental perspective on working and money, because the person perceives the control (the necessity) in some thing outside of his/her control.

2. Exotelic. Exotelic is the fancy way to describe this observer perspective, but let's again not be fancy anymore. Let's use the less fancy but more descriptive word to describe this perspective—**Environmental**. This observer perspective is relative to and controlled by the environment. The environment is people, places, and things *outside of your intentional control.* You *have to* do environmental experiences. For example, "I shop because my wife makes me" is an environmental observer perspective on shopping, because the person doing the shopping (no relation to me!) perceives the control in some other entity besides himself—and that entity is his wife. With this example, you are probably wondering if a person can be confused about which exact observer perspective he/she is having relative to a life circumstance. And the answer is yes—people can be, and quite often are, confused about interpreting their observer perspectives—hence the publication of this book! ☺ So the husband in the previous example may be saying, "I want to be shopping with my wife," an obvious Selfish observer perspective, but in reality this is the last place he wants to be (he wants to be any place else) and knows in his heart of hearts this is the place he has to be (if he wants to be married for longer than 8.2 years). This "observer-perspective confusion" is the primary case of *happiness confusion.* Thus, not only may people be confused or wrong about interpreting their observer perspectives, these observer perspectives may be outside of people's immediate conscious awareness.

3. Autotelic. Autotelic is the fancy way to describe this observer perspective, but let's use the less fancy, but more descriptive word to describe this perspective—**Action**. This observer perspective is relative to the *experience* itself. Neither you nor the environment is in control of the action experience. You do these experiences for no other reason than the experience itself. "Let's go out to eat"—it doesn't matter where, when, how, or even if you're hungry—the key to this statement is the experience of eating itself. My children and I like playing a game we coined "Monster" in the swimming pool. The goal of the game is simple: my children have to "topple the monster." In other words, they have to get me on my back. In the (numerous) times we've played this game, they've never toppled the monster. They certainly try, but Rayen's and Sember's combined weight is no match for the monster's weight (and then some). But guess whether they enjoy—heck, *love*—playing Monster, even though they've never met their goal. Guess whether they want to play Monster every time I set foot in the pool—even though they've never met their goal? Guess how motivated they are to play this game? Even though… Okay, I think you get my point. The motivation that comes from action-based goals can take you a long way—such a long way that non-action based goals are more likely to be achieved secondarily. Let's pretend you're climbing Mount Everest—Okay—BOOM! You *are* climbing Mount Everest. Let's also pretend you're climbing Mount Everest not because you want to get to the top (selfish) or even because of the fame and fortune it will bring (environmental); instead, you're climbing Mount Everest (or could be climbing just about any other mountain) for the mere sake of climbing. In an action sense, as long as you're climbing, it doesn't matter if you get to the top or not. One more guess—guess whether you are likely to get to the top because you are focusing on action-based goals instead of non-action based goals?

Since I told you reading has an impact on emotions, I should also tell you that writing has an impact on our emotions, too. Research has demonstrated writing in two different manners leads to positive psychological and physical benefits. One manner is writing a gratitude journal. A gratitude journal is a diary of sorts, in which you write in every day (or at least once per week) about the people, places, and things that you are grateful for. The more detailed and introspective your writing is—that is, writing in active voice, and explaining *why* you're grateful—the greater the benefits. These benefits include making you happier and increasing your levels of physical energy (Emmons & McCullough, 2003; Sheldon & Lyubomirsky, 2006). The other manner is writing using the Pennebaker expressive writing paradigm (Pennebaker, 2006). The Pennebaker expressive writing paradigm, as described by Laura King (2001), is simply writing for 20 minutes about your best possible future self. Imagine everything goes right for you in the coming years—all your hard work pays off—what would your life look like relative to family, friends, employment, etc.? Again, this writing should be detailed and introspective while being overly optimistic. People who write in this fashion for four consecutive days gain significant increases in happiness (King, 2001). Writing in an intentionally positive manner has lasting beneficial effects on your emotions—and in **Chapter Six**, I'll show you how this type of writing is associated with living longer!

An Empirical Demonstration of the Three Independent Observer Perspectives: Let Science Show Us

You've been working hard—learning a lot of new information about reading, writing, and happiness in a very short amount of time. I think it is time for a break—what do you think? I say we take a break and go on a bike ride. The bike ride I'm thinking of will combine psychophysical time dilation and the three just-mentioned observer perspectives. Doesn't this sound fun? On this bike ride, our perception of time and positive emotions will be relative to ourselves, our bikes, the park we may be riding in, other people within the park, and any number of a thousand other people, places, and things a bike ride may bring. The three observer perspectives are interdependent of one another and may be shifting among the three possible observer perspectives (selfish, environmental, and action) during (and then re-defining) the experience. Keeping the potential for observer-perspective shift in mind, the people, places, and things we are exposed to during our bike ride are defined relative to whatever observer perspective we may have of them:

1. **Selfish.** Relative to self, we may be saying (implicitly or otherwise), "I like bike riding," "I want to go bike riding," or "Bike riding is enjoyable."
2. **Environmental.** Relative to environment, we may be saying (implicitly or otherwise), "I ride my bike because my doctor has recommended this activity for my cardiovascular health," "I have to go bike riding," or "My bike costs $2,000; I'd better use it!"
3. **Action.** Relative to having the experience itself, we may be saying (implicitly or otherwise), "I'm exercising," "I'm riding," or "I'm bicycling."

As the people, places, and things associated with our bike ride change relative to the three observer perspectives, so too should our perception of time:

1. Selfish. If we took a mostly selfish-observer perspective, we would be relatively accurate in our judgments about the amount of time passing from experience inception to experience completion (i.e., bike ride beginning to ending). The positive emotion we would likely be feeling when taking a selfish perspective is happiness; if negative, then we would likely be sad. At ride ending, when asked about the amount of time the bike ride took (actual time: 30 minutes), if we took a selfish-observer perspective, then we'd most likely report the bike ride lasting about 30 minutes and, if we were feeling positive, say something like "I liked it"; and if negative, "It saddened me to find out how out of shape I am..."

2. Environmental. If we took a mostly environmental-observer perspective, we would overestimate the amount of time passing from experience inception to experience completion (i.e., bike ride beginning to ending). The positive emotion we would likely be feeling when taking an environmental perspective is pleasure; if negative, then we would likely be in pain. At ride ending, when asked about the amount of time the bike ride took (actual time: 30 minutes), if we took an environmental-observer perspective, we'd most likely report the bike ride lasting significantly more than 30 minutes and, if we were feeling positive, say something like, "I felt good;" and if negative, "I was in a lotta pain out there."

3. Action. If we took a mostly action-observer perspective, we would underestimate the amount of time passing from experience inception to experience completion (i.e., bike ride beginning to ending). The positive emotion we would be likely feeling when taking an action perspective is contentment; if negative, then we would be likely depressed. At ride ending, when asked about the amount of time the bike ride took (actual time: 30 minutes), if we took an action-observer perspective, then we'd most likely report the bike ride lasting significantly less than 30 minutes and, if we were feeling positive, "I could have gone on forever;" and if negative, "...that could have gone on forever."

FLOW AND THE ACTION-OBSERVER PERSPECTIVE—ONE AND THE SAME?

A comprehensive review of the psychology research literature will yield all of the just-described observer perspectives (e.g., see Csikszentmihalyi, 1990 for environmental and action; Gibson, 1979 for action; James, 1890 for environmental and selfish; Rotter, 1966 for environmental and selfish; Skinner, 1974 for environmental; Tulving, 1983 for selfish; Watson, 1928 for environmental). However, no one has recognized putting these perspectives together to build a single theory to define positive emotions—until now.

Being Theory uses these three observer perspectives in combination with perceived time to objectively measure and distinguish happiness, pleasure, and contentment. The environmental-observer perspective by itself is like the classic Behaviorist school of thought within psychology, which states control is within someone (or something) other than self (i.e., external locus-of-control); and the selfish-observer perspective by itself is like the classic Cognitive school of thought within psychology, which states control is within self (i.e., internal locus-of-control). Because these two schools of thought have been at the basis of the science of psychology since nearly its inception, the observer perspectives associated with these schools need no further explanation here. However, if you would like to learn more about a school of thought (Functionalism) that incorporates both the environmental- and selfish-observer perspectives, then read William James' (the Father of American Psychology) *Principles of Psychology* (1890)—a book that is as relevant today in its theories of human behavior as it was nearly 120 years ago.

Because psychology has only recently addressed the action-observer perspective, it deserves further explanation. Mihaly (pronounced, ME HI) Csikszentmihalyi (pronounced, CHICK SENT ME HIGH) and his theory of flow have brought the most attention to the "autotelic experience" as being worthy of scientific inquiry. You may be familiar with, or even have read, Csikszentmihalyi's 1990 best-selling book on the topic, *Flow: The Psychology of Optimal Experience.* In Csikszentmihalyi's description and definition of flow, he explicitly uses the word autotelic to show what flow is: "...a particular type of experience...so engrossing...that it becomes autotelic, that is, worth doing for its own sake..." (1999, p. 824); "The key element of an optimal experience is that it is an end in itself" (1990, p.67); in fact, he actually uses the words—flow and autotelic—interchangeably: "The autotelic experience, or flow, lifts the course of life to a different level" (1990, p. 69); "My own addition to this list is the concept of the autotelic experience, or flow, and of the autotelic personality" (1999, p. 824). Further, Csikszentmihalyi uses the word "exotelic" to show what flow is not: "...activities done for external reasons..." (1990, p. 67). Csikszentmihalyi does not *explicitly* use the word endotelic or selfish, although he does discuss "motives" as they relate to "intrinsic...considerations" (1999, p. 824).

An autotelic or action experience is indeed what Csikszentmihalyi says it is: any activity having a purpose in itself (*Webster's Ninth New Collegiate Dictionary*, 1985); an exotelic or environmental experience is indeed what Csikszentmihalyi says it is, too: any activity done for reasons beyond one's intentional control; and, although Csikszentmihalyi does not mention it explicitly, an endotelic or selfish experience is any activity done for reasons within one's intentional control. However, like other scientists not recognizing the differences among happiness, pleasure, and contentment, Csikszentmihalyi does *not* make (or recognize) the distinction among these types of experiences in his definition of flow. Instead, he uses a combination of these experiences to define and describe flow, which makes flow anything but a model for "autotelic" experience—it makes flow a model for "mixed" experiences. Csikszentmihalyi's own words show this lack of distinction. Being Theory does not make this mistake; Being Theory recognizes the observer perspectives as being different from one another. Csikszentmihalyi starts erroneously combining observer perspectives in his initial example of what an "autotelic" experience is in the book, *Flow: The Psychology of Optimal Experience*:

> Teaching children in order to turn them into good citizens is not autotelic… (1990, p. 67).

So far, so good—this is correct; indeed, this is actually an example of an environmental experience—rules, laws, statutes, mores, etc., outside of one's self and mostly beyond one's control, define a "good citizen." But then he says:

> …whereas teaching them because one enjoys interacting with children is (autotelic; 1990, p. 67).

This is incorrect. This is an example of a selfish experience—"one enjoys" is defined relative to self and one is in control of the activity—in order for this to be an autotelic experience, the line would have to be changed to something like: …whereas teaching them *for the experience of teaching* is. If teaching children is going to be an autotelic/action experience, then one must be teaching for the experience of teaching alone—or, to put it in Csikszentmihalyi's own words (1990, p.67), "…an end in itself," not because of external influences ("good citizens") or internal influences (one's own enjoyment).

Csikszentmihalyi then goes onto to describe flow as having features that are *selfish*, "…we do feel in *control* of our actions, masters of our own fate." (1990, p. 3); "Because optimal experience depends on the ability to *control* what happens in consciousness moment by moment…" (p. 5); "…the way is through *control* over consciousness." (p. 22); "…freely invested to *achieve* a person's *goals*…" (p. 40); "…as long as *we are in control* of what is happening to us." (p. 108), as well as features that are *environmental*, "…is the ability *to find rewards* in the events of each moment." (1990, p. 19); "…activities that are goal-directed and *bounded by rules*." (p. 49). (Italics added.)

The paradoxes of flow ≠ A model of positive emotions

Because **Flow Theory** mixes observer-perspective definitions, it is incapable of distinguishing between any of the experiences interdependently associated with these perspectives. Csikszentmihalyi appears to recognize this fundamental problem when he reports equivocal data that the single-mindedness of Flow Theory cannot explain. In one instance, he states, "This brings up one of the paradoxes of flow: one has to be in control of the activity to experience it, yet one should not try to consciously control what one is doing" (1999, p. 825). This is *not* a paradox when one recognizes the observer-perspective experiences as being different from one another. In this instance, the "paradox" can be simply explained by an observer-perspective shift between a selfish, "in control," experience and an action, "not try to consciously control," experience. Thus, any one experience is likely to have some percentage of selfish-, environmental-, and action-observer perspectives within it. Repeat: any one experience is likely to have some percentage of selfish-, environmental-, and action-observer perspectives within it. However, this is beyond a paradox, and better described as being impossible, when one jumbles these three observer perspectives together as Flow Theory does.

In another instance, Csikszentmihalyi reports:

> One of the most common descriptions of optimal experience is that time no longer seems to pass the way it ordinarily does...in general, most people report that time seems to pass much faster. But occasionally the reverse occurs: Ballet dancers describe how a difficult turn that takes less than a second in real time stretches out for what seems like minutes: "Two things happen. One is that it seems to pass really fast. I see that it's 1:00 in the morning, and I say: 'Aha, just a few minutes ago it was 8:00.' But then while I'm dancing...it seems like it's been much longer than maybe it really was." (1990, p. 66).

Csikszentmihalyi explains this paradox by saying, "The safest generalization to make about this phenomenon is to say that during the flow experience the sense of time bears little relation to the passage of time as measured by the absolute convention of the clock" (1990, p. 66). This may be the "safest" thing to say, but it is not an accurate thing to say. Csikszentmihalyi cannot see this phenomenon for what it really is, because Flow Theory "ties" his hands together. This phenomenon really involves two different types of experiences: one environmental, "a difficult turn" and one action, "dancing." As we have already seen in our discussions of time earlier in this chapter, when people are in action experiences (e.g., reminiscing with a long-lost friend), they lose track of time—time passes fast; and when people are in environmental experiences (e.g., the dentist is pulling out an impacted molar!), then time passes slowly. When we model this as Being Theory does, using two observer perspectives, the phenomenon is easily explainable. When we model the phenomenon from a flow perspective, it is equivocal and as Csikszentmihalyi puts it, a "paradox."

In yet another instance, Csikszentmihalyi discusses the "paradox of work."

> In our studies we have often encountered a strange inner conflict in the way people relate to the way they make their living. On the one hand, our subjects usually report that they have had some of their most positive experiences while on the job. From this response it would follow that they would wish to be working, that their motivation on the job would be high. Instead, even when they feel good, people generally say that they would prefer not to be working, that their motivation on the job is low. The converse is also true: when supposedly enjoying their hard-earned leisure, people generally report surprisingly low moods; yet they keep on wishing for more leisure. (1990, pp. 157–158).

Again, because Flow Theory so narrowly defines positive emotions, it doesn't allow Csikszentmihalyi to see this work phenomenon for what it really is—anything but a paradox, and instead, a combination of observer perspectives. As we found in **Chapter Three**, work (employment) is associated with happiness; leisure is not—however, as a part of the development of Happy Ignorance (**Chapter Two**), people are environmentally taught the stereotypical reverse, that work *is not* associated with happiness and leisure *is*. By late childhood/early adolescence, this environmental training has selfish effects—people start saying aloud that they *don't like* work and that they *do like* leisure. In spite of this environmental training and selfish "understanding," work situations still yield more action perspectives than leisure situations. Thus, people's senses are not fooled—during work situations people are aware of the positive, action emotions—and report it as so; during leisure situations people are aware of the lack of positive, action emotions—and report it as so. However, before and after these situations, people's selfish-observer perspectives of these situations kick in and they report the opposite as what they actually experienced. This is not a paradox; this is a perfect example of the second part of *happiness confusion*: pleasure (leisure) makes you believe you want happiness, when all you really want is contentment (work). This is also a nice example of observer perspectives being outside of our immediate awareness.

Mihaly's misunderstandings

A clue as to why Csikszentmihalyi defines flow in the way that he does is in his statement, "Of course, we never do anything purely for its own sake. Our motives are always a mixture of intrinsic (selfish) and extrinsic (environmental) considerations" (content within parentheses added; 1999, p. 824).[3] This statement shows Csikszentmihalyi doesn't really believe in autotelic/action experiences, and is stuck in the traditional Cognitive (intrinsic) and Behaviorist (extrinsic) schools of thought. Apparently, Csikszentmihalyi has never just "shot the shit," gone for a car drive without intended destination or reason, stopped to smell the flowers—no matter if they were weeds or roses—or done something just for "the Helluvit." All kidding and vulgarisms aside, Csikszentmihalyi's own data (more than 10,000 interviews) show hundreds of examples of human behavior *without*

3 Another reason why Csikszentmihalyi may be defining flow the way he that he does (by mixing observer-perspective experiences together) relates to the purpose of the present paper—Csikszentmihalyi fails to distinguish among the positive emotions of happiness, pleasure, and contentment. He switches amongst the emotions and groups them together as if they mean the same thing (e.g., "...pleasure and happiness as the touchstone..." [p. 821, 1999]; "...pleasure and happiness would come from increased affluence..." [p. 821, 1999]); these emotions are distinguished from one another through recognition of the observer-perspective experiences being interdependent of one another.

intrinsic or extrinsic motives: "My hand seems devoid of myself, and I have nothing to do with what is happening" (1999, p. 825); "I am totally absorbed in what I am doing" (1999, p. 824); "Perception and understanding have come to a stop and spirit moves where it wants" (1990, p. 150); "What I care about is the Way, which goes beyond the skill" (1990, p. 150); "I may be flying a complicated airplane, rushing through space, but in this cabin I'm surrounded by simplicity and thoughts set free of time" (1990, p. 206)...

Csikszentmihalyi's bias may come from his linear, stimulus-response approach to behavior: in responding to criticisms on his theory of flow, he addresses one of his critics in an *American Psychologist* article by saying, "In human psychology it is quite common for causes also to be consequences and vice versa" (2000, p. 1163). This antiquated approach to behavior requires a stimulus (whether it be intrinsic or extrinsic) in order for an organism to have a response or behave (see **Figure 17a**). However, we've already seen with the modeling of the facial-feedback hypothesis in **Chapter Three** (**Figure 6**), this approach doesn't coincide with how humans or other higher-order, biological organisms actually behave (Powers, 1973)—most biological systems (e.g., the peripheral and central nervous systems, the endocrine system, the immune system, and the hormonal system) are best modeled using, nonlinear, negative-feedback (control) systems (Campbell & Reece, 2005; Martini, 2006). From a control-theoretic perspective (Powers,

Figure 17. Linear **(a)** and negative **(b)** feedback models of behavior.

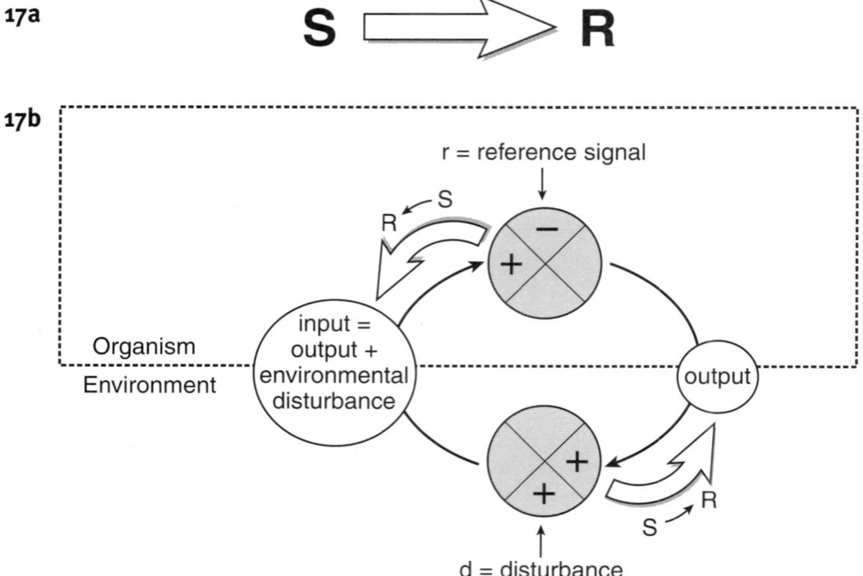

1973; 1989), the stimulus-response approach is associated with secondary, reflexive behavior, whereas what the organism is primarily—or intentionally—doing is controlling his/her perceptual input (i.e., environmental disturbances [stimuli: intrinsic and extrinsic stimuli] + organism output [behaviors]). In order for this control to occur, it does *not* require an intrinsic or extrinsic stimulus; mere output (autotelic, action, activity, "doing") from the organism (and possibly changing reference signals, what the organism wants) is enough to allow for perceptual control (see **Figure 17b**). Whoa! That's a mouthful. What exactly did I just say? Well, let's first thank Csikszentmihalyi, and then we'll break down exactly what a "control-theoretic perspective" to behavior is relative to Control Theory.

THANK YOU

Csikszentmihalyi has done the science of psychology a great service by bringing attention to the autotelic/action experience; however, Flow Theory does not capture the autotelic/action experience as an independent human experience. Being Theory does. Being Theory distinguishes among selfish, environmental, and action experiences. Being Theory *uses* the three observer perspectives in combination with perceived time and voice in a control-theoretic framework to objectively measure and distinguish happiness, pleasure, and contentment.

It is quiz time again! Let's see if you've learned anything else (good) yet. Here it is...

◇ Quiz

1. **A Self Awareness Test measures happiness by assuming:**
   a. That your friends know more about your happiness than you do.
   b. That you know more about your own happiness than anyone else.
   c. The grass is always greener on the other side of the fence—especially when there's a sewer on the other side.

2. **Social comparison theory shows, one way to make yourself happy is:**
   a. To compare your own personal attributes to someone who has personal attributes that are more than your own.
   b. To compare your own personal attributes to Oscar Madison.
   c. To compare your own personal attributes to someone who has personal attributes that are less than your own.

3. **A Memory Test measures happiness by assuming:**
   a. That memories of your past have an impact on your present happiness.
   b. That memories of your past have no impact on your present happiness.
   c. That your memory lasts longer than a fish's.

4. **Which of the following areas of the brain is most associated with being happy?**
   a. That little thingamajig just above my ear.
   b. The right frontal lobe.
   c. The left frontal lobe.

5. **Consuming dark chocolate is associated with increasing:**
   a. My waistline.
   b. Oxytocin—a hormone associated with "feeling good."
   c. Nestles' profits.

You'll find the answers in **Appendix Four**. Well? How did you do? If you didn't score a perfect 5 again, I want you to go back to page 1 and re-read....

Finally!

As I said in **Chapter One**, it seems a book about happiness, pleasure, and contentment should actually define exactly what these terms mean. Well, I think you're finally ready for some definitions—not because you've learned enough yet (you can always learn more!), but because I believe you've forgotten enough about the definitions of happiness you've developed since childhood. So, without further ado, here are working definitions of happiness, pleasure, and contentment.

Happiness. Happiness varies relative to our selfish-observer perspective. It is mostly within our intentional control—that is to say, happiness is mostly controlled by higher-order faculties within our central nervous system, and is dependent to varying degrees upon our self-esteem, autonomy, hope, optimism, extraversion, subjective health, self-respect, and self-control. As mentioned in our recipe from **Chapter Three**, friendships, marriage, social relationships in general, spirituality/religiosity, and work are some of the categories of research that are most associated with happiness. Joy, enjoyment, jubilation, glee, and delight may be words we use to describe our happiness. Happiness is based centrally and is associated with higher-order centers of the brain and is mostly lateralized within the left hemisphere (e.g., left temporal, left pre-frontal, and left frontal lobes; Lane, Reiman, Bradley, Lang, Ahern, Davidson, & Schwartz, 1997; Pelletier, Bouthillier, Levesque, Carrier, Breault, Paquette, Mensour, Leroux, Beaudoin, Bourgouin, & Beauregard, 2003, see **Figures** 7 and **18**). Due to the adaptability and plasticity of the brain, happiness is objectively fleeting, but nowhere, as we will see, in terms of pleasure's short life: happiness-inducing stimuli such as jobs, religions, friends, faiths, spouses, and one's weight may induce happiness for several weeks to years before habituation is complete (see **Figure 19a**). Habituation occurs for even winning the lottery! As I mentioned before, giving you $100,

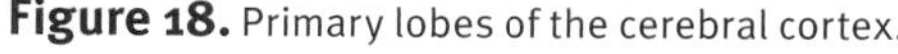
Figure 18. Primary lobes of the cerebral cortex.

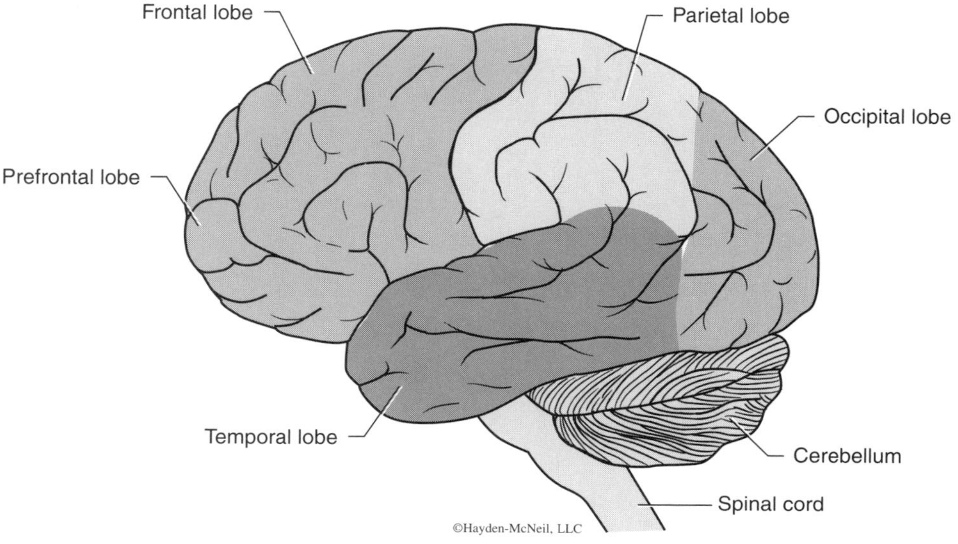

$100,000, or even $1,000,000 may put a smile on your face for a moment or two, *but it ain't gonna last,* and we both know, eventually, you'll be asking me for more!

Philip Brickman and his colleagues at the University of Michigan studied lottery winners and found within a year after winning the lottery, the winners were no happier than they were before winning the lottery, and many of the winners were actually unhappier than they were before the lottery. Based on these results, Brickman modeled happiness as a treadmill (The Hedonic Treadmill; Brickman & Campbell, 1971; Brickman, Coates, & Janoff-Bulman, 1978), similar to **Vicious Cycle Two**, described in **Chapter Two**. Imagine running on a treadmill, and as you are running, the treadmill begins to incline slowly, so you'd have to run faster and faster in order to stay in the same place on the treadmill; else you'd be falling off. By analogy, in order for you to keep the same level of happiness, you'll need to be doing more and more of whatever you're currently doing for happiness. Thus, if work brings you happiness, then as with the inclining treadmill, you'll have to work more and more in order for work to continue bringing you happiness. Further, the hedonic treadmill predicts that the greatest happiness comes from the newest things (things you've most recently met or obtained); the least—if any at all—happiness comes from the oldest things (things that you've known or possessed the longest). Thus, one thing that people will do to get happiness from something that has been bringing them happiness for an extended period (e.g., a spouse) is replace it (e.g., an extramarital affair).

Figure 19. Habituation timelines for happiness- (19a), pleasure- (19b), and contentment- (19c) inducing experiences. X-axis equals time; Y-axis equals level of the particular positive emotion.

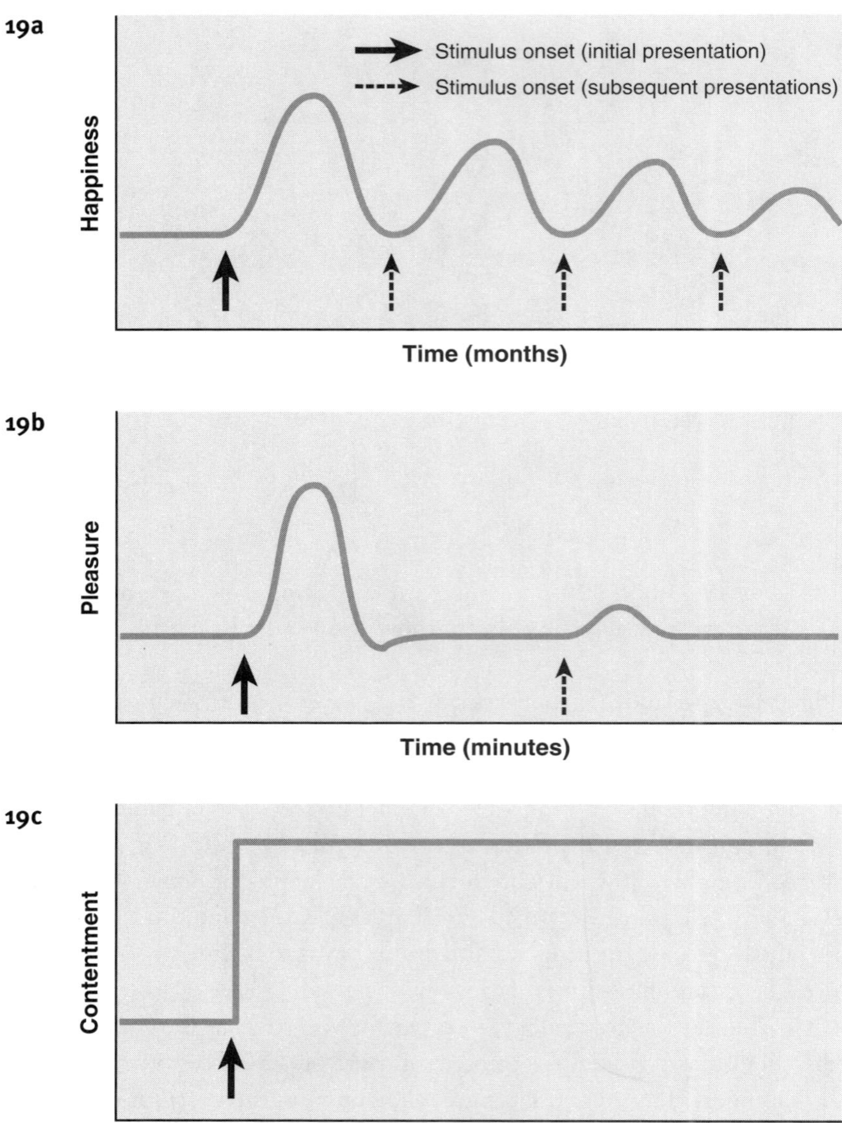

For example, when a job is "getting old," you can go onto the next job…and the next job, and the next job, and the next… Or, if a relationship is "getting old," then you can get into a new relationship…and then another new relationship, and then another… Does this sound like anyone you know—maybe even yourself? The hedonic treadmill, combined with excitation transfer, leaves us with the fact that whomever you are currently with is the one person you are least likely to be (pleasurably) attracted to. The point is that you can attempt to get happiness from not only the ingredients that compose the Happiness and You recipe, but also from just about anything you set your mind to. However, within the recipe or not, you will habituate to *whatever* thing brings you happiness.

> Blessed is the man who expects nothing, for he shall never be disappointed.
>
> (Alexander Pope)

Selecting, and ultimately, achieving goals causes this above-described habituation. For example, a person may set a series of short- and long-term goals at work:

"I want to get my current work project completed within the next week."

"I want to start a humanitarian-giving campaign at work within the next month."

"I want to get a raise before the end of the year."

"I want to get a promotion within three years."

The person's level of happiness will directly vary relative to how close he/she is to completing the goals. The closer the person is to achieving a goal, the happier he/she will be. However, this phenomenon does not occur in a simple, linear fashion because once a goal is achieved, levels of happiness quickly drop off. People are often surprised to find out that what brought on happiness was not actually achieving the goals, but instead was working towards them (see **Figure 19a**). With this habituation comes the human's want (more complex than need) for more of the happiness-inducing things or goals. However, working towards the same goals is not likely to bring happiness again, and if it does, it will be at a significantly reduced level. As the brain develops a tolerance for a drug it is repeatedly exposed to (an example of pleasure), so too will the brain develop a tolerance for happiness-inducing things that come in contact with it repeatedly.

Happiness is a higher-order, learned emotion. Ontogenetically and phylogenetically (a fancy word meaning development *between* the species), happiness is likely the newest of the three described emotions. Animals are likely to be contentment and pleasure seeking, but not happy. Happiness is based upon morals and ethics. (With morals defined as how *you* judge experiences relative to being right or wrong, good or bad—morals are only relative to *you*; your pure conscience.

Ethics are defined as how organizations that you're a part of judge experiences relative to being right or wrong, good or bad—ethics are only relative to the organizations you're involved in. For example, you're not born with rules, laws, or commandments; instead, all these ethical concepts are associated with organizations such as families, churches, religions, governments, professions, sports, etc.) Thus, what brings on happiness is individually and culturally specific.

Within the laboratory or within your own experiences, happiness is reliably distinguished from pleasure and contentment based upon:

1. It taking a selfish-observer perspective.
2. You accurately estimating the length of time the experience lasts.
3. You slowly, but surely, adapting to the emotions associated with the experience.

The opposite of happiness is sadness. Thus, all that was just discussed about happiness may be discussed about sadness but with dilatory effects—that is, a negative (–27 to –1) SEA-weighting score.

> How strange would appear to be this thing that men call pleasure! And how curiously it is related to what is thought to be its opposite, pain! . . . Wherever the one is found, the other follows up behind.
>
> (Plato, *Phaedo*, fourth century B.C.)

Pleasure. Pleasure varies relative to our environmental-observer perspective. It is mostly outside of our intentional control—that is to say, pleasure is mostly controlled by our peripheral nervous system; lower-order forms of our central nervous system (e.g., the various parts of the limbic system: amygdala, cingulate gyrus, fornix, hippocampus, hypothalamus, thalamus, mammillary body, pineal gland, and the pituitary gland, see **Figure 20**); and other people, places, and things. Bliss, ecstasy, rapture, elation, and euphoria may be words we use to describe our pleasure. Feeding, sexual behavior, and, to a lesser extent, sleeping, are the most studied objective behaviors associated with pleasure. Because pleasure is based at the periphery, specifically, the muscles and sensory end organs (i.e., eyes, ears, skin, nose, and tongue), it is objectively fleeting. We quickly adapt to pleasurable sights, sounds, caresses, flavors, kisses, smells, "runner highs," etc. (see **Figure 19b**), and thereby no longer "feel" the pleasure they originally brought us. With this swift adaptation comes our *need* (more basic than want) for *more* of the pleasure-inducing stimulus, whether this stimulus be another person (e.g., we demand more from our lover so that he/she can make us feel like he/she "used to" make us feel), a place (e.g., we need to ride the roller coaster three, four, five... times in a row to gain the exhilaration we used to gain from a single ride), or a

Figure 20. The structures of the limbic system.

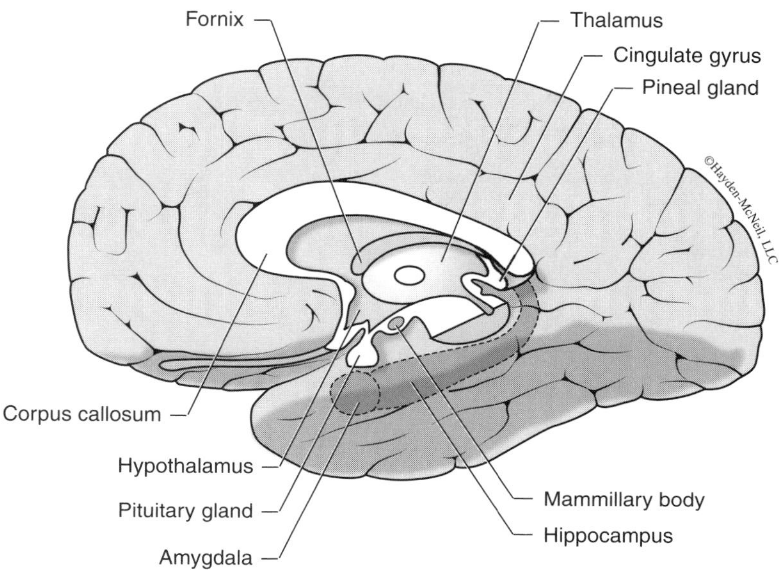

thing (e.g., we need to drink six, seven, eight…cans of beer to get that "buzz" we used to get from drinking a single can).

In addition to gaining more of the pleasure-inducing stimulus, there is another method we can use to get the "original pleasure" back. This method involves getting *different* pleasure-inducing stimuli. So, we don't demand more from our lover—we just simply replace him/her with another; we don't go repeatedly on the same roller coaster, we find another one to ride; and we no longer merely drink alcohol, we smoke some weed instead. Replacing one pleasure-inducing stimulus for another may be the most natural method of getting our "original pleasure" back. This may be best illustrated by the Coolidge Effect. The Coolidge Effect comes from a story about Calvin Coolidge (the 30th President of the United States) and his wife. This story may or may not be true—but if it isn't, it should be! A farmer was leading Mr. and Mrs. Coolidge on a tour of a government-owned chicken farm. Mrs. Coolidge recognized with all the chickens on the farm, there appeared to be only one rooster. She confirmed her observation by asking the farmer, "How many times a day does that *one* rooster perform his 'duty'?" "Dozens," the farmer replied. With a wink of her eye Mrs. Coolidge asked the farmer to share this information with Mr. Coolidge. The farmer did just that, and when he did, Mr. Coolidge thought for a moment, then asked the farmer, "Does the rooster get a *new* hen each time to perform his 'duty'?" "Yes," the farmer replied. With a wink of his eye—Mr. Coolidge asked the farmer to share this information with Mrs. Coolidge (Bermant, 1976).

The Coolidge Effect occurs not only in chickens, but in most other higher-order organisms—including humans. The Coolidge Effect directly affects the refractory period following an ejaculation/orgasm. For a man, the refractory period is the time between ejaculations—which, by the way, are mostly controlled by the spinal cord; for a woman, the refractory period is the time between orgasms—which, by the way, are mostly controlled by the brain. Although the refractory period is generally different for a man and a woman (the man's is longer; the woman's is shorter and may even be zero—i.e., multiple orgasms), the refractory period is physiologically alike for a man and a woman in it increasing in length of time with each new ejaculate/orgasm. That is, with each new ejaculation/orgasm, we quickly adapt to the pleasure-inducing stimulus, and require more of that stimulus (a longer period of time) in order to ejaculate/orgasm again. For example, if a man and a woman were having sexual intercourse, and the man ejaculates for the first time, it may take him 10 or 20 minutes before he is able to ejaculate again with her. In order for him to ejaculate a third time with her, the refractory period may be 30 or 40 minutes in length. In order for him to ejaculate a fourth time with her, it will likely take him over an hour. The steady increase in the length of the refractory period between subsequent ejaculations/orgasms occurs for women as well (Lester & Gorzalka, 1988). The Coolidge Effect keeps the length of the refractory period the *same* between subsequent ejaculations/orgasms. The Coolidge Effect does this through having a *new* mate for each ejaculation/orgasm. There appears to be no limit to pleasure brought on by this method (Beamer, Bermant, & Clegg, 1969).

Pleasure and how long it lasts is ironic because it is often rationally clear to us that the experiences brought about by pleasure-inducing stimuli are objectively fleeting in (physical) time; however, our perception (in psychophysical time) about the amount of time these experiences last (and the length of time they will continue to have a positive effect after the experience has passed) is often overestimated. For example, although any single human orgasm actually lasts only between 10 and 30 seconds (Levin & Wagner, 1985), people likely report "...that orgasm lasted *forever*!" As another example of this, notice how two people who are "falling in love" with one another talk about one another, "We'll be in-love *forever*!" "It is as if we've known one another *forever*!"

Pleasure is a lower-order emotion that is by nature; thus, it will rarely be completely inhibited by any of the higher-order (i.e., central nervous system: the brain and spinal cord, especially the frontal and temporal cortices) faculties. Because pleasure is by nature, it (by itself) is neither moral nor immoral. Nor is pleasure ethical or unethical. What gives you pleasure is likely to give pleasure to any other human being in any other culture.

> The beauty I *feel* relative to my peripheral nervous system today, will be the beauty I *describe* relative to my central nervous system tomorrow. (Me)

One of the clearest examples of the temporal characteristics of pleasure is associated with "catching a glimpse" of a new love. As I mentioned in describing the Excitation Transfer Theory, early within passionate, romantic relationships, lover's autonomic nervous systems sympathetically respond to something as simple as the lovers seeing one another. Lovers often interpret these responses as evidence for the potential of a long-term relationship, when in fact these responses are evidence for sensory adaptation—they eventually diminish or disappear. This is a perfect example of **Vicious Cycle One**; people get stuck doing pleasure-inducing activities (sex) with the false intention of these activities leading to happiness (long-term relationship). As counterintuitive as this may be, the truth of the matter is (*the truth hurts!*), possessing attributes associated with pleasure (e.g., sexual appeal) is not at all predictive of possessing attributes associated with happiness (social adeptness, optimism, friendliness).

Within the laboratory or within your own experiences, pleasure can be reliably distinguished from happiness and contentment based upon:

1. It taking on an environmental-observer perspective.
2. You overestimating how long the experience lasts.
3. You rapidly adapting to the emotions associated with the experience.

The opposite of pleasure is pain. Thus, all that was just discussed about pleasure may be discussed about pain but with dilatory effects—that is, a negative (–27 to –1) SEA-weighting score.

> If you want to improve, be content to be thought foolish and stupid. (Epictetus)

Contentment. Contentment varies relative to our action-observer perspective. It is not necessarily within or outside of our control—that is to say, contentment is not dependent upon our self or *other* people, places, or things. Fulfillment, satisfaction, and gratification may be words we use to describe our contentment. Contentment is beyond, or "a propos," pleasure and happiness—it is action or activity and not a *thing.* Since there is nothing (no people, places, or things) for the peripheral or central nervous system to adapt or habituate to (because there is no one *thing* within activity), contentment by itself is satisfying. If we were to "find" contentment within the brain, we would likely find it within the corpus callosum or (anterior and posterior) commissures, which connect the left and right hemispheres of the brain. Thus, contentment is not lateralized to any one hemisphere of the brain. Contentment is objectively enduring because it is *about* the nervous systems (see **Figure 19c**). With no adaptation or habituation comes no need for us to seek more contentment-inducing things. Our perception about the amount of time an action experience lasts, and how long we will continue to have positive effects from the experience after the experience has passed, is most often underestimated because there is nothing within the action experience that time can be relative to. Any *specific* action can induce or be associated with contentment: digging, painting, running, talking, thinking, driving, walking, learning, torturing, teaching, writing, building, etc. Contentment transcends our rational understanding of morality and ethics, and is therefore neither (im)moral or (un)ethical. For example, from a moralistic (selfish-observer) and ethical (environmental-observer) perspective, the actions of "killing" and "saving" are radically different from one another; from a strict action-observer perspective, a person is just as likely to be content with either one of these actions. Contentment is by nature and ontogenetically and phylogenetically the second oldest of the three presently described emotions—having developed shortly after the capacity for pleasure. Because it is by nature, like pleasure, what brings you contentment is likely to bring contentment to any other human being in any other culture.

Reorganization of pleasure and happiness states is dependent upon contentment—in other words, if you want more/better happiness, and more/better pleasure within your life, then you're going to have to figure out what makes you content.

Within the laboratory or within your own experiences, contentment is reliably distinguished from pleasure and happiness based upon:

1. It taking on an action-observer perspective.
2. You underestimating how long the experience lasts.
3. You never adapting to the emotions associated with the experience.

The opposite of contentment is depression. Thus, all that was just discussed about contentment may be discussed about depression but with dilatory effects—that is, a negative (–27 to –1) SEA-weighting score.

In 353 words, tell me what the heck is Being Theory

As an introduction to Being Theory—what this book is really all about—let's walk through nine basic attributes of Being Theory. I'll expand upon the details of Being Theory later on within this chapter—for now, I just want you to be aware of what Being Theory has to say about your positive emotions.

1. Being Theory posits (this is a fancy word meaning "states") you have the capacity for pleasure and contentment at birth, and develop the ability to be

happy through your childhood and adolescence while decreasing your ability to be content by adulthood. Your capacity to be content increases in late adulthood.

2. Being Theory distinguishes among the positive emotions of happiness, pleasure, and contentment.
3. Being Theory posits happiness is within your control; but positive emotions, like pleasure and contentment are not; the environment controls pleasure and actions control contentment.

4. Being Theory posits you setting goals and following goals is important to obtain and cultivate pleasure and happiness; however, you setting goals and following goals is less important for your contentment (and creativity, see cartoon above) and may even impede it.
5. Being Theory posits your morals and ethics affect your happiness, and have no effect on your pleasure and contentment.
6. Being Theory posits happiness is relative to particular parts of your life, whereas pleasure and contentment are likely to occur in any part of your life. Parts of life provide the framework for our human experience. We rationally frame events (good, bad, and everything in between) in our lives around these parts. Although we certainly think about "life in general," we are most likely to think about "life" around its significant parts, such as the parts associated with our family, work, friendships, possessions, home, etc.
7. Being Theory posits using active and passive voice affects your positive emotions.
8. Being Theory posits your perception of time slows during pleasure, is about the same during happiness, and speeds up during contentment.
9. Being Theory posits that you'll habituate slowly to experiences that bring happiness, quickly to experiences that bring pleasure, and *never* to experiences that bring contentment.

Figure 21. Being Theory: A three-level, hierarchical control-theoretic model of happiness, pleasure, and contentment lateralized within the left hemisphere.

i = input; o = output; r = reference signal; d = disturbance

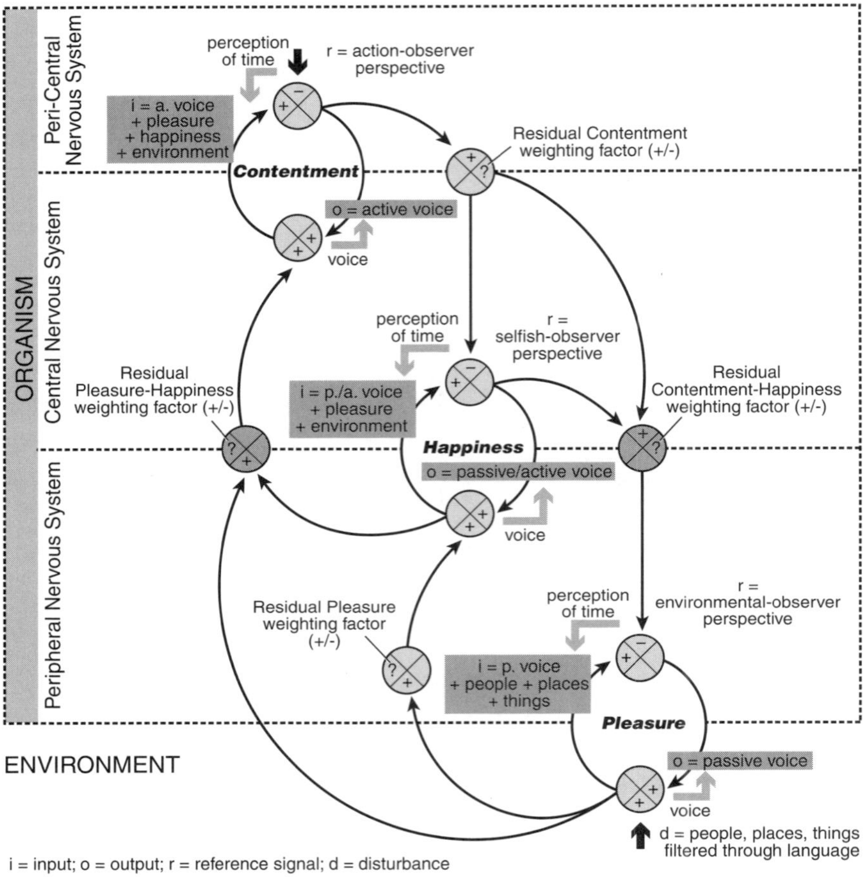

A picture is worth a thousand words. Figure 21 is a diagram of Being Theory's predictions about the interplay of positive emotions. It shows how happiness, pleasure, and contentment may be designed within the nervous systems—lateralized within the left hemisphere. It is hierarchically organized by three negative feedback control loops. A negative feedback control loop has four parts: a reference signal, output, disturbance, and input.

A reference signal within a negative feedback loop, abbreviated r, in **Figure 21**, defines what the control system *wants* to do. The reference signal is the control system's intentions or intended goals. Observer perspectives serve as the reference signals within Being Theory. Thus, happiness' reference signal is the selfish-observer perspective, pleasure's reference signal is the environmental-observer perspective, and contentment's reference signal is the action-observer perspective.

Further, the environmental-observer perspective and output from the emotions of contentment and happiness determine the reference signal for the control loop associated with pleasure. The selfish-observer perspective and output from the emotion of contentment determine the reference signal for the control loop associated with happiness. And the action-observer perspective by itself determines the reference signal for the control loop associated with contentment.

Output within a negative feedback loop, abbreviated o, in **Figure 21**, defines what the control system is *actually doing* in order to achieve the reference signal. Voice serves as the output within Being Theory. Thus, happiness' output is some combination of passive and active voice, pleasure's output is passive voice, and contentment's output is active voice.

A disturbance within a negative feedback loop, abbreviated, d, in **Figure 21**, defines the control system's environment—with environment being anything that affects the control system's output. Because happiness, pleasure, and contentment are organized in an hierarchical fashion—that is, pleasure is subordinate to happiness and happiness is subordinate to contentment, they each have different disturbances, but the disturbances are additive upon one another. Contentment's disturbance is composed of happiness' and pleasure's disturbances; happiness' disturbance is composed of pleasure's disturbance, and pleasure's disturbance is only its own environment because it is the most subordinate control system. Pleasure's disturbances are other people, places, and things. Happiness' disturbances are memories (labeled in **Figure 21**, residual weighting factor) of pleasures associated with other people, places, and things. Contentment's disturbances are a combination of memories (labeled in **Figure 21**, residual weighting factors) of pleasure and happiness associated with other people, places, and things.

Input within a negative feedback loop, abbreviated, i, in **Figure 21**, defines what the control system is perceiving. The control system is perceiving the addition of the control system's output and disturbances. Psychophysical time serves as the measure for input within Being Theory. Thus, psychophysical time for happiness' input is equal to physical time, psychophysical time for pleasure's input is greater than physical time, and psychophysical time for contentment's input is less than physical time.

Are you still with me? So what does this all mean? Well, first of all it means you have a really cool graphic to put up on your refrigerator (**Figure 21**). And second of all it means a lot for your emotions.

For happiness, it means your happy experiences are generally interdependent upon experiencing pleasure. You can experience happiness without directly experiencing pleasure—but previous experiences of pleasure (pleasure-memory), in part, mediate these happy experiences (residual pleasure weighting factor, see **Figure 21**). Being happy, in part, determines what pleasure means to you. Also, previous experiences of being content and happy (contentment-happiness memory), in part, mediate what pleasure means to you (residual contentment-happiness weighting factor, see **Figure 21**).

For pleasure, it means you directly experience pleasure without ever experiencing happiness and contentment.

For contentment, it means your experiences of contentment are generally interdependent upon happiness and pleasure. You can experience contentment without directly experiencing pleasure and happiness—but previous experiences of pleasure and happiness (pleasure-happy memory), in part, mediate these content experiences (residual pleasure-happiness weighting factor, see **Figure 21**). Being content, in part, determines what happiness means to you. Also, previous experiences of being content (contentment memory), in part, mediate what happiness means to you (residual contentment weighting factor, see **Figure 21**).

Figure 22 is a diagram of Being Theory's predictions about the interplay of negative emotions. It shows how sadness, pain, and depression may be designed within the nervous systems—lateralized within the right hemisphere. It is hierarchically organized by three negative feedback control loops—and is parallel in its anatomical structure and functioning to the negative feedback control loops that define positive emotions.

Being Theory: The details

Okay. Remember when I was treating you like a first grader and teaching you about nouns and verbs—and I promised you I wouldn't being doing this for very long? Well, be prepared to be treated like a graduate student now, because you are about to learn the details of Being Theory.

Ready?

Psychophysical and physical time. As already stated above, the basis of Being Theory is psychophysical and physical time. This basis has the following three assumptions:

1. When experiencing happiness, people will perceive the experience as lasting about the same amount of time as it really does last.
2. When experiencing pleasure, people will perceive the experience as lasting longer than the amount of time it really does last.
3. When experiencing contentment, people will perceive the experience as lasting shorter than the amount of time it really does last.

The relationship between a person's perception of time and his/her positive emotions is bi-directional. For example, if a person shifts from being happy to content, then his/her perception of time will shift from being veridical to one of underestimation. And if a person's perception of time shifts from being veridical

Figure 22. Being Theory: A three-level, hierarchical control-theoretic model of sadness, pain, and depression lateralized within the right hemisphere.

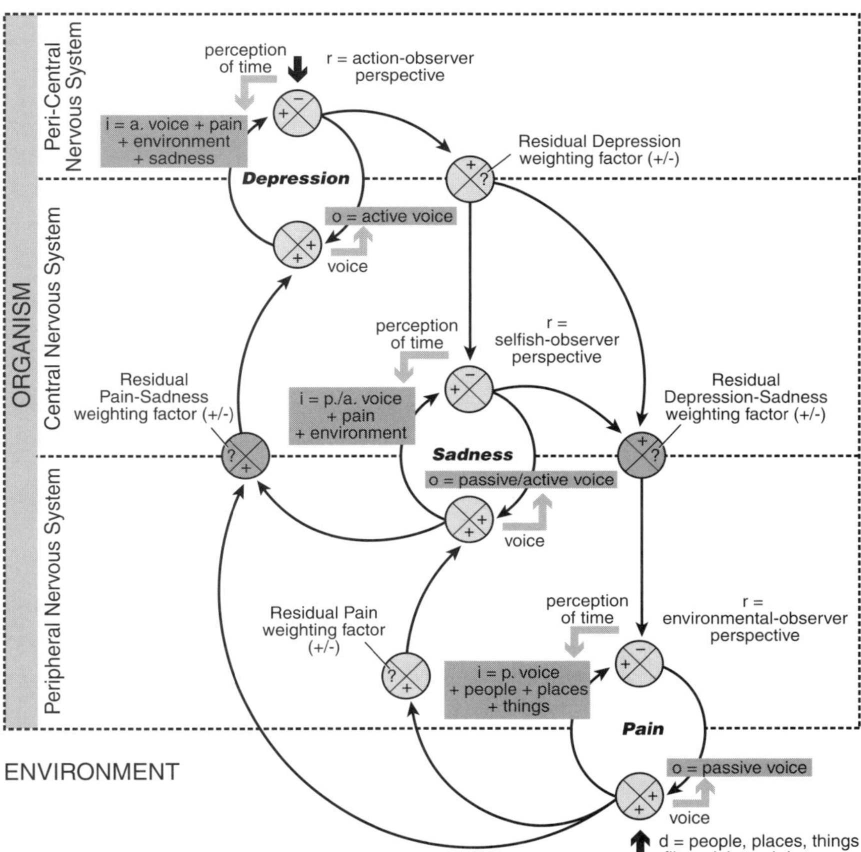

to being one of underestimation, then that person's emotional state, if positive, will shift from being happy to content. (If the person was in a negative state of emotion, then this psychophysical shift in time will cause him/her to change from being sad to being depressed.)

Observer perspective. Time is interdependent upon observer perspective within Being Theory, that is, psychophysical time shifts relative to observer perspective. If a person shifts his/her observer perspective, then his/her perception of time shifts; if a person's perception of time shifts, then his/her emotional state shifts too. Being Theory assumes selfish-, environmental-, and action-observer perspectives exist: people taking selfish-observer perspectives perceive life situations within their control—"I want to work." People taking environmental-observer perspectives perceive life situations outside their control—"My boss makes me work." People taking action-observer perspectives perceive nothing controlling the life situation—"I am working." Rarely does one have an experience that is purely defined by one observer perspective. Instead, people typically have a portion of each of the three perspectives within life's various parts. The person who is involved in the part of life, and the part of life itself, control a so-called **observer-perspective shift**. The observer-perspective shift occurs when the relative proportions of the three observer perspectives change for a particular part of life. For example, for me, writing is mostly about the selfish-observer perspective, but when I am writing to meet a deadline set by my publisher, an observer-perspective shift occurs for the writing part of my life from being mostly about the selfish-observer perspective (I like to write) to being mostly about the environmental-observer perspective (I have to write). People can be aware of their observer-perspective shifts; people can also be aware of their actual observer perspectives; however, people, most likely, are unaware of their shifts and perspectives.

Observer perspective ratios/Selfish, Environmental, Action (SEA) scores. Being Theory supposes *overall* feelings of happiness, pleasure, and contentment are dependent upon the length of time people have each of the observer perspectives during their life, whereas, *specific* feelings of happiness, pleasure, and contentment are dependent upon the length of time people have each of the observer perspectives during a specific part of life. The next chapter is about exploring the most typical parts of life. These parts of life include situations involving long-term partners, family, friends; situations of being alone, at work, and at home; and parts of life associated with health, learning, playing, money, and possessions. For example, let's say we analyze the relatively simple situation within the "home part of life" that has you kicking back by yourself, drinking some beers, and watching a football game on television. The game lasts four hours. Of the four hours, in no certain order, you spend one hour and 24 minutes channel surfing, looking for something you really want to see (selfish-observer perspective); you spend two hours knowing there is nothing you can do to make your team win (environmental-observer perspective); and you spend 36 minutes thinking about playing (action-observer perspective). Your observer-perspective ratio for watching this football game would be 35 : 50 : 15, which means 35% (1 hour and 24 minutes divided into 4 hours) of your time was selfish, 50% (2 hours divided into 4 hours) of your time was environmental, and 15% (36 minutes divided into 4 hours) of your time was action. Thus, an observer-perspective ratio is simply **percentage of time spent within a part of life that is Selfish : percentage of time spent within a part of life that is Environmental : percentage of time spent within a part of life that is Action**, or in shorthand:

$$\%S : \%E : \%A$$

Taken together, the percentages associated with the respective observer perspectives yield your level of potential emotions. So, another term for an observer-perspective ratio is simply a SEA score, with S representing the selfish-observer perspective, E representing the environmental-observer perspective, and A representing the action-observer perspective. Hereafter, I will use the term SEA score when I'm talking about observer-perspective ratios. Why? Two reasons: 1) It is an easy mnemonic or catchphrase to remember, and 2) This alone ought to sell a serious number of books—I can see it now, a national craze, "hey dude(tte), what's your SEA score?"

In all seriousness, knowing your SEA scores *will* get you a step closer to your ideal positive emotions, true happiness. So remember, you can never break apart a SEA score; however, when analyzing a SEA score, happiness (and its opposite, sadness) is associated with the selfish-observer perspective, S; pleasure (and its opposite, pain) is associated with the environmental-observer perspective, E; and contentment (and its opposite, depression) is associated with the action-observer perspective, A.

How do you know whether the S is representing happiness or its opposite; E is representing pleasure or its opposite; A is representing contentment or its opposite? Well, it is time to use your SEA-weighting score. The SEA-weighting score tells you:

1. *The polarity of your emotions.* That is, whether your emotions are likely to be positive (happiness, pleasure, contentment; standardized scores ranging from +1 to +27) or negative (sadness, pain, depression; standardized scores ranging from –1 to –27).

   and

2. *The intensity of your emotions.* That is, higher absolute value (drop the +/– sign) SEA-weighting scores equal stronger emotions and lower absolute value SEA-weighting scores equal weaker emotions.

For example, if you have a SEA score of 56:34:10 and a SEA-weighting score of +4, then you should most often feel happy (S: 56), but not too intensely (SEA-ws = +4—absolute value, 4). Less often and to a lesser extent, you should get some pleasure (E: 34) and contentment (A: 10), but these feelings may be so weak that you likely may not even be aware of them. As another example, if you have a SEA score of 26:58:16 and a SEA-weighting score of –22, then you should expect to feel intensely (SEA-ws = –22, absolute value = 22) in pain (E: 58). Much less often, you'll feel at times intensely sad (S: 26) and depressed (A: 16). So are you ready to be quizzed on SEA and SEA-weighting scores? Hint, hint...

It is sufficient to say that increasing the amount of time associated with a particular observer perspective (i.e., increasing one of the numbers within the SEA score) will increase the probability of the emotion associated with that observer perspective to occur; however, it is not necessary, because the observer perspectives are interdependent upon one another. Specifically, changing one observer perspective will have effects on the other two perspectives. For example, if a person has a SEA score of 10 : 70 : 20 and a SEA-weighting score of +17, then this person is likely gaining a lot of relatively intense pleasure. If the E part (70) of the SEA score changes, this does not necessarily change pleasure to happiness or pleasure to contentment, because this change depends on "where" the energy from the E part of the SEA score is going to. If it is going to the S part of the SEA score, then the potential for happiness will increase; if it is going to the A part of the SEA score, then the potential for contentment will increase; and lastly, if it is going to both the S and A part of the SEA score, then there may be minimal or no changes in emotions—and this of course is assuming the SEA-weighting score stays the same. I'll be expanding upon this discussion in **Chapters Five** and **Six**.

As I hinted to—It is quiz time! It is quiz time!! It is quiz time!!!

Quiz

1. **The S in the SEA score is most associated with predicting which of the following emotions?**
   a. Er, is boredom an emotion?
   b. Fear.
   c. Happiness.

2. **The E in the SEA score is most associated with predicting which of the following emotions?**
   a. Pain.
   b. Happiness.
   c. The joy of the New England Patriots losing a Super Bowl?

3. **The A in the SEA score is most associated with predicting which of the following emotions?**
   a. Mashed potatoes—sooner or later this is going to be a correct answer!
   b. Contentment.
   c. Pleasure.

4. **What two items on the SEA-weighting instrument did not come from the Happiness and You recipe?**
   a. Lavern and Shirley.
   b. Peanut Butter and Jelly.
   c. Sleep and Exercise.

5. **What emotion is a person with a SEA score of 35:55:10, and a SEA-weighting instrument score of –14, most likely to have?**
   a. Happiness.
   b. Pain.
   c. Nausea.

6. **What emotion is a person with a SEA score of 30:30:40, and a SEA-weighting instrument score of +23, most likely to have?**
   a. Happiness.
   b. Contentment.
   c. Itchiness.

Answers for this quiz can be found in **Appendix Four**. You got six out of six—didn't you?

WHAT ELSE DO SEA SCORES TELL US?

SEA scores, in concert with their corresponding SEA-weighting scores, tell us a lot about emotions. Additionally, SEA scores also tell us about human characteristics, especially when the SEA scores are excessively high or low.

Selfish part of the SEA score: Let's begin with the selfish part of the SEA score. Regardless of its corresponding SEA-weighting score, people with excessive selfish parts of their SEA scores—we'll put some specific numbers to "excessive" in the next chapter (**Table 3**)—can be described by some combination of the following 10 characteristics:

- overly subjective
- egotistical
- constantly feeling overwhelmed
- tired
- unrealistically high expectations
- obsessive
- perfectionist
- easily disappointed
- lonely
- controlling

People with exceptionally low selfish parts of their SEA scores—we'll put some specific numbers to "exceptionally low" in the next chapter (**Table 3**)—can be described by some combination of the following 10 characteristics:

- significantly underwhelmed
- searching for things that are meaningful
- overly confused
- overly malleable
- overly pliable
- overly flexible
- co-dependent
- undecided
- a follower
- a conformist

Environmental part of the SEA score: Regardless of its corresponding SEA-weighting score, people with excessive environmental parts of their SEA scores—we'll put some specific numbers to "excessive" in the next chapter (**Table 3**)—can be described by some combination of the following 10 characteristics:

- chronically feeling out of control
- exhausted
- depressed
- chronically bored
- markedly low expectations
- overly realistic
- overly cynical
- constantly feeling trapped
- overly defensive
- feelings of having no autonomy

People with exceptionally low environmental parts of their SEA scores—we'll put some specific numbers to "exceptionally low" in the next chapter (**Table 3**)—can be described by some combination of the following 10 characteristics:

- overly naïve
- immature
- egotistical
- narcissistic

- constant feelings of being alone
- disassociating from reality
- solipsistic (this is the second time I've used this word—have you looked it up yet?)
- anti-social
- unfriendly
- unrealistic

Action part of the SEA score: Regardless of its corresponding SEA-weighting score, people with excessive action parts of their SEA scores—we'll put some specific numbers to "excessive" in the next chapter (**Table 3**)—can be described by some combination of the following 10 characteristics:

- manic
- having loose associations
- not following implicit and explicit rules, regulations, and/or laws
- having very emotional, intense and strong—but at the same time very *short-term* relationships
- creative
- undisciplined
- short-sighted
- self-destructive
- unfaithful
- artistic

People with exceptionally low action parts of their SEA scores—we'll put some specific numbers to "exceptionally low" in the next chapter (**Table 3**)—can be described by some combination of the 10 following characteristics:

- grounded in self
- grounded in environment
- focused on people
- focused on places
- focused on things
- dissatisfied
- unhappy
- discontent
- objective
- object driven

For those of you who are children or know one or two of them—a quick word of warning

Let's go back to our children and the developmental phenomenon of contentment recognition transitioning to happy ignorance. We are born with contentment recognition SEA scores ranging from about 5 : 20 : 75 to about 5 : 40 : 55, and SEA-weighting scores in the mid to high positive range (SEA-ws: +12 to +20). As happy ignorance begins developing, the SEA scores are stood on their proverbial heads, and by late childhood/early adolescence they range from about 10 : 40 : 60 to about 30 : 50 : 20, and their SEA-weighting scores drop to near zero and below (see **Figure 23**). Note, the adolescent knows more about who he/she is than when he/she was a child—but not *a lot* more. That is, his/her self-concept (imbedded within the selfish-observer perspective, S) has increased, but only to 30. The adolescent's actions are much more dependent upon the environment (an environmental-observer perspective, E, of 40 to 50 from the childhood range of 20 to 40). And what composes an adolescent's environment is radically different from that of the child's. The child's environment is mostly composed of parents and siblings, whereas the adolescent's environment is mostly composed of peers (and the peer pressure that comes along with these peers), friends, external rewards (praise, public recognition, money), and the media. Okay—ready for the warning? At no other time during our lifespan are we more susceptible to the influences of the media than during our adolescence. The adolescent is at his/her most vulnerable to media influences because of the high levels of potential pleasure (environmental-observer perspectives, E, greater than 40) driving and

Figure 23. Typical SEA scores and SEA-weighting scores for infancy/childhood through late childhood/adolescence.

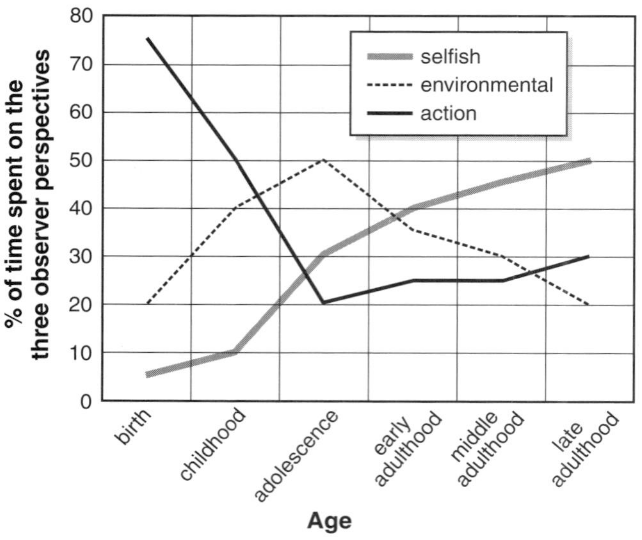

motivating his/her actions. As an example of this, cigarette companies know that 50% of adolescents who start smoking before age 20 will continue to smoke for 16 to 20 years, whereas only about 10% of adults who start smoking will continue to smoke this long (Moody, Memon, Sugathan, El-Gerges, & Al-Bustan, 1999). The media feeds on this potential pleasure motivating behavior by bombarding the adolescent with sensationalistic images and sounds of pleasure paired with products or whatever else they are trying to sell (classical conditioning all over again: CS + US pairings): beer paired with breasts; cologne paired with sex; Mountain Dew paired with the X-Games/extreme sports; McDonalds paired with the latest and greatest music; the military paired with adventure and the unknown; cigarettes paired with beauty... This makes clear that it is a misnomer to think adolescents are selfish and egocentric—they are not! They are environmental—and easily influenced by forces beyond themselves. Thus, this is one of the most important times of our lifespan to boost egos, build self-esteems and self-concepts, and increase the selfish parts of SEA scores. In **Chapter Six**, I will show you how to transform environmental parts of the SEA scores to selfish ones.

USING SEA SCORES TO INTERPRET THE HAPPINESS AND YOU RECIPE

Let's end this chapter by looking at the ingredients within the Happiness and You recipe relative to SEA scores. As I'm sure you were aware, when you were reading about the ingredients within the Happiness and You recipe, there were conditions on each of the ingredients in order for them to be included within the recipe. Relative to SEA scores, Being Theory perfectly explains these conditions. By changing the SEA scores associated with each of the ingredients, and having a positive SEA-weighting score, we can make the ingredients part of a Happiness and You recipe (high selfish part of the SEA score)—or a Pleasure and You recipe (high environmental part of the SEA score), or a Contentment and You recipe (high action part of the SEA score).

Now we get to answer the question posed to you on several occasions earlier in this book: What do you want: Happiness, Pleasure, or Contentment? Or, maybe you want some combination of all of them? It follows, then, to continue our recipe analogy from **Chapter Three**: if I was a chef and I wanted to make you happy, then I would take each of the ingredients described in **Chapter Three** to make sure you had a high positive SEA-weighting score, then I would make the selfish part of your SEA scores the highest relative to the other two parts. For example, with a positive SEA-weighting score, if we took the ingredient money, and we had your experiences with your money be, relatively speaking, mostly within your control (SEA: 46 : 29 : 25), then happiness would be the most likely positive emotion you would be experiencing.

If we took the ingredients described in **Chapter Three** to make sure you had a high positive SEA-weighting score, and I made the environmental part of your SEA scores the highest relative to the other two parts, then we would have a 10-ingredient recipe for Pleasure and You. For example, with a positive SEA-weighting score, if we took the ingredient friendships, and we had your experiences with your friends be, relatively speaking, mostly out of your control (SEA: 30 : 50 : 20), then pleasure would be the most likely positive emotion you would be experiencing.

If we took each of the ingredients described in **Chapter Three** to make sure you had a positive SEA-weighting score, and I made the action part of your SEA scores the highest relative to the other two parts, then we would have a 10-ingredient recipe for Contentment and You. For example, with a positive SEA-weighting score, if we took the ingredient spirituality, and we had your experiences with your spirituality be, relatively speaking, mostly about the experience itself (SEA: 34 : 21 : 45), then contentment would be the most likely positive emotion you would be experiencing.

Of course, the best recipe for your life is not going to be one that is purely by happiness, pleasure, or contentment, but instead is going to be a recipe that combines each of the above recipes. And this recipe will likely be relative to specific parts of your life. In the next chapter, we'll measure your SEA scores for eleven parts of your life and introduce some SEA scores for these parts of life that are associated with true happiness.

In summary

Before we measure your SEA scores within different parts of your life in the next chapter, let's summarize what a SEA score tells you:

1. **It tells you about your emotions...**
   S: The probability your experiences within a part of life will be happy (sad).*
   E: The probability your experiences within a part of life will be pleasurable (painful).*
   A: The probability your experiences within a part of life will bring you contentment (depression).*

2. **It tells you how long your positive/negative emotions will last/how quickly you will adapt to the positive/negative emotions...***
   S: A few months to a few years.
   E: A few moments to a few months.
   A: Endless.

* Positive or negative emotions as determined by your SEA-weighting score.

a. the intensity of your emotions, with higher absolute value standardized scores equaling stronger emotions and lower absolute value scores equaling weaker emotions;

   and

b. whether the emotions are likely to be positive (standardized scores ranging from +1 to +27) or negative (standardized scores ranging from –1 to –27).

For example, if your Playing SEA score is 56 : 34 : 10 and your SEA-weighting score is +4, then when you are at play, you should most likely expect to feel happy (S: 56), but not too intensely (SEA-ws: |+4| = 4), to a lesser extent, you should get some pleasure (E: 34), but again not too intensely because of the small SEA-weighting score.

3. **It tells you about your control of an experience...**
   S: You are in control.
   E: Some other person, place, or thing is in control.
   A: The experience is in control, no thing or nothing is in control.

4. **It tells you about how long you might live...**
   I'm serious! See **Chapter Six** for the details...

Chapter Five

You Probably Don't Need to Change Your Whole Life, You Just Have a Few Things You Want to Work On

It's a "part of life"

As **Chapter Three** is a cookbook of sorts, containing a recipe for gaining positive emotions, this chapter is a workbook of sorts, containing a method to measure positive emotions. I warned you some 130 pages ago that reading this book *requires* your active participation. Well, this chapter is no exception to the rule, for it requires you becoming aware of *your* current levels of happiness, pleasure, and contentment. After reading **Chapter Four**, you know that more than anything else, your happiness, pleasure, and contentment are dependent upon SEA-weighting scores—the substance of your life, and SEA scores—your combined Selfish, Environmental, and Action observer perspectives. The question now is, where exactly are these SEA scores?

SEA scores are within life's various parts. Parts of Life provide the framework for our human experience. We rationally frame events—good, bad, and everything in between—in our lives around these parts. These parts are so engrained within our everyday language, we might not even recognize them. For example, I'm sure you've said many a times, something to the extent of, "it's just a part of life." And we often distinguish between at least two of the more obvious parts of life when we talk about trying to keep our "work life" separate from our "home life." Although we certainly think about our lives "in general," we most likely think about our lives around significant, specific parts—such as parts associated with our *family, work, friendships, possessions, home,* and even *food*. This type of thinking begins very early on in our development. While dining out at a restaurant with my family, my oldest daughter, Sember, who was seven at the time, stopped eating while most of her food was still on her plate. I told her to finish eating and she said she was "full." So I said "okay, I guess we don't have to order dessert." Without pause, Sember did not start eating what was left on her plate; instead she said, "The *'food' part of me* is full; the *dessert part of me* is empty—I can still eat dessert." How can I argue with that logic? We had dessert...

We may answer the question, "Are you happy?" with a simple "yes" or "no" response; the better, more meaningful question is not the general "Are you happy?" question, but specific questions structured by life's various parts, "Are you happy with the amount of *money* you have or make?" "Are you happy with your *leisure time*?" "Are you happy with your *spouse*?" etc. Indeed, when we perceive our life to be "wonderful" or for it to "suck," we usually have very specific parts of our lives to celebrate or blame for these perceptions. This chapter will ask *you* about happiness, pleasure, and contentment relative to *your* parts of life.

Introspecting

In all the classes I teach, I require my students to write papers called "introspections." The term introspection simply means "to look inward—to self examine." The papers I assign my students require them to go beyond describing who they are—the papers require my students to break down who they are. By introspecting, my students end up writing papers that are open, honest, meaningful—and their bases are true. The most important word to use while introspecting is "why." For example, without thinking—and without true meaningfulness—anybody can answer the above-stated, non-introspective question, "Are you happy?" This is analogous to the typical greeting of "How are you doing?" A yes or no response to these questions is descriptive, but it tells us practically nothing beyond the response itself. However, thinking is required—meaningfulness is required—to answer the introspective questions, "*Why* are you happy?" or "*Why* are you unhappy?" Answers to these questions most often lead to specific parts of life: "I am happy because of *work* and my *family*..." Or, "I am unhappy because of my *friend*..." Of course the introspection doesn't end here, but continues with yet another "why" and yet another answer to it: "Why are you happy with your *work* and *family*...?" "Why are you unhappy with your *friend*?" Introspection only ends when the basis of the issue—the truth of the issue—is addressed. And you know how much I like truth.

If you ever want to find the real, true meaning behind any of your emotions, behaviors, cognitions, or perceptions, then simply ask the question "Why?" Why am I in this relationship? Because I love her. Why do you love her? What is your definition of love? Why is this your definition of love...? Ironically, and unfortunately, as we age, we are reinforced *not* to use the word why. Most young children, interestingly, at about the same age as happy-ignorance's beginnings (~3 years of age), have bountiful levels of curiosity with "why" as their favorite question word—if not even their favorite word, period. But exasperated parents (redundant), eventually begin answering the question with the prototypical responses of "because" or "that's just the way it is" or the absolute classic "because mommy/daddy said so!" My graduate school's psychology department took a similar philosophy in teaching its student clinical psychologists. Their philosophy was to *never* use the word "why" with clients. The psychology department believed the "why" word only built walls between the clinician and client and it made clients feel defensive. Indeed, the why word is powerful in not only finding meaning in one's behaviors, but also in making one defensive!

Let's pretend your best friend just bought a new Chevrolet Suburban and comes over to your house to show it off. What do you say? **A:** Wow! That's great! Congratulations! Or **B:** *Why* did you buy a (gas-guzzling) Suburban? So what do you think? Might there be any differences in the defensiveness your friend may be feeling relative to your **A** response as compared to your **B** response? Why also makes *us* defensive when we use it on *ourselves*. Why? Because through the use of the word "why," we find things out about ourselves that are meaningful and significant, which is great in one sense: "Hurray, I can use this insight to make my life better and happier!" But it is horrible, and often times even depressing, in another sense: "Damn, I wish I knew this about myself before I got married—or before I picked this major—or before I chose this occupation—or before I bought this Suburban!" Insights gained from introspections over the short term are often emotionally painful; however, over the long term, these insights are emotionally strengthening.

Parts is parts

Parts of life do *not* cause happiness, pleasure, and contentment. Repeat, parts of life do *not* cause happiness, pleasure, and contentment—SEA-weighting scores combined with SEA scores do. However, with this said, some parts of life—take for instance marriage and family—are more likely to be *associated* (or to use the technical term, correlated) with positive emotions than other parts of life, like your savings (Campbell, Converse, & Rodgers, 1975). Without question, parts of life define our nervous systems. Our nervous systems operate relative to and because of our various parts of life. Now, what *exact* parts of life define our nervous systems is questionable. Some parts of life, like family and friendships, are relatively obvious and become part of our nervous systems by instinct. Whereas other parts of life, like religion and money, are not as obvious, less instinctual, and most likely become part of our nervous systems through learning.

What parts of life define you and your nervous systems? Yes, I'm really asking—and I'm really interested to hear what you come up with. If you compartmentalized your life, what parts would you have? A review of the research literature on this topic reveals there to be almost as many ideas about the number and types of life parts as there are people writing about them—and there a lot of people writing about them.

For example, Stephen Covey (1990), of *The 7 Habits of Highly Effective People* fame, argues life is composed of ten parts (family, money, work, possessions, pleasure, friend, enemy, church, self, and spouse), and uses these parts as a framework to facilitate "success" within people. Thomas Holmes and Richard Rahe (1967), who developed the classic "Social Readjustment Rating Scale," which measures stress within people's lives (see **Table 2**), theorize there to be nine parts of life (marriage, family, health, work, money, self, home, friendships, and leisure).

Table 2. The Social Readjustment Rating Scale, Holmes & Rahe (1967).

Life event	Value
1. Death of a spouse	100
2. Divorce	73
3. Marital separation	65
4. Jail term	63
5. Death of a close family member	63
6. Personal injury or illness	53
7. Marriage	50
8. Fired at work	47
9. Marital reconciliation	45
10. Retirement	45
11. Change in health of family member	44
12. Pregnancy	40
13. Sex difficulties	39
14. Gain of a new family member	39
15. Business readjustments	39
16. Change in financial state	38
17. Death of a close friend	37
18. Change to different line of work	36
19. Change in no. of arguments with spouse	35
20. Mortgage over $50,000	31
21. Foreclosure of mortgage	30
22. Change in responsibilities at work	29
23. Son or daughter leaving home	29
24. Trouble with in-laws	29
25. Outstanding personal achievements	28
26. Wife begins or stops work	26
27. Begin or end school	26
28. Change in living conditions	25
29. Revision of personal habits	24
30. Trouble with boss	23
31. Change in work hours or conditions	20
32. Change in residence	20
33. Change in school	20
34. Change in recreation	19
35. Change in religious activities	19
36. Change in social activities	18
37. Loan less than $50,000	17
38. Change in sleeping habits	16
39. Change in no. of family get-togethers	15
40. Change in eating habits	15
41. Vacation	13
42. Holidays	12
43. Minor violations of laws	11

Use only events that have taken place in your life in the last 12 months. Add values to the right of each item to obtain your total score.

Your potential for mental and physical illness in the near future:

For a score that is less than 149: Low
For a score that is between 150 and 200: Mild
For a score that is between 201 and 299: Moderate
For a score that is greater than 300: High

Mortimer Adler (1984), one of the most popular and well-published philosophers of the 20th century, argued for six parts of life: sleep, which also includes eating, drinking, eliminating, cleansing, and exercising; labor, which includes working to earn your livelihood; leisure, which includes working for some purpose other than earning your livelihood; play, which includes amusing yourself; idling; and resting. Lastly, Angus Campbell (Campbell, Converse, & Rodgers, 1975) is the only known scientist in the research literature to have examined life satisfaction relative to different parts of life. He studied life satisfaction relative to marriage, family life, neighborhood, health, friendships, housework, job, life in the United States, life in the city or county of residence, non-work, housing, standard of living, usefulness of education, amount of education, and savings.

We can debate all day (and the next) about which of these theorists (or others) is closest to the truth about the number and types of life parts that define our nervous systems—but let's save that debate for another book. In this book, let's just call it a draw, and combine the best from each of the aforementioned theories. This results in the following eleven parts of life: Learning, Playing, Possessions, Family, Home, Friendships, Partner, Money, Work, Health, and Self. I'll be using these parts of life in this chapter and for the remainder of this book.

As an aside, these eleven parts of life (Learning, Playing, Possessions, Family, Home, Friendships, Partner, Money, Work, Health, and Self) are ordered chronologically for our cognitive (consciousness) development. That is, we Learn before we Play, we Play before we Possess, we Possess before we (understand) Family, we (understand) Family before we (understand) Home, we (understand) Home before we (understand) Friendships, we (understand) Friendships before we (understand) long-term Partnership, we (understand) long-term Partnership before we (understand) Money, we (understand) Money before we (understand) Work, we (understand) Work before we (understand) our Health, and the last thing we can fully understand is our Self. Although the parts of life cognitively develop in this strict chronology, this does not mean you could not be working before having a friend—or have money before a family. In fact, you can possess any of the parts of life in any order. Only the *cognitive understanding* of the parts of life follows this strict chronological order.

How are the parts of life related to one another?

I need to make mention of two things about the parts of life. The first thing is that some of the parts of life may be more significant to you than other parts of life. That is okay. It is normal to judge some parts of life as better or worse than other parts of life. Some people may even deny having all eleven parts of life. If this is the case for you, no problem—focus on the parts of life that you think are relevant to you. Most people, however, do have all eleven parts of life, and judge the parts with differing levels of personal significance. The second thing is to recognize the eleven parts of life are not independent of one another. Instead, they are interdependent upon one another and blend into one another. You may use some of the same terms to describe and do the same things within more than one part of life. For example, Family may blend into Work… Work may blend into Money… Money may blend into Possessions… Possessions may blend into Playing… Playing may blend into Health… Health may blend into Home… Home may blend into Family… And so on, and so forth. Although parts of life are not independent of one another, they allow us—at a minimum, to implicitly structure and frame our lives.

I just cannot get away from drawing figures of negative feedback control loops—or for that matter, *you* just cannot get away from these figures! ☺ **Figure 24** is a series of eleven hierarchically arranged control systems composed of three negative feedback loops each. I've drawn this figure for several reasons.

The first and probably most important reason is so you can put this too on your refrigerator, thereby impressing your friends on just how damn intelligent you are to understand such a complicated figure.

The second reason is that, as I said earlier, these parts of life define your nervous system, so this figure shows how the parts of life may be modeled as your nervous system. You likely have one series of control systems for positive emotions that is left lateralized and one series of control systems for negative emotions that is right lateralized.

The third reason is, this provides you with a graphical representation of how I just mentioned that each of your parts of life (represented by the eleven hierarchical control systems) have an impact on every other part of your life.

The last reason, related to the third reason, is to show how each part of life has a *different* impact on every other part of life. In the figure, the closer a part of life is to another part of life (e.g., Learning is adjacent to Playing), the greater the impact these parts of life have on one another—the way we learn has a tremendous impact on the way we play. Further, when viewing **Figure 24**, parts of life above are superordinate—and generally in control of parts of life below. Thus, if something affects the learning part of life, then all other parts of life will be affected too.

It's quiz time—again!

Figure 24. A model of happiness/sadness, pleasure/pain, and contentment/depression defined by eleven hierarchically arranged control systems composed of three negative feedback loops.

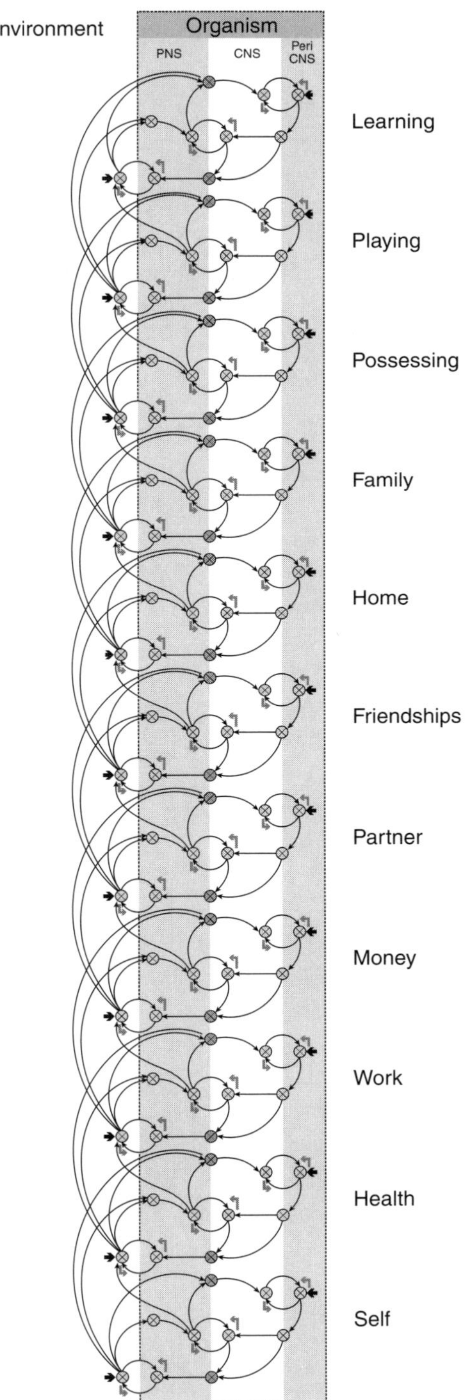

Quiz

1. **In addition to predicting emotions, the SEA score predicts other things about your life. For example, the Selfish part of a SEA score predicts the emotions you gain from an experience will likely last:**
   a. A few months to a few years.
   b. A few moments to a few months.
   c. Until you're through reading this book.

2. **In addition to predicting emotions, the SEA score predicts other things about your life. For example, the Environmental part of a SEA score predicts the emotions you gain from an experience will likely last:**
   a. Until the end of a M*A*S*H rerun.
   b. A few moments to a few months.
   c. Forever.

3. **In addition to predicting emotions, the SEA score predicts other things about your life. For example, the Action part of a SEA score predicts the emotions you gain from an experience will likely last:**
   a. Until you run out of money.
   b. A few months to a few years.
   c. Forever.

4. **In addition to predicting emotions, the SEA score predicts other things about your life. For example, the Selfish part of a SEA score predicts who/what is controlling your experiences?**
   a. You.
   b. Other people, places, and things.
   c. The little person in your head.

5. **In addition to predicting emotions, the SEA score predicts other things about your life. For example, the Environmental part of a SEA score predicts who/what is controlling your experiences?**
   a. Tony the Tiger.
   b. Other people, places, and things.
   c. The experience itself.

6. **In addition to predicting emotions, the SEA score predicts other things about your life. For example, the Action part of a SEA score predicts who/what is controlling your experiences?**
   a. You.
   b. Bishop George Berkeley—can we say solipsism?!
   c. The experience itself.

Refer to **Appendix Four** for the answers... Surely you scored a 6/6 again!

How is this chapter going to work?

The remaining part of this chapter is organized by first having a quiz for each of the eleven parts of life (Lucas & Kaylor, 2005). Each of the "life-part quizzes" has between 20 and 32 questions—and should only take you 10 or fifteen minutes to complete. All you need to do to complete a quiz is select one of three possible answers for each quiz question. After completing a quiz, you will be able to calculate your SEA score for the respective part of life the quiz is associated.

By no means are you required to complete all eleven life-part quizzes. Instead, you may just pick and choose to complete the life-part quizzes associated with the parts of life you are most interested in examining/changing relative to your positive emotions of happiness, pleasure, and contentment. The eleven life-part quizzes begin on the following pages:

Following each quiz, there are answers and scoring instructions. Answers for the quizzes are marked **s**elfish, **e**nvironmental, or **a**ction.

Following the SEA scoring sheet, I ask for *your* definition of the part of life, then I provide an operational definition for it. An operational definition is an agreed-upon, succinct but detailed definition of a measure. So, the definitions I give for each part of life are intentionally short, detailed, and sweet. Well—maybe not sweet. I provide the definitions so that you can compare *your* definition for a particular part of life to the one used to develop these quizzes.

This chapter ends with discussions about what your specific SEA scores mean relative to different parts of your life. The final chapter will show you how to change your SEA scores for more happiness—less sadness; more pleasure—less pain; and more contentment—less depression.

Instructions for calculating your SEA score for a particular part of life

To get an estimate of what your SEA score is for a particular part of life, first record your answers to the 20–32 questions about the part of life you're interested in examining. And, c'mon, there's really no point for you to be taking any of these quizzes, if you are not going to be honest with your answers. So for goodness' sake, answer the questions honestly—you don't have to share them with anybody else but yourself! And if you cannot be honest with yourself, then... Well, you need a lot more than this book can provide—maybe you need to call me?!

The questions that comprise these quizzes are about typical life experiences, so you'll find most of the questions' content related to your own personal experiences. If a question is about an experience you have not had, then please answer the question by considering what you think you would *actually* do—not what you would *ideally* do. (And yes, if you are a narcissist—these are two different things!)

The quizzes' questions have three possible answers. Please be sure to read all three of a question's answers before making your selection. You may choose *only* one of these three answers. Many questions may have more than one answer that you will want to choose. With these questions, as with all the questions on the quizzes, choose the *one* answer that best fits with what you would do relative to the question's described situation. Remember, do *not* base your answers on your ideal behaviors; base your answers on what you would really do within the questions' described situations.

LEARNING QUESTIONS

1. **If I don't understand something, I most likely:**
   a. Ask somebody to explain the "something" to me.
   b. Study harder at coming to an understanding of the "something."
   c. Leave it at that—Some things are better left not understood.

2. **If someone is trying to teach me something, then:**
   a. I better be interested in the content.
   b. It doesn't matter how interesting the content or teacher is—I'm interested in learning for its own sake.
   c. The person teaching the content better be interesting.

3. **When learning, I have to:**
   a. Be interested in the content.
   b. There is no "have-tos" for me in learning.
   c. Be in a "learning" mood.

4. **The best curriculum for the classroom:**
   a. Allows for students' experiences to be mostly within the instructor's control.
   b. Allows for students' experiences to happen without any particular person, place, or a thing to be in control.
   c. Allows for students' experiences to be mostly within their control.

5. **I have class at 11 a.m. and when I am pulling my car into the school parking lot at 10:55 a.m., it begins down-pouring rain. I do *not* have an umbrella. What do I do?**
   a. I get out of my car and go to class.
   b. I wait to see if the rain is going to stop.
   c. I look around my car for something that I could use as an umbrella.

6. **When do I learn best?**
   a. When I'm alone.
   b. When I'm with others.
   c. When I'm caught up within the learning experience.

7. **What is my definition of school?**
   a. Learning.
   b. Something that I had to do.
   c. Something that I enjoyed doing.

8. **What is my definition of an ideal teacher?**
   a. Someone who becomes a part of the topic they are teaching.
   b. Someone who finds out what I want to learn and then teaches that.
   c. Someone who gets me excited about the topic he/she is teaching.

9. **What am I most interested in learning?**
   a. Things that I like.
   b. Things that are important.
   c. Anything.

10. **Who is the most important person involved in my learning?**
    a. There is no single person that is most important in my learning.
    b. Me.
    c. Whomever is teaching me about what I am learning.

11. **What am I most likely to be distracted by when I'm learning?**
    a. Myself.
    b. Others.
    c. The learning itself.

12. **What is my definition of education?**
    a. Something I'm going to be doing for a lifetime.
    b. Something that is dependent upon whether or not I am in school.
    c. Something that is dependent upon me wanting to learn.

13. **What typically happens when I'm faced with a difficult problem?**
    a. I begin thinking about possible solutions to solve it.
    b. I begin solving it.
    c. I find other people and/or resources to help me solve it.

14. **What would I have to say about a student who gets all "As" for grades?**
    a. He/she does a lot of thinking for its own sake.
    b. He/she obviously was born intelligent and/or he/she has had a very positive learning environment.
    c. He/she obviously works hard at his/her school work.

15. **When is learning boring to me?**
    a. When I'm not interested in the subject matter.
    b. Learning cannot be boring.
    c. When the subject matter itself is not interesting.

16. How does time pass when I'm learning?
  a. Quickly.
  b. Slowly.
  c. The same as it does when I'm not learning.

17. When studying for a test:
  a. I prefer to prepare alone.
  b. I prefer to prepare with a group of fellow classmates.
  c. Being alone or with others does not impact my studying.

18. My feeling about someone getting a college degree is:
  a. That a college degree is necessary in today's job market.
  b. Getting a degree is not necessarily significant for life's education.
  c. That it is up to the individual as to decide whether or not a college degree is significant relative to life's education.

19. The most important goal of a college education is:
  a. Learning in an area that I enjoy.
  b. Learning something that I can use for employment.
  c. Learning.

20. The most likely reason a student would make an "F" in a college class is:
  a. Because he/she didn't study.
  b. Because the class was too difficult for that student.
  c. Because making low grades is part of the educational experience.

Scoring instructions

Use the selfish, environmental, and action Learning answers below to tally your Learning SEA score.

Selfish, environmental, and action Learning answers

1. a. environmental b. selfish c. action
2. a. selfish b. action c. environmental
3. a. selfish b. action c. environmental
4. a. environmental b. action c. selfish
5. a. action b. environmental c. selfish
6. a. selfish b. environmental c. action
7. a. action b. environmental c. selfish
8. a. action b. selfish c. environmental
9. a. selfish b. environmental c. action
10. a. action b. selfish c. environmental
11. a. selfish b. environmental c. action
12. a. action b. environmental c. selfish
13. a. selfish b. action c. environmental
14. a. action b. environmental c. selfish
15. a. selfish b. action c. environmental
16. a. action b. environmental c. selfish
17. a. selfish b. environmental c. action
18. a. environmental b. action c. selfish
19. a. selfish b. environmental c. action
20. a. selfish b. environmental c. action

Learning scoring

Selfish: $\frac{\text{Total number of selfish responses}}{20} \times 100$

Environmental: $\frac{\text{Total number of environmental responses}}{20} \times 100$

Action: $\frac{\text{Total number of action responses}}{20} \times 100$

Learning SEA score = ____ : ____ : ____

Before I give you the definition of learning that was used to develop these questions and answers, I want you to tell me what your definition of learning is... Really. What is it—to learn? To help guide your thoughts about learning, come up with answers on a piece of paper to the following questions:

- Where are you most likely to learn?
- Does everyone—children and adults, learn?
- Do children learn differently than adults? How?
- Who learns more—children or adults? Why?
- Is learning always a good thing? Why?
- Give one example of you—learning.

Now that you have a more explicit idea about your definition of learning, take a look at the definition of learning that was used to develop the "learning" questions and answers. The learning part of life is composed of your emotions, behaviors, cognitions, and perceptions *changing* relative to you being exposed to other people, places, or things. With the exception of maturational (or developmental) change, just about any change in your life—whether you are aware of it or not, is learning. This change can also come from self-reflection or introspection. Key elements of your learning include:

- Having some awareness of the things you do not understand.
- Definition of teacher and teaching.
- Definition of school, education in general, and higher education in particular.
- Ability to take in new information (encoding).
- Obstacles to learning.
- Best practices for learning.
- The effects of your personal control on learning.
- Perception of time possibly being affected during the learning process.

Playing questions

1. **When I am involved in a project during my leisure time, I:**
    a. Enjoy the sense of accomplishment that comes with completing my project.
    b. Get input from others regarding my project.
    c. Lose myself in the project.

2. **What I love most about my favorite pastime is:**
    a. Being totally focused on what I am doing.
    b. That I choose what to do with my time.
    c. That others choose what to do with my time.

3. **What is the main reason I listen to music?**
    a. Because it is something I like to do.
    b. By listening to pop(ular) music, I can find out what others are listening to.
    c. For the sake of being a part of the music.

4. **What types of activities do I do to relax?**
    a. I spend time alone, or sleep.
    b. I do whatever I feel like doing at the moment.
    c. I spend time with my friends, or get a relaxation treatment (like a massage).

5. **Which of the following games would I most likely prefer during my leisure time?**
    a. Any game would do, as long as I get to play.
    b. A board game (e.g., Monopoly, Clue, checkers, chess, etc.).
    c. Some game in which I get to make up the rules.

6. **When I have free time, I can be typically found doing:**
    a. Nothing in particular.
    b. Sports, hobbies, crafts by myself.
    c. Sports, hobbies, crafts with friends or family.

7. **Recreation is:**
    a. Something that everybody should do.
    b. Something that people should do if they want.
    c. Part of life.

8. **I find myself on a boat with friends that are water skiing. Assume that I've never water skied before, and my friends are asking me to ski. What do I do?**
   a. I ski for the sake of skiing.
   b. I ski because my friends obviously are expecting me to.
   c. I ski because I might find that I actually like skiing.

9. **The best kind of vacation:**
   a. Is filled with activities and events that were scheduled before the vacation.
   b. Has me planning the daily activities and events during the vacation itself.
   c. Has me taking everything in as it comes along.

10. **Which of the following would be the most relaxing for me?**
   a. Practicing Yoga poses, techniques, and meditations to improve my health and well-being.
   b. Surfing the Internet or channel surfing the TV.
   c. Writing in my diary.

11. **When I start a project during my spare time:**
   a. I'm not really too concerned about completing the project; I'm more concerned about just doing it.
   b. I'm likely to finish it as quickly as possible.
   c. Depending upon my responsibilities, the project gets done in due time.

12. **Which of the following statements is the most true?**
   a. Playing can happen any time in any place.
   b. I decide when to play and when to work.
   c. There is a proper time and place for playing, and that time and place is not necessarily within my control.

13. **I find myself climbing a mountain. What's the most important thing about this climb?**
   a. That I get to the top of the mountain.
   b. That I climb within my climbing abilities.
   c. That I am climbing.

14. **I like to read:**
   a. Things that are of interest to me.
   b. Anything.
   c. Things that are popular (e.g., New York best-seller's list, Top 100 best novels ever written, etc.).

15. The most likely reason I would go dancing is:

a. For the social aspect of being at a dance club.
b. To dance.
c. To have fun.

16. I work in the yard or garden:

a. Because I enjoy seeing the improvements I make.
b. So my neighbors and friends will notice my effort.
c. I've never really been aware of any particular reasons why I'm working in the garden.

17. Why might I build a piece of furniture for my home rather than buy one?

a. To save money.
b. To build a piece of furniture.
c. For the satisfaction that comes with building something myself.

18. You have enlisted the help of a friend to build an entertainment unit for yourself. What is most important in making the experience fun?

a. Making sure the job is completed correctly.
b. Working together will be fun; how the job is completed is less important.
c. Making sure that I remain in control of the project.

19. When I am reading, time seems to go by:

a. Fast.
b. Slow.
c. The same as when I'm not reading.

20. When I play video games:

a. I'm always aware of my score, overall performance, etc.
b. I don't pay attention to anything in particular.
c. I focus on myself having a good time.

SCORING INSTRUCTIONS

Use the selfish, environmental, and action Playing answers below to tally your Playing SEA score.

Selfish, environmental, and action Playing answers

1. a. selfish b. environmental c. action
2. a. action b. selfish c. environmental
3. a. selfish b. environmental c. action
4. a. selfish b. action c. environmental
5. a. action b. environmental c. selfish
6. a. action b. selfish c. environmental
7. a. environmental b. selfish c. action
8. a. action b. environmental c. selfish
9. a. environmental b. selfish c. action
10. a. environmental b. action c. selfish
11. a. action b. selfish c. environmental
12. a. action b. selfish c. environmental
13. a. environmental b. selfish c. action
14. a. selfish b. action c. environmental
15. a. environmental b. action c. selfish
16. a. selfish b. environmental c. action
17. a. environmental b. action c. selfish
18. a. environmental b. action c. selfish
19. a. action b. environmental c. selfish
20. a. environmental b. action c. selfish

Playing scoring

Selfish: $$\frac{\text{Total number of selfish responses}}{20} \times 100$$

Environmental: $$\frac{\text{Total number of environmental responses}}{20} \times 100$$

Action: $$\frac{\text{Total number of action responses}}{20} \times 100$$

Playing SEA score = ____ : ____ : ____

Before I give you the definition of playing that was used to develop these questions and answers, I want you to tell me what your definition of playing is… Really. What is it—to play? To help guide your thoughts about playing, come up with answers on a piece of paper to the following questions:

- Where are you most likely to play?
- Does everyone—children and adults—play?
- Who plays more—children or adults?
- Why does this one group—children or adults—play more?
- If adults do, in fact, play less than children, what replaces play in adulthood?
- Is it irresponsible to play as an adult?
- Give one example of you playing.

Now that you have a more explicit idea about your definition of playing, take a look at the definition of playing that was used to develop the "playing" questions and answers. The playing part of life is mostly composed of your experiences associated with leisure, recreation, and relaxation. These experiences are the opposite of work-life experiences because you are not "required to do" whatever you are doing for the experiences to exist—often you have a great sense of control within the playing part of life. The playing part of life is associated with words like hobby, sport, game, job, pastime, entertainment, amusement, and recreation. If the following are not related to the work part of your life, then they are likely associated with your playing part of life: cleaning, organizing, washing, facilitating life's most typical objects: houses, gardens, cars, relationships, careers, etc. Key elements of you playing include:

- Personal or home projects.
- Pastimes.
- Free time.
- Reading.
- Music (listening to or making).
- Relaxing.
- Games.
- Recreation.
- Vacation.
- Doing things that have no explicit goals.
- Perception of time possibly being affected when you're playing.

POSSESSIONS QUESTIONS

1. **I shop:**
   a. Because I have to.
   b. Because it feels good.
   c. For something to do.

2. **When I'm shopping for something:**
   a. I tend to lose track of time.
   b. Time seems to slow down.
   c. Time goes by like it does when I'm not shopping for something.

3. **My house was on fire (and I knew every person was out of the house but me) and I picked up one item as I was leaving. What would that item be?**
   a. I'd grab my most cherished item.
   b. I'd grab whatever was on the way out of the house.
   c. I'd grab my important documents.

4. **Who is happiest?**
   a. Societies that do not even include possessions as being related to happiness.
   b. Societies that put a lot of importance on possessions.
   c. Societies that do not put a lot of importance on possessions.

5. **How many pairs of shoes do I own?**
   a. I have no idea.
   b. Just enough that I need.
   c. Too many!

6. **My most favorite possession:**
   a. Is forever changing.
   b. Is something I knew I would obtain.
   c. Was thrust upon me.

7. **People usually collect things:**
   a. Because it makes them feel good.
   b. Because they like the things they're collecting.
   c. For the sake of collecting itself.

8. **The happiest people are likely to have:**
   a. The most possessions.
   b. Possessions have no relationship to happiness.
   c. The least possessions.

9. **What is the greatest reason my possessions exist?**
   a. I like them.
   b. There is no particular reason—life is simply made up of gaining and losing possessions.
   c. I have to have them.

10. **With shelter, food, and water provided, which of the following would be most vital to my survival if I was on a deserted island for one year?**
    a. I could survive with anything or nothing beyond the necessities described above.
    b. I'd need a lot more than the necessities described above.
    c. I'd want a lot more than the necessities described above.

11. **What is my most prized possession?**
    a. Something a loved one gave to me.
    b. Something I got for myself.
    c. I don't prize possessions.

12. **What is in my wallet/purse?**
    a. The basics: identification, money, checks, credit cards, etc.
    b. I have no idea.
    c. The basics and beyond: identification, money, checks, credit cards, photos, personal items, etc.

13. **What is within my most personal physical space?**
    a. Mostly things that others have obtained for me.
    b. Mostly things that I just picked up by myself or with others along the way.
    c. Mostly things that I have obtained on my own.

14. **If someone looked in my car and trunk, he/she would likely see:**
    a. Mostly personal items.
    b. I don't keep track of what is in my car and trunk.
    c. Mostly items for car maintenance and emergency situations.

15. **Concerning my tastes in personal possessions:**
    a. I go with whatever feels right at the moment, rather than seek out any specific trendy item or think about what I like.
    b. I'm always up with the latest trends, features, etc.
    c. I know what I like, and don't necessarily follow the latest trends.

16. **When it comes to selecting clothing:**
    a. I wear whatever is within reach when I'm getting dressed.
    b. I'm most influenced by my own personal preferences.
    c. I tend to be fashion conscious and follow the trends.

17. **If you had the power to do one of the following things, which of the following things would you do?**
    a. Make my family happy.
    b. Make me happy.
    c. Happiness is not a thing.

18. **I would define an attractive living environment as:**
    a. One that I've furnished with beautiful and comfortable items.
    b. One that makes visitors feel at home.
    c. There are many ways to define an "attractive living environment," many of which have nothing to do with beauty and comfort relative to me and my visitors.

19. **If I had a complete collection of a favorite item, and one of the items was ruined in some way:**
    a. I would need to replace the missing item so as to complete the collection.
    b. I would want to replace the missing item.
    c. I would have an incomplete collection.

20. **My favorite aspect of shopping is:**
    a. Finding just what I'm looking for.
    b. Finding a great buy.
    c. The act of shopping itself.

Scoring instructions

Use the selfish, environmental, and action Possessions answers below to tally your Possessions SEA score.

Selfish, environmental, and action Possessions answers

1. a. environmental b. selfish c. action
2. a. action b. environmental c. selfish
3. a. selfish b. action c. environmental
4. a. action b. environmental c. selfish
5. a. action b. selfish c. environmental
6. a. action b. selfish c. environmental
7. a. environmental b. selfish c. action
8. a. environmental b. action c. selfish
9. a. selfish b. action c. environmental
10. a. action b. environmental c. selfish
11. a. environmental b. selfish c. action
12. a. environmental b. action c. selfish
13 a. environmental b. action c. selfish
14. a. selfish b. action c. environmental
15. a. action b. environmental c. selfish
16. a. action b. selfish c. environmental
17 a. selfish b. environmental c. action
18. a. selfish b. environmental c. action
19. a. environmental b. selfish c. action
20. a. selfish b. environmental c. action

Possessions scoring

Selfish: $\frac{\text{Total number of selfish responses}}{20} \times 100$

Environmental: $\frac{\text{Total number of environmental responses}}{20} \times 100$

Action: $\frac{\text{Total number of action responses}}{20} \times 100$

Possessions SEA score = ____ : ____ : ____

Before I give you the definition of possessions that was used to develop these questions and answers, I want you to tell me what your definition of possessions is... Really. What is it to possess? To help guide your thoughts about possessions, come up with answers on a piece of paper to the following questions:

- How does shopping—especially in a society that is as rich as America—fit into your definition of possessions?
- How does sentimentality fit into your definition of possessions?
- Do possessions have to be materialistic?
- Within relationships and families, are people one another's possessions? My daughter... My husband...

Now that you have a more explicit idea about your definition of possessions, take a look at the definition of possessions that was used to develop the "possessions" questions and answers. The possessions part of life is composed of the materialistic world of which you have ownership (or you *believe* to have ownership). In addition to things within your possession, the possessions part of life also may include: people and places—whatever objects (organic or inorganic) used to define your "owned" environment may be included. Possessions are not to be confused with the money part of life, as items within the possessions part of life may not have any monetary value. Sentimentality may be an important concept within this life category. Key elements of your possessions include:

- Having a personal definition of a "prized possession."
- A significant positive correlation between your possessions and what the society in which you are living reinforces you to possess—in other words, fad items have an impact on you.
- Possessions include at least one collection of some sort.
- An understanding that one part of your self (important or not) is defined by your possessions.
- Shopping.
- Perception of time possibly being affected when you are with your possessions.

Family questions

1. **The aspect of having a pet that I do (or would) enjoy the most is:**
   a. My pet making me happy.
   b. Me making my pet happy.
   c. Being with my pet.

2. **Which one of the following best fits my definition of family?**
   a. People I love.
   b. Any loving environment.
   c. People who love me.

3. **Which of the following is the most likely thing I find myself doing with my family?**
   a. Nothing in particular.
   b. Usually something in particular that I planned.
   c. Usually something in particular that my family planned.

4. **When I am away from my family:**
   a. I find myself contacting my family more than my family contacting me.
   b. Contacting one another never has been anything that I've paid much attention to.
   c. I find my family contacting me more than me contacting my family.

5. **Family can be:**
   a. Anybody that is biologically related to me.
   b. Anybody that I love.
   c. Anybody.

6. **The love I have for my family is:**
   a. Unconditional.
   b. Conditional upon what I do to them.
   c. Conditional upon what they do to me.

7. **I'm on a family vacation—I'm most likely to be:**
   a. Doing things that my family likes doing.
   b. Doing things that I like doing.
   c. Doing things that my family and I are not likely to be immediately aware of liking or not liking until after we've done these things.

8. **My relationship with my mother mostly is (was):**
   a. Kept intact by me.
   b. Neither of us ever have (had) to expend energy to keep our relationship intact.
   c. Kept intact by her.

9. **My mother raised me to:**
   a. Love myself.
   b. Be loving.
   c. Love others.

10. **Children:**
    a. Define who their parents are.
    b. Are defined by their parents.
    c. Are as defined by their parents as they are defining their parents.

11. **The time I spend with my family passes by:**
    a. Quickly.
    b. Slowly.
    c. No different from time passing by in any other situation.

12. **For what reason might I quarrel with a family member?**
    a. A personal insult.
    b. I don't need a reason to quarrel with a family member.
    c. An incident involving another family member.

13. **I am spending the evening with my family. What do I enjoy most?**
    a. Spending time with my family; what we do is not important.
    b. Spending time doing something I enjoy.
    c. Spending time watching others have fun.

14. **What is the most important thing I can do for my family?**
    a. Provide emotional and/or financial support.
    b. Be dependable and loyal.
    c. Be with them.

15. **If two or more members of my family have a disagreement and are not speaking with each other, I:**
    a. Try to help resolve the disagreement.
    b. I do nothing; disagreements are a natural part of family relationships.
    c. I decide to intervene based on the grief it causes other family members.

16. A member of your family goes on a trip. You:
   a. Make sure you have all the contact information for that person.
   b. Assume that some other member of your family has that person's information.
   c. Wish the family member "bon voyage."

17. The primary component necessary to maintain loving relationships within my family is:
   a. Loving them.
   b. Me keeping in touch with everyone.
   c. Having everyone keep in touch with you.

18. Who would be most likely to be considered "part of my family?"
   a. Someone who is giving towards my family.
   b. Someone who my family is giving towards.
   c. Someone who does not get caught up with the giving and taking that goes on within familial relationships.

19. My relationship with my father is (was):
   a. Neither of us have (had) to expend energy to keep our relationship intact.
   b. Kept intact by me.
   c. Kept intact by him.

20. My father raised me to:
   a. Love myself.
   b. Love others.
   c. Be loving.

SCORING INSTRUCTIONS

Use the selfish, environmental, and action Family answers below to tally your Family SEA score.

Selfish, environmental, and action Family answers

1. a. environmental b. selfish c. action
2. a. selfish b. action c. environmental
3. a. action b. selfish c. environmental
4. a. selfish b. action c. environmental
5. a. environmental b. selfish c. action
6. a. action b. selfish c. environmental
7. a. environmental b. selfish c. action
8. a. selfish b. action c. environmental
9. a. selfish b. action c. environmental
10. a. selfish b. environmental c. action
11. a. action b. environmental c. selfish
12. a. selfish b. action c. environmental
13. a. action b. selfish c. environmental
14. a. environmental b. selfish c. action
15. a. selfish b. action c. environmental
16. a. selfish b. environmental c. action
17. a. action b. selfish c. environmental
18. a. environmental b. selfish c. action
19. a. action b. selfish c. environmental
20. a. selfish b. environmental c. action

Family scoring

Selfish: $\frac{\text{Total number of selfish responses}}{20} \times 100$

Environmental: $\frac{\text{Total number of environmental responses}}{20} \times 100$

Action: $\frac{\text{Total number of action responses}}{20} \times 100$

Family SEA score = ____ : ____ : ____

Before I give you the definition of family that was used to develop these questions and answers, I want you to tell me what your definition of family is... Really. What is the definition of family? To help guide your thoughts about family, come up with answers on a piece of paper to the following questions:

- What is it to have a family?
- Do you have to be biologically/legally related to someone, to call him or her family?
- What are the differences in the relationships between family and friends?
- Does proximity—physical distance—have a significant impact on family?

Now that you have a more explicit idea about your definition of family, take a look at the definition of family that was used to develop the "family" questions and answers. The family part of life is composed of kin that may or may not be biologically related to you. This kin has labels such as: father, son, mother, daughter, brother, sister, uncle, aunt, cousins, grandparent, nephew, niece, etc. Relationships with kin are likely to have a component of commitment. Kin are likely to live in close proximity with one another. Key elements of your family include:

- Definition of kin, including domestic animals and pets.
- Having an understanding about what an ideal family is.
- Kin doing many activities with one another.
- Knowing when your kin are separated on short-term or long-term bases, there is an effort to stay in contact with one another.
- Kin loving one another.
- Mother being a significant part (not necessarily good or bad part) of your kin.
- Father being a significant part (not necessarily good or bad part) of your kin.
- Children and your childhood being significant parts (not necessarily good or bad parts) of your kin.
- Fighting occurring among your kin.
- Perception of time possibly being affected when you are with your kin.

Home questions

1. **Home is:**
   a. Where I feel comfortable.
   b. Where my loved ones are.
   c. Anyplace.

2. **When I am at home:**
   a. I'm typically with friends and family.
   b. I'm typically alone with my thoughts.
   c. I'm never really aware of the amount of time that I spend alone or with friends and family at home.

3. **The best thing about being at home is:**
   a. It allows me to do what I want to do.
   b. There is no particular "best" thing about being at home.
   c. I do what I want to do.

4. **The people I live with at home:**
   a. Regardless of whether or not we get along, they are significant for being a part of my home.
   b. I mostly get along with.
   c. Mostly get along with me.

5. **My biggest worry about home is:**
   a. I don't worry about home.
   b. Losing my home.
   c. Me wanting some home other than the one I currently have.

6. **Which of the following words comes closest to the first word that comes to my mind when I hear the word "home"?**
   a. Family.
   b. Playing.
   c. Owning.

7. **When I spend a weekend at home, my time feels:**
   a. Short.
   b. Long.
   c. No different from time spent during any other days of the week not spent at home.

8. **My comfort at home is dependent upon:**
   a. Being able to do anything.
   b. Me.
   c. The people and things that live with me.

9. **"Home is where the heart is," may be a correct statement if:**
   a. The "heart" is within me.
   b. The "heart" is beating.
   c. The "heart" is within my family and friends.

10. **Homes are happy when:**
    a. They are filled with action and goings-on.
    b. They are filled with family and friends.
    c. They are filled with people who want to be happy.

11. **Most of the things on the walls of my home are:**
    a. Pictures/Photos of family and friends.
    b. Relatively random items that I've put up for one reason or another.
    c. Posters, paintings, pictures, photographs, etc., of things that I like.

12. **Why might it be beneficial to keep my kitchen clean and orderly?**
    a. Because I want to keep my kitchen clean and orderly.
    b. Because someone who sees the kitchen messy may think I am a messy or unclean person.
    c. I don't associate any particular benefits to keeping my kitchen clean and orderly.

13. **What makes a "house" a "home?"**
    a. Having my personal belongings in a house makes it a home.
    b. There is no particular difference between a "house" and a "home"; they are both places where people live.
    c. The people who live there make a house a home.

14. **Why is home improvement a billion-dollar industry in the U.S.?**
    a. There is likely no one reason.
    b. Because people like to do-it-themselves.
    c. Because it is socially important to have an attractive home.

15. **Which is the most important room in the home?**
    a. The bedroom, because it is the most personal room.
    b. The living room/den, because it is the room most people will see.
    c. Although rooms are important in a home, I don't think any one room in a home is more important than another.

16. **Why might I prefer to own a home rather than rent one?**
    a. Because I want something I can call my own.
    b. I don't assign any particular value to either renting or owning a home.
    c. For the tax benefit.

17. **In which room do I most often sleep, and why?**
    a. In my bedroom, because that's where I'm supposed to sleep.
    b. In my bedroom, because that's where I'm most comfortable sleeping.
    c. I sleep wherever I am when I'm tired.

18. **What is the best benefit of knowing my neighbors?**
    a. Knowing anybody is beneficial in itself.
    b. They can help me whenever I need something.
    c. Knowing neighbors is basic for building healthy communities.

19. **If someone was to look around my bedroom, he/she would see:**
    a. All kinds of things...some unusual, some not.
    b. Things that reflect my personality.
    c. Things that one would find in most bedrooms.

20. **My ideal home includes:**
    a. Having a home filled with things I cherish and enjoy.
    b. Having a home filled with things that would make my friends and family comfortable.
    c. Nothing in particular.

Scoring instructions

Use the selfish, environmental, and action Home answers below to tally your Home SEA score.

Selfish, environmental, and action Home answers

1. a. selfish b. environmental c. action
2. a. environmental b. selfish c. action
3. a. environmental b. action c. selfish
4. a. action b. selfish c. environmental
5. a. action b. environmental c. selfish
6. a. environmental b. action c. selfish
7. a. action b. environmental c. selfish
8. a. action b. selfish c. environmental
9. a. selfish b. action c. environmental
10. a. action b. environmental c. selfish
11. a. environmental b. action c. selfish
12. a. selfish b. environmental c. action
13. a. selfish b. action c. environmental
14. a. action b. selfish c. environmental
15. a. selfish b. environmental c. action
16. a. selfish b. action c. environmental
17. a. environmental b. selfish c. action
18. a. action b. selfish c. environmental
19. a. action b. selfish c. environmental
20. a. selfish b. environmental c. action

Home scoring

Selfish: $\frac{\text{Total number of selfish responses}}{20} \times 100$

Environmental: $\frac{\text{Total number of environmental responses}}{20} \times 100$

Action: $\frac{\text{Total number of action responses}}{20} \times 100$

Home SEA score = ____ : ____ : ____

Before I give you the definition of home that was used to develop these questions and answers, I want you to tell me what your definition of home is... Really. What is the definition of home? To help guide your thoughts about home, come up with answers on a piece of paper to the following questions:

- How does the term stress fit into your definition of home?
- What is it to have a home?
- Is home a physical location—is home equal to house?
- What are some things that people are most likely to do within their home that they may not do anyplace else?
- Is it necessary for home to have social component?

Now that you have a more explicit idea about your definition of home, take a look at the definition of home that was used to develop the "home" questions and answers. The home part of life is composed of the shelters in which you feel most comfortable and at peace with yourself. The home part of life may include such physical things as: houses, apartments, condominiums, trailers, etc., but is less about the physical shelter and more about how you feel within this physical shelter. Shelter is defined relative to the place sheltering you from the stresses and expectations of the outside world more so than the place sheltering you from the physical elements. You're most likely to be your "true" self within your home. The family part of life is positively correlated with the home part of life. Key elements of your home include:

- Comfort.
- Socialization.
- A place where most of your stresses are most likely to be worked out.
- A place where you can have pure control, volition, and ownership.
- It being defined by you.
- Definition of happiness being likely best understood relative to home.
- Having a very clear definition of home.
- Home being composed of different physical locations (e.g., rooms).
- Neighbors defining a significant part of your home.
- Perception of time possibly being affected when you are home.

Friendship questions

1. **When I'm with my friends:**
   a. Time goes by fast.
   b. Time goes by slowly.
   c. Time goes by like any other time when I'm not with my friends.

2. **A friend calls on the telephone and asks if I'd like to go out to eat with him/her. My most likely response would be:**
   a. My response would depend on my schedule as to whether I could go.
   b. Yes.
   c. My response would depend upon whether I like the restaurant my friend is inviting me to—and other factors such as who else is going, whether I'm hungry, etc.

3. **My definition of a "best" friend is:**
   a. Someone who I find has a lot in common with me.
   b. Someone who finds me very attractive.
   c. Anyone has the potential to be a best friend.

4. **One of the worst things a friend could do to me is:**
   a. Lie.
   b. Tell a lie about me.
   c. Tell a lie about him/herself.

5. **One of the best attributes a friend has is:**
   a. Giving me things that I want.
   b. Giving.
   c. Giving me things that are important to him/herself.

6. **The most typical situation involving me and my friends is:**
   a. Us hanging out—doing nothing in particular.
   b. Us doing something I like doing.
   c. Us doing something they like doing.

7. **When getting in contact with my friends:**
   a. I've never really noticed who initiates the contacts.
   b. I initiate contact with my friends more often than they do me.
   c. My friends initiate contact with me more often than I do them.

8. I run into a friend that I haven't spoken to in years. What happens?
   a. We'd likely have a lively conversation—time is insignificant when it comes to friendship.
   b. I'd feel guilty about not having been in touch with my friend for so long.
   c. We'd likely have a conversation; however, it would be a difficult one since so much time had passed.

9. I share an intimate secret with a friend. I probably did this because:
   a. It makes me feel better about myself.
   b. There is unlikely to be any reason why things like this happen.
   c. Situations with friends just seem to cause things like this to happen.

10. A friend promises to get me tickets to one of my favorite leisure events, but never delivers on his/her promise. What is the most likely reason for my friend's failure?
   a. I don't see this as a "failure." It is the thought that counts.
   b. Probably something outside of my friend's control negated the possibility of him/her getting the tickets.
   c. I probably set my expectations too high on actually getting the tickets.

11. If I had a financial windfall, then my friendships would:
   a. Change—not sure whether they would change for the better or worse, but they would definitely change.
   b. I would not let my friendships change.
   c. Things like money do not affect my friendships.

12. My best friend cancels plans for the evening at the last minute. What do I do?
   a. I see if another friend wants to do something.
   b. I take it in stride; sometimes things just don't work out.
   c. My plans for the evening are ruined—I don't do anything.

13. A close friend betrays a confidence. What would most people do in this situation?
   a. Most people's responses would be dependent upon the reason for the betrayal.
   b. Because of the close friendship, most people's responses would be minimal.
   c. Most people's responses would be dependent upon their own personality traits.

14. **When making plans with my friends, I most likely:**
    a. Make suggestions based on what I feel like doing.
    b. Am open to whatever happens.
    c. Go along with what the group wants to do.

15. **Most people that I know:**
    a. Like or dislike me based upon things I have done to them.
    b. Have no particular feelings of like or dislike towards me.
    c. Like or dislike me based upon things they have done to me.

16. **When forming new friendships, I:**
    a. Wait to see if the other person is interested in forming a friendship with me.
    b. Try to assess whether or not the person would make a good friend.
    c. Get caught up in the beauty of a friendship's formative stages.

17. **For what behavior would I most likely end a friendship?**
    a. No one behavior would end a friendship.
    b. Being betrayed.
    c. Having to betray my friend.

18. **If money were no object, what kind of vacation would I plan for myself and a best friend?**
    a. I would probably pick something that I think we would both enjoy.
    b. Being together on vacation would be great; what we did would be less important.
    c. I would let my best friend pick whatever he/she wanted to do.

19. **Some people just seem to make friends wherever they go. The best explanation for this is:**
    a. Some people are just naturally attractive.
    b. Some people seek friends wherever they go.
    c. There's likely no one explanation for this phenomenon.

20. **The neighbors with whom I'm most likely to become friendly are:**
    a. Any neighbors are potential friends.
    b. Those who act friendly toward me.
    c. Those who I perceive as being nice people.

SCORING INSTRUCTIONS

Use the selfish, environmental, and action Friendship answers below to tally your Friendship SEA score.

Selfish, environmental, and action Friendship answers

1. a. action b. environmental c. selfish
2. a. environmental b. action c. selfish
3. a. selfish b. environmental c. action
4. a. action b. selfish c. environmental
5. a. selfish b. action c. environmental
6. a. action b. selfish c. environmental
7. a. action b. selfish c. environmental
8. a. action b. selfish c. environmental
9. a. selfish b. action c. environmental
10. a. action b. environmental c. selfish
11. a. environmental b. selfish c. action
12. a. selfish b. action c. environmental
13. a. environmental b. action c. selfish
14. a. selfish b. action c. environmental
15. a. selfish b. action c. environmental
16. a. environmental b. selfish c. action
17. a. action b. environmental c. selfish
18. a. selfish b. action c. environmental
19. a. environmental b. selfish c. action
20. a. action b. environmental c. selfish

Friendship scoring

Selfish: $$\frac{\text{Total number of selfish responses}}{20} \times 100$$

Environmental: $$\frac{\text{Total number of environmental responses}}{20} \times 100$$

Action: $$\frac{\text{Total number of action responses}}{20} \times 100$$

Friendship SEA score = _____ : _____ : _____

Before I give you the definition of friendships that was used to develop these questions and answers, I want you to tell me what your definition of friendships is… Really. What is the definition of friendships? To help guide your thoughts about friendships, come up with answers on a piece of paper to the following questions:

- What is it to be in a friendship?
- What are the differences between short-term friendships and long-term friendships?
- Is there a limit on the number of friends one can have?
- How does the term acquaintance fit into your definition of friend?
- Do you necessarily have to "like" your friends?

Now that you have a more explicit idea about your definition of friendships, take a look at the definition of friendships that was used to develop the "friendships" questions and answers. The friendships part of life is composed of short-term and long-term relationships you have had throughout your lifetime. These relationships may be simply defined by time (*we've known one another a long time*) or proximity (*we live next door to one another*), but are more likely associated with some significantly developed emotional bond and thus friendships do not need concurrent time or space. Like the family part of life, friendships likely include a component of commitment. Key elements of your friendships include:

- There being a public part of your friendships.
- Having a definition of a best friend.
- There being an understanding that your friendships have good and bad parts to them.
- A significant part and number of your activities being defined by your friendships.
- There being some type of ongoing verbal and/or non-verbal (e.g., thinking about) component to your friendships.
- Friendships having an understood basis and beginning.
- Novel environments often breeding friendships.
- Perception of time possibly being affected when you are with your friends.

Partner Questions

1. **When I'm spending time with my partner:**
   a. Time seems to fly by.
   b. Time seems to slow down.
   c. Time seems as it does any other time when I'm not with my partner.

2. **The most important aspect of a loving relationship is:**
   a. Me loving my partner.
   b. My partner loving me.
   c. Loving.

3. **The success of a long-term loving relationship is mostly based upon:**
   a. Not any one thing.
   b. Me working on the relationship.
   c. Both of us working on the relationship.

4. **One of the best aspects of falling in love is:**
   a. Someone loving me.
   b. Having someone to love.
   c. The experience of loving.

5. **My definition of unconditional love is:**
   a. Loving no matter what the circumstances.
   b. Unconditional love may exist, but it is dependent upon my lover unconditionally loving me, too.
   c. There is no way I can say truthfully that I could love someone no matter what the circumstances.

6. **My life partner is stricken with a physical condition that leaves him/her unable to care for him/herself. What would happen to the relationship?**
   a. My commitment is forever: I'd stay to the end with my life partner.
   b. The relationship would be dependent upon my life partner's wishes.
   c. No physical condition would significantly impact the relationship.

7. **When making love:**
   a. I'm in control of having an orgasm.
   b. Orgasms are not a necessary part of making love.
   c. My partner is in control of me having an orgasm.

8. **My partner and I have an argument. The argument is most likely due to:**
    a. Not any one thing in particular—having arguments is just part of relationships.
    b. My partner.
    c. Me.

9. **Falling in love is determined by:**
    a. Me.
    b. The person who is attracted to me.
    c. No person (including me) determines whether or not I fall in love.

10. **Marriage is:**
    a. Largely determined by factors outside the control of the people involved in it (e.g., society, family, traditions, religion, etc.).
    b. Part of the flow of long-term relationships.
    c. A person's decision to make a long-term commitment.

11. **My memories of previous sexual experiences:**
    a. Are memories I don't want to forget.
    b. Will be with me forever.
    c. Come and go, but are usually not about any one person, place, or thing.

12. **Which of the following most closely describes what I enjoy most about having sex with my partner?**
    a. Knowing my partner wants to please me sexually.
    b. The act of having sex itself.
    c. Pleasing my partner sexually.

13. **What do I most enjoy when falling in love with someone?**
    a. The romantic things my lover does for me.
    b. The romantic things I do for my lover.
    c. The feelings associated with falling in love.

14. **On a day-to-day basis, which of the following best describes my ideal relationship with my partner?**
    a. My partner sharing his/her life experiences with me.
    b. Sharing.
    c. Me sharing my life experiences with my partner.

15. **My partner and I have gotten into an argument. The most likely next step will involve:**
    a. Our conflicts tend to resolve themselves over time.
    b. My partner approaching me to resolve the conflict.
    c. Me approaching my partner to resolve the conflict.

16. **My partner calls during the day and says he/she can get tickets to a concert for that night. My response would most likely be yes, if:**
    a. Just being asked would determine my decision.
    b. My partner wants to go.
    c. I want to go.

17. **My partner calls to cancel plans for the evening because he/she has to work late. I:**
    a. Am likely disappointed.
    b. Think about what else I can do for the evening.
    c. Am not affected; things come up.

18. **What do I most enjoy about spending special occasions with my partner?**
    a. The feeling of happiness that I bring to my partner.
    b. Being together.
    c. The feeling of happiness that my partner brings to me.

19. **What would be the most difficult aspect of losing my partner in death?**
    a. Me not being with my partner anymore.
    b. The experience of my partner and I no longer being together.
    c. My partner not being with me anymore.

20. **"Growing old with someone" means:**
    a. Sharing your life with someone.
    b. Someone sharing his/her life with you.
    c. Being with someone...nothing more, nothing less.

Scoring instructions

Use the selfish, environmental, and action Partner answers below to tally your Partner SEA score.

Selfish, environmental, and action Partner answers

1. a. action b. environmental c. selfish
2. a. selfish b. environmental c. action
3. a. action b. selfish c. environmental
4. a. environmental b. selfish c. action
5. a. action b. environmental c. selfish
6. a. selfish b. environmental c. action
7. a. selfish b. action c. environmental
8. a. action b. environmental c. selfish
9. a. selfish b. environmental c. action
10. a. environmental b. action c. selfish
11. a. selfish b. environmental c. action
12. a. environmental b. action c. selfish
13. a. environmental b. selfish c. action
14. a. environmental b. action c. selfish
15. a. action b. environmental c. selfish
16. a. action b. environmental c. selfish
17. a. environmental b. selfish c. action
18. a. selfish b. action c. environmental
19. a. selfish b. action c. environmental
20. a. selfish b. environmental c. action

Partner scoring

Selfish: $\frac{\text{Total number of selfish responses}}{20} \times 100$

Environmental: $\frac{\text{Total number of environmental responses}}{20} \times 100$

Action: $\frac{\text{Total number of action responses}}{20} \times 100$

Partner SEA score = ____ : ____ : ____

Before I give you the definition of partner that was used to develop these questions and answers, I want you to tell me what your definition of partner is... Really. What is the definition of partner? To help guide your thoughts about partner, come up with answers on a piece of paper to the following questions:

- How does the term "unconditional" fit into your definition of partner and spouse?
- What is it to have a partner or spouse? What good things does it bring to a person? What bad things does it bring to a person?
- Is the term "forever" realistic or idealistic when it comes to how long partners/spouses "should be" together?
- Which of the following Venn diagrams, with the circles representing the people involved in the relationship, defines the healthiest long-term relationship?

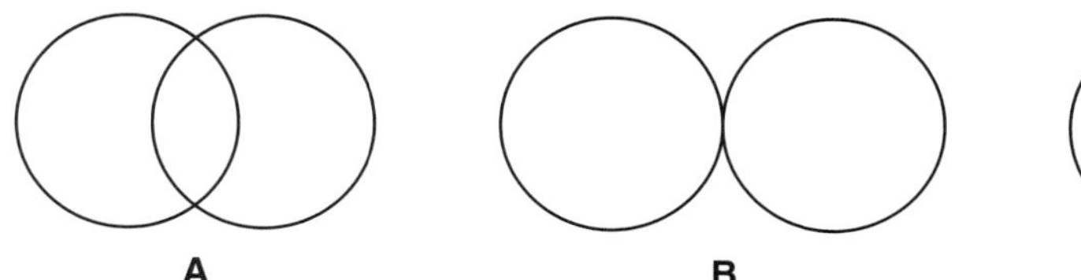
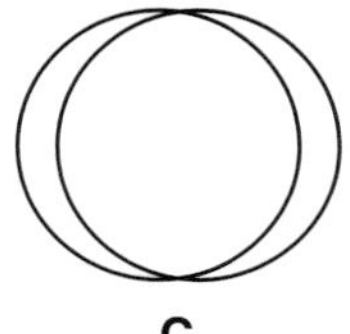

Now that you have a more explicit idea about your definition of partner, take a look at the definition of partner that was used to develop the "partner" questions and answers. The partner part of life is composed of your romantic or companionate dyad-relationships that have some degree of personal significance of time or feelings of love/lust or thoughts of commitment. Key elements of your partners include:

- You deeming your partner as more important than most any other thing in your life.
- There being an actual or expected longevity associated with the relationship with your partner.
- You perceiving good things about your partner.
- The relationship with your partner being perceived as being unconditional.
- There being intimacy, sexuality, or sensuality involved in the relationship with your partner.
- Arguments or disagreements being part of the relationship with your partner.
- The relationship with your partner having a relatively unique and memorable beginning.
- Marriage (legal or otherwise) being part of the definition of the relationship with your partner.

- The relationship with your partner being—in part—built from experiences with past spouses/lovers/partners.
- Although the relationship with your partner may not be an ideal one, there is an ideal relationship in mind in which the current relationship may be compared.
- You doing a lot (if not the majority) of life's activities with your partner.
- Your partner and yourself being dependent upon one another.
- Loss of your partner coming at great emotional distress.
- Your perception of time possibly being affected when you are with your partner.

MONEY QUESTIONS

1. **While out on a walk, I see a $100 bill in the street. What do I do?**
   a. I continue walking.
   b. I stop to pick it up because it is money.
   c. I stop to pick it up because I want it.

2. **When eating in a restaurant with company, I look outside the restaurant's window and see a $20 bill. It is raining outside and I'm not finished eating. What do I do?**
   a. I wait for the rain to stop and/or finish eating, and then go and get the 20 dollars.
   b. As soon as I see it, I go and get it.
   c. Money is not something worth getting wet or hungry over, so I continue eating and enjoying my company.

3. **I am at the grocery store and find an envelope with money in it. What do I do?**
   a. I would ask if anyone had reported having lost money.
   b. I would count the money.
   c. I would turn in the money at customer service.

4. **Money is important:**
   a. Money per se has no importance.
   b. Because I like it.
   c. Because it allows me to be happy.

5. **The amount of money a person makes:**
   a. Defines how hard that person works.
   b. Defines how lucky that person is.
   c. Defines nothing significant about that person.

6. **Who is happiest?**
   a. A person who works who never really pays any attention to how much money he/she will make over his/her lifetime.
   b. A person living off an inheritance of $1,000,000.
   c. A person who works 40 hours per week that knows he/she will make $1,000,000 over his/her lifetime.

7. **"Money makes the world go round" is a correct catchphrase if money is:**
   a. Something I'm in control of.
   b. Something that I've been given a lot of.
   c. Something that is for giving.

8. **A distant relative passes away, and surprises me by leaving me a large sum of money. What do I do with the money?**
   a. Give it away—keep up the surprises!
   b. It depends on what's going on in my life as to what I'd be doing with it.
   c. Save some of it and spend some of it.

9. **How important is money in my life?**
   a. It is very important, because I buy the things I want with money.
   b. The society that I live in is a token economy based upon money more than anything else, thus it has to be very important.
   c. Money is no more important than any other thing in my life.

10. **What would I do if my income was suddenly cut in half?**
    a. Panic because I would not have a way to pay my bills.
    b. Continue on—this is a part of life.
    c. Worry about maintaining my lifestyle.

11. **If I won the lottery, my first consideration would be:**
    a. The security it would provide me.
    b. The things I want to buy.
    c. Claiming the winnings.

12. **How important is money to my overall happiness?**
    a. Money is no more important to my happiness than any other thing in my life.
    b. I determine how money is associated with my happiness.
    c. Money determines how happy I am.

13. **People who have large incomes:**
    a. Are really no different than anyone else.
    b. Must have personal qualities that led to success.
    c. Must get lucky breaks.

14. When I get paid, the first thing I do with the money is:
   a. Pay my bills or buy necessities.
   b. Splurge on something for myself.
   c. Nothing in particular.

15. If I've decided to donate money to a charity, I:
   a. Do a bit of research and determine who needs the donation most urgently.
   b. Donate; which charity gets the donation is less important that the act of donating itself.
   c. Pick my favorite charity and make the donation.

16. You make a bad investment and lose a moderate sum of money. You:
   a. Do nothing; this is part of the ups and downs of investing.
   b. Try to figure out why the company(ies) you invested in are so financially poor.
   c. Make a plan to recoup your losses.

17. You discover that someone you know is very wealthy. Does your relationship with that person change?
   a. Yes; I'd be thinking of that person in terms of the discrepancy between our incomes.
   b. Yes; I'd be thinking of all the personal items that person can afford and must possess.
   c. No; money makes no difference in my relationships with my friends.

18. The main reason to save money is:
   a. To fund my retirement.
   b. For the sake of saving.
   c. To know that I have money.

19. How a person spends money:
   a. Tells something about that person's living environment.
   b. Tells nothing important about the person.
   c. Tells something about that person's self-control.

20. I am awarded a large raise in pay. I:
   a. Feel proud of myself.
   b. Do nothing out of the ordinary; I continue in my current activity.
   c. Begin to consider how the increase will affect my lifestyle.

Scoring instructions

Use the selfish, environmental, and action Money answers below to tally your Money SEA score.

Selfish, environmental, and action Money answers

1. a. action b. environmental c. selfish
2. a. environmental b. action c. selfish
3. a. selfish b. action c. environmental
4. a. action b. selfish c. environmental
5. a. selfish b. environmental c. action
6. a. action b. environmental c. selfish
7. a. selfish b. environmental c. action
8. a. action b. environmental c. selfish
9. a. selfish b. environmental c. action
10. a. environmental b. action c. selfish
11. a. environmental b. selfish c. action
12. a. action b. selfish c. environmental
13. a. action b. selfish c. environmental
14. a. environmental b. selfish c. action
15. a. environmental b. action c. selfish
16. a. action b. environmental c. selfish
17. a. environmental b. selfish c. action
18. a. environmental b. action c. selfish
19. a. environmental b. action c. selfish
20. a. selfish b. action c. environmental

Money scoring

Selfish: $\frac{\text{Total number of selfish responses}}{20} \times 100$

Environmental: $\frac{\text{Total number of environmental responses}}{20} \times 100$

Action: $\frac{\text{Total number of action responses}}{20} \times 100$

Money SEA score = ____ : ____ : ____

Before I give you the definition of money that was used to develop these questions and answers, I want you to tell me what your definition of money is... Really. What is the definition of money? To help guide your thoughts about money, come up with answers on a piece of paper to the following questions:

- What is it to be rich? What is it to be poor?
- Which of the following two scenarios would you rather have? Why? Be honest! I'm watching you!
    1. You, making $150,000 per year, and all your friends, family, and neighbors making $300,000 per year

       or

    2. You, making $75,000 per year, and all your friends, family, and neighbors making $50,000 per year

Now that you have a more explicit idea about your definition of money, take a look at the definition of money that was used to develop the "money" questions and answers. The money part of life is composed of your associations with money in particular and other societal tokens of reinforcement and reward in general. For example, the money part of life may also include credit and debt within your life. Key elements of your money include:

- Rewards and achievements being associated with your money.
- What you are doing for money's sake.
- Whether conscious or not, you wondering whether money is or you are in control of your life.
- Income.
- In whatever society you live, money being perceived as one of life's most important elements.
- Perception of time possibly being affected when you are dealing with money.

Work questions

1. **If I suddenly came into a lot of money, under what circumstances would I continue to work at my job?**
   a. If I really enjoyed my job.
   b. If my job provided something that made my life better or easier.
   c. Continuing to work at my job is not dependent upon my financial situation.

2. **When a training seminar is offered at work:**
   a. I'll go if it is a requirement.
   b. I'll go for the sake of going.
   c. I'll go if it is something of interest to me.

3. **When deciding whether or not to take part in an activity at work that is beyond my usual duties:**
   a. I consider how interesting the activity is to me.
   b. I agree to go, just for the experience.
   c. I consider how my co-workers will view my choice.

4. **When I have a boring task to complete at work:**
   a. I recognize that by definition, some part of work has to be boring.
   b. I've never noticed my work to be boring.
   c. I recognize the task is boring because I'm making it so—I try and change my attitude about it.

5. **I work:**
   a. For the sake of working.
   b. Because I enjoy it.
   c. Because I have to make a living.

6. **How would *not* getting an annual pay raise affect my job morale?**
   a. Depends if I like my job or not.
   b. Money has no impact on my morale at work.
   c. It would decrease it.

7. **The best thing about my work is:**
   a. It allows me to do what I want to do.
   b. The money.
   c. Having something to do.

8. **My co-workers:**
   a. I mostly get along with.
   b. Regardless of whether or not we get along, they are significant for being a part of work.
   c. Mostly get along with me.

9. **I've just done a wonderful job on a project at work, but my boss fails to notice it. What do I do?**
   a. Rewards are unnecessary for a job well done.
   b. Find a way to make sure my boss will notice.
   c. If a reward is meant to be, then it will happen on its own.

10. **Which of the following statements about how prestigious occupations are is the most accurate?**
    a. It depends on whether or not I'm in one of the occupations—the occupation that I am in is the most prestigious!
    b. Most prestigious: Physician; Average prestigiousness: Construction Worker; Least prestigious: Fast-food Employee
    c. Any occupation may be more/less prestigious than any other occupation depending upon what the individual is doing within the particular occupation.

11. **My biggest worry about work is:**
    a. Losing my job.
    b. I don't worry about work.
    c. Getting bored.

12. **If I didn't have to work, then I'd be:**
    a. Still working.
    b. Happy!
    c. I don't have to work if I don't want to work.

13. **Which of the following is the most significant thing for me at work?**
    a. Salary, fringe benefits.
    b. Liking what I do.
    c. Doing what I do.

14. Which of the following words comes closest to the first word that comes to my mind when I hear the word "work."
  a. Play.
  b. Money!
  c. Myself.

15. An 8-hour day at work typically feels like:
  a. 8 hours.
  b. Less than 8 hours.
  c. More than 8 hours.

16. I am late for a meeting at work and there is a lot of traffic. What do I do?
  a. I make opportunities to move through the traffic.
  b. I don't attempt to move through the traffic; traffic is part of driving.
  c. I move through the traffic as the opportunities arise.

17. Regarding my work and home lives:
  a. When I have to, I bring work home.
  b. I try to keep them separated.
  c. Thoughts and activity flow freely, regardless of the setting.

18. I'm in a meeting and, once again, my supervisor takes credit for one of my good ideas. I most likely:
  a. Take it as it comes—that is just a part of work.
  b. Tactfully confront my supervisor regarding his/her behavior.
  c. Feel angry and mistreated.

19. I have to go to the bank during my lunch hour at work. As I'm waiting in a long line, I'd most likely be:
  a. Watching the clock to make sure I won't be late returning to work.
  b. People-watching or looking at the lobby décor.
  c. Wondering why I waited until now to run my errand.

20. Sometimes when I'm doing work that I don't enjoy at my job:
  a. I think this may not be the "right" job for me.
  b. I think about how I can make this particular work more interesting.
  c. I work and find that time passes very quickly.

SCORING INSTRUCTIONS

Use the selfish, environmental, and action Work answers below to tally your Work SEA score.

Selfish, environmental, and action Work answers

1. a. selfish b. environmental c. action
2. a. environmental b. action c. selfish
3. a. selfish b. action c. environmental
4. a. environmental b. action c. selfish
5. a. action b. selfish c. environmental
6. a. selfish b. action c. environmental
7. a. selfish b. environmental c. action
8. a. selfish b. action c. environmental
9. a. environmental b. selfish c. action
10. a. selfish b. environmental c. action
11. a. environmental b. action c. selfish
12. a. action b. environmental c. selfish
13. a. environmental b. selfish c. action
14. a. action b. environmental c. selfish
15. a. selfish b. action c. environmental
16. a. selfish b. action c. environmental
17. a. environmental b. selfish c. action
18. a. action b. selfish c. environmental
19. a. environmental b. action c. selfish
20. a. environmental b. selfish c. action

Work scoring

Selfish: $\frac{\text{Total number of selfish responses}}{20} \times 100$

Environmental: $\frac{\text{Total number of environmental responses}}{20} \times 100$

Action: $\frac{\text{Total number of action responses}}{20} \times 100$

Work SEA score = ____ : ____ : ____

Before I give you the definition of work that was used to develop these questions and answers, I want you to tell me what your definition of work is... Really. What is the definition of work? To help guide your thoughts about work, come up with answers on a piece of paper to the following questions:

- What is it to have to work? Would you work if you did not have to?
- What do you make of research that demonstrates people are happier at work than on vacation, but are not aware of it?
- What are the bad things about work?
- What are the good things about work?
- What are differences between working at home versus working on the job?

Now that you have a more explicit idea about your definition of work, take a look at the definition of work that was used to develop the "work" questions and answers. The work part of life is mostly composed of experiences that have you being paid for whatever you are doing for the experiences to exist, or experiences that have you "required to do" whatever you are doing for the experiences to exist. Often, the work part of life has some combination of these two aforementioned types of experiences, and you do not have any great sense of control over either of them. The work part of life is associated with words like: job, profession, career, occupation, and livelihood. Additionally, the work part of life may be associated with maintaining (e.g., cleaning, organizing, washing, facilitating) life's most typical objects: houses, gardens, cars, relationships, careers, etc. Key elements of your work include:

- Money, rewards, and/or external reinforcement being intimately involved.
- Having structured goals and activities.
- Boredom.
- Recognizing good things about working.
- Recognizing bad things about working.
- Often contemplating about why you work.
- Society reinforcing the idea that work is something not to be enjoyed.
- A significant social element—for example, fellow employees.
- The perception of time possibly being affected when you are working.

HEALTH QUESTIONS

1. **I'm about to leave my house to go jogging for some exercise when it begins to rain outside. What do I do?**
   a. Wait for it to stop raining.
   b. Whether or not I go jogging is based upon whether or not I like jogging in the rain.
   c. Go jogging.

2. **When I worry:**
   a. I don't pay it much attention—worrying is part of living.
   b. I try to find a solution to resolve my worry.
   c. I wonder about the external factors that created my worry.

3. **It is easiest for me to sleep when:**
   a. I'm with someone.
   b. I'm alone.
   c. I'm sleepy.

4. **If I was told that I had a serious medical condition, the first thing I would do is:**
   a. Get a second opinion.
   b. Consider my situation.
   c. Find all the information I could regarding the condition.

5. **When I am depressed:**
   a. Bad moods don't affect me much.
   b. I want to be alone.
   c. I want my friends to bring me out of it.

6. **My physical health is largely dependent upon:**
   a. My general attitude.
   b. Not any one thing in particular; instead it is more dependent on just being active.
   c. The environment and my own genetics.

7. **My mental health is largely dependent upon:**
   a. The environment and my own genetics.
   b. My general attitude.
   c. Not any one thing in particular; instead it is more dependent on just staying active.

8. **My diet is mostly composed of:**
   a. Food that is good for me.
   b. Food that I like.
   c. Food that is around when I'm hungry.

9. **The number of hours of sleep I get each night is mostly due to:**
   a. When I decide to go to sleep and get up.
   b. Natural sleep processes.
   c. What my work, family, and/or leisure schedule demands.

10. **I exercise:**
    a. Because I like staying in shape.
    b. For the sake of exercising itself.
    c. Because it is associated with being healthy.

11. **I expect to live:**
    a. Whatever the life expectancy of a person with my demographics is.
    b. One day at a time.
    c. Based upon how I live my life, I'm going to either live well beyond or well below the average life expectancy of a person with my demographics.

12. **My motivation to have a healthy lifestyle mostly comes from:**
    a. Me.
    b. Living itself is motivating.
    c. Fear of the alternative—sickness and death.

13. **If I were to go on a diet, then I'd stay on it:**
    a. Indefinitely.
    b. Until I got bored of it.
    c. It depends upon whether or not the diet was yielding any worthwhile results.

14. **Which of the following do I agree with the most?**
    a. Health is mostly mind over matter.
    b. Health is mostly matter over mind.
    c. Health is mostly about the activity of mind and matter.

15. What I dislike most about feeling ill is:

a. My feelings associated with illness are not necessarily negative. Whether I'm sick or not, I feel like I want to feel.

b. Nothing; I see occasional illness as part of life.

c. Not being able to do the normal things I do in my life.

16. What do I consider to be the main benefit of maintaining a healthy lifestyle?

a. Being healthy.

b. Knowing that I have attained good physical and mental health.

c. Looking healthy to others.

17. When I attain a health goal:

a. I go onto the next goal—health is not about attaining goals but is instead about working towards them.

b. I look and feel good.

c. Others recognize how good I look and feel.

18. When I have a headache:

a. I think about what I can do to relieve it.

b. I think about what someone (e.g., physician) or something (e.g., medication) can do to relieve it.

c. Relief of the pain is not an issue.

19. When I come down with a cold, what am I most likely to do:

a. See my doctor and/or take medication to fight it.

b. My daily routines really don't change when I have a cold.

c. I'll slow down a bit, get more sleep, and maybe take a day or two off of work.

20. The most important factor in determining my overall health and well-being is:

a. My positive outlook.

b. A combination of factors whose whole is more important than the sum of any individual factors.

c. My friends and family.

Scoring instructions

Use the selfish, environmental, and action Health answers below to tally your Health SEA score.

Selfish, environmental, and action Health answers

1. a. environmental b. selfish c. action
2. a. action b. selfish c. environmental
3. a. environmental b. selfish c. action
4. a. environmental b. action c. selfish
5. a. action b. selfish c. environmental
6. a. selfish b. action c. environmental
7. a. environmental b. selfish c. action
8. a. environmental b. selfish c. action
9. a. selfish b. action c. environmental
10. a. selfish b. action c. environmental
11. a. environmental b. action c. selfish
12. a. selfish b. action c. environmental
13. a. action b. selfish c. environmental
14. a. selfish b. environmental c. action
15. a. selfish b. action c. environmental
16. a. action b. selfish c. environmental
17. a. action b. selfish c. environmental
18. a. selfish b. environmental c. action
19. a. environmental b. action c. selfish
20. a. selfish b. action c. environmental

Health scoring

Selfish: $\frac{\text{Total number of selfish responses}}{20} \times 100$

Environmental: $\frac{\text{Total number of environmental responses}}{20} \times 100$

Action: $\frac{\text{Total number of action responses}}{20} \times 100$

Health SEA score = ____ : ____ : ____

Before I give you the definition of health that was used to develop these questions and answers, I want you to tell me what your definition of health is... Really. What is the definition of health? To help guide your thoughts about health, come up with answers on a piece of paper to the following questions:

- What is well-being?
- What is it to be healthy?
- Come up with the ingredients that are necessary to live a healthy life. Be prepared to tell me why the ingredients are included within your *Healthy Life Recipe* and how much of each ingredient is necessary.

Now that you have a more explicit idea about your definition of health, take a look at the definition of health that was used to develop the "health" questions and answers. The health part of life is composed of your physical and psychological well-being. Physical and psychological well-being changes relative to your ability to do the activities you want to do. Specifically, your health is dependent upon the correlation between the total number of activities you *want* to do and the total number of activities that you actually *can* do, or, for that matter, *are doing*. The more positive this correlation, the healthier you are. Key elements of your health include:

- Having preventative measures against illness.
- Physical exercise.
- The total amount of stress, worry, or depression in your life (see **Table 2**).
- Sleeping patterns.
- Contemplations of death.
- Contemplations of physical and mental well-being.
- Diet.
- Levels of motivation.
- Behaviors associated with sickness.
- Life goals.

Self questions

1. **If I went to a party by myself and was meeting many people for the first time, then how would I be behaving?**
    a. My behavior would be reflective of my personality.
    b. My behavior would be reflective of the behavior of others.
    c. My behavior would be reflective of me enjoying the party.

2. **I am:**
    a. Conscientiously always on time.
    b. Constantly losing track of time.
    c. On time for important events.

3. **Who is in control of my life?**
    a. Me.
    b. Others.
    c. No one.

4. **When it comes to decisions of a religious or spiritual nature:**
    a. I listen to my heart and mind for meaning.
    b. The actual contemplating about my beliefs or the possibilities for my beliefs brings me meaning.
    c. I weigh factors like my upbringing, scientific facts, and specific teachings for meaning.

5. **When someone is in distress:**
    a. I ask the person if he/she would like me to help him/her.
    b. I help.
    c. Depending upon whether or not I think I can help the person, I help or not.

6. **In the middle of a painting project, I find a place to be painted that no one other than myself will ever see. What do I do?**
    a. Paint it—It is a part of the painting project.
    b. Paint it—I know it is there.
    c. Don't paint it—If no one other than myself is going to know about it, then there is really no point.

7. **I am most likely to fantasize about:**
    a. Having sex.
    b. Nothing in particular.
    c. Relationships.

8. **My own embarrassment mostly comes from:**
   a. Me doing something stupid.
   b. The people I do the embarrassing thing in front of.
   c. Being embarrassed is just another activity in life; it isn't necessarily related to my own shortcomings or those around me who may be judging those shortcomings.

9. **When I'm alone:**
   a. I think.
   b. I think about things that are within my control.
   c. I think about the stressors within my life.

10. **My private feelings are:**
    a. Completely my own.
    b. A direct result from people, places, and things within my life.
    c. Ever changing.

11. **Which of the following metaphors best fits a description of my life?**
    a. A river with me swimming against its current.
    b. A river.
    c. A river with me floating with its current.

12. **My behavior:**
    a. Is controlled by nothing in particular.
    b. Is mostly controlled by the environment.
    c. Is mostly under my control.

13. **When I'm by myself:**
    a. Time goes by slowly.
    b. Time goes by as it goes by when I'm with others.
    c. I typically lose track of time.

14. **When I'm watching TV by myself, I:**
    a. Channel surf a lot.
    b. Find something I like, and watch it.
    c. Hope there is something on that is good to watch.

15. **If I was on a deserted island for one year:**
    a. I'd use the time alone to focus on my own thoughts and needs.
    b. Family, friends, and loved ones from back home would fill my thoughts.
    c. Play time!

16. **When I'm writing, I'm most likely to be focused on:**
    a. What I want to write about.
    b. Writing.
    c. Who I'm writing for.

17. **Spirituality is defined as:**
    a. Something personal.
    b. A process.
    c. Something between me and my place of worship (e.g., a church, synagogue, forest, library, etc.).

18. **What's the most important lesson one can learn in life?**
    a. Life is what you make of it.
    b. Life is fitting in.
    c. Life is living for the day.

19. **Religion is defined as:**
    a. Something personal.
    b. A process.
    c. Something between me and my place of worship (e.g., a church, synagogue, forest, library, etc.).

20. **Do I ever find myself singing out loud with the radio?**
    a. Yes, but only if I am alone.
    b. Yes, if I'm in the mood.
    c. Yes.

21. **What would be the most important reward associated with being a musician?**
    a. The fun that comes with living a creative life.
    b. Playing music is its own reward.
    c. Money and fame.

22. **I masturbate:**
    a. When I've got nothing better to do.
    b. For pleasure.
    c. Relative to fantasies.

23. When walking by myself, I fall down. What is the first thing I do after the fall?

a. See if I am hurt.
b. See if anyone saw me fall.
c. Get up and continue on my way.

24. Which of the following do I think is most important?

a. Feeling happy in my life.
b. Living life.
c. Being seen as successful.

25. What is the main benefit of being honest?

a. Honesty is its own benefit.
b. The feeling that I am an honest person.
c. Having others see me as an honest person.

26. How do I determine what is "right"?

a. I decide based on my own moral code.
b. I decide based on what others (e.g., laws, rules, ethics, etc.) have deemed as being "right."
c. I don't view the world in "rights" and "wrongs."

27. I come across someone lying on the ground. How do I decide what to do?

a. I don't think, I act.
b. I assess the situation and then determine what I need to do.
c. I look for help; two heads are better than one.

28. While on a walk by myself, I come across a letter in the street that someone has dropped. It has not yet been mailed. What do I do?

a. I would drop it in the nearest mailbox.
b. I would continue walking.
c. If the letter looked interesting, I would open it and read it, and then drop it in the nearest mailbox.

29. I am driving on the highway and pass someone with a flat tire. What would I do?

a. If the person needed help, I would stop.
b. I would assess the situation before deciding to stop and help.
c. The decision to stop and help is not dependent upon any one factor.

30. Whenever really good or bad things happen in my life:

a. I don't contemplate the cause of such outcomes; good and bad things mostly happen without cause.

b. I wonder how my choices affected the good or bad outcome.

c. I attribute the good or bad outcome to forces beyond my control (e.g., fate, chance, higher power, etc.).

31. Where am I most likely to find a beautiful experience?

a. In a place that I feel most comfortable.

b. Any place.

c. In a place that most people would find beautiful.

32. What are coincidences?

a. Just random events.

b. Meaningful events relative to me.

c. Meaningful events determined by something beyond me.

Scoring instructions

Use the selfish, environmental, and action Self answers below to tally your Self SEA score.

Selfish, environmental, and action Self answers

1. a. selfish b. environmental c. action
2. a. selfish b. action c. environmental
3. a. selfish b. environmental c. action
4. a. selfish b. action c. environmental
5. a. selfish b. action c. environmental
6. a. action b. selfish c. environmental
7. a. selfish b. action c. environmental
8. a. selfish b. environmental c. action
9. a. action b. selfish c. environmental
10. a. selfish b. environmental c. action
11. a. selfish b. action c. environmental
12. a. action b. environmental c. selfish
13. a. environmental b. selfish c. action
14. a. action b. selfish c. environmental
15. a. selfish b. environmental c. action
16. a. selfish b. action c. environmental
17. a. selfish b. action c. environmental
18. a. selfish b. environmental c. action
19. a. selfish b. action c. environmental
20. a. selfish b. environmental c. action
21. a. selfish b. action c. environmental
22. a. action b. environmental c. selfish
23. a. selfish b. environmental c. action
24. a. selfish b. action c. environmental
25. a. action b. selfish c. environmental
26. a. selfish b. environmental c. action
27. a. action b. selfish c. environmental
28. a. environmental b. action c. selfish
29. a. environmental b. selfish c. action
30. a. action b. selfish c. environmental
31. a. selfish b. action c. environmental
32. a. action b. selfish c. environmental

Self scoring

Selfish: $\dfrac{\text{Total number of selfish responses}}{32} \times 100$

Environmental: $\dfrac{\text{Total number of environmental responses}}{32} \times 100$

Action: $\dfrac{\text{Total number of action responses}}{32} \times 100$

Self SEA score = ____ : ____ : ____

Before I give you the definition of self that was used to develop these questions and answers, I want you to tell me what your definition of self is… Really. What is the definition of self? To help guide your thoughts about self, come up with answers on a piece of paper to the following questions:

- Is there something unique about each one of us that allows us to have a self?
- Where is self? Is self in mind? In body?
- What is it to be alone? Can one ever be truly alone?
- Is there such a thing as a non-social situation?
- What is the result of your island experience?

Okay, are you ready to get away? Are you ready to be by your*self*? I'm putting you on an island for 10 years. You can have anything you want on this island, with one exception. The things that you can have—have no *social* significance to them. Thus, you can have mansions, racetracks, cars, the best food, drink, computers (no Internet), etc., *but*, you *cannot* have any humans, pets, books (because they're written by humans), phones (no communication), Internet, email, televisions, tape recorders, radios, etc.

My question: What/Who would you be at the end of the 10 years? What would happen to you?

Now that you have a more explicit idea about your definition of self, take a look at the definition of self that was used to develop the "self" questions and answers. The self part of life is composed of situations in which you are physically or mentally alone. These are "I'm by myself" situations. Any feelings, thoughts, perceptions, or behaviors occurring in concert with no one but yourself is the self part of life. There may be other people involved within a self part of life, but the other people are likely to not have any significant amount of control of the situation or experience. Fantasies and dreams are examples of the self part of life.

Personal ideas about life in general and human behavior in particular are other examples of the self part of life. Key elements of your self include:

- Masturbating and fantasizing.
- Thinking, reading, and writing in general.
- Doing activities in public, but alone.
- Contemplations of spirituality and religion.
- Contemplations of morality and ethics.
- Being embarrassed.
- Contemplations of self-control, habits, addictions, determinism, and indeterminism.
- Contemplations of life's meaning, survival, and basic necessities.
- Contemplations of beauty.
- Singing and listening to music.
- Altruism and helping behavior.
- The perception of time possibly being affected when you are by yourself.

YOUR HAPPINESS SEA PROFILE

Now that you know your SEA score for at least one part of your life—if not *all* eleven parts of your life, and you have your SEA-weighting score in hand, the question is: What do you do with this knowledge? Let's start by applying this knowledge to **Figure 25**, "Your Happiness SEA profile," so that your SEA scores are all together in a single place. **Figure 25** also has a place—right in the middle—for your SEA-weighting score. Isn't that nice?

Figure 25. Your happiness SEA profile.

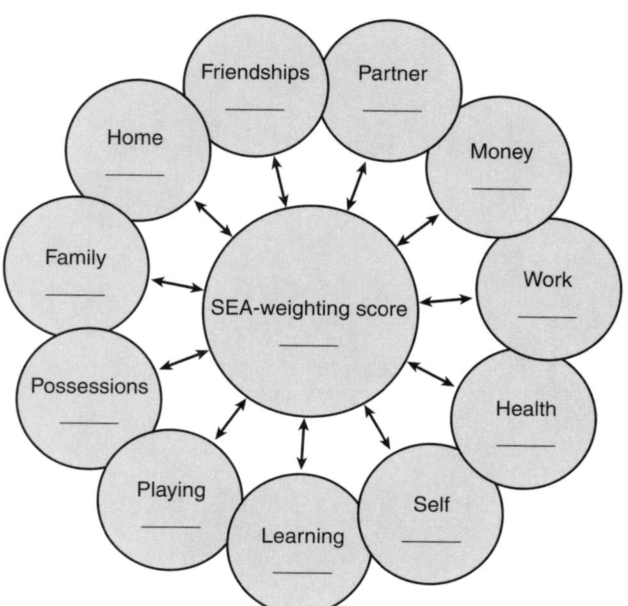

Table 3. Average SEA scores for each of the eleven parts of life.

Parts of Life	SELFISH				ENVIRONMENTAL				ACTION			
	Low End of Range	High End of Range	Standard Deviation	Average	Low End of Range	High End of Range	Standard Deviation	Average	Low End of Range	High End of Range	Standard Deviation	Average
Learning	30	54	11.6	**42**	18	41	12.2	**30**	17	38	10.1	**28**
Playing	31	49	8.9	**40**	17	37	10.1	**28**	21	42	10.3	**32**
Possessions	31	53	11.3	**42**	18	38	9.7	**29**	18	39	11.1	**29**
Family	20	39	9.7	**30**	15	36	10.9	**25**	32	58	12.8	**45**
Home	26	49	11.5	**38**	29	54	12.2	**42**	9	31	11.0	**20**
Friendships	13	34	10.0	**24**	22	43	9.9	**33**	30	56	12.6	**43**
Partner	18	39	10.2	**30**	15	38	11.5	**26**	31	56	12.4	**44**
Money	24	47	11.1	**35**	24	45	10.5	**35**	18	42	10.7	**30**
Work	25	50	12.0	**38**	20	51	15.4	**36**	13	38	12.8	**26**
Health	28	52	11.9	**40**	16	41	12.3	**30**	18	42	12.1	**30**
Self	36	61	11.9	**50**	17	39	11.3	**28**	13	31	9.2	**22**

n = 204; Mean age = 25.2, lo age = 17, hi age = 71; 35% male, 65% female; Lucas, Kaylor, Burgess, & Nigh, 2007.

For comparison sake, **Table 3** has average SEA scores for each of the eleven parts of life (Lucas, Kaylor, Burgess, & Nigh, 2007). Let's use these average part-of-life SEA scores, gathered from 204 participants who had an average age of 25.2 (minimum = 17, maximum = 71), to make comparisons to your parts-of-life SEA scores. You'll also note that **Table 3** has the significance ranges for the SEA scores—if your SEA score falls within the significance range, then it is not significantly different from average. If your SEA score is outside of the significance range, then it may be interpreted as being excessive or exceptionally low.

Okay, I've got my SEA-weighting scores and my SEA scores... Should I change my SEA score? Should I stay the same? Should I care? What if I really want to change—how would I go about doing it? In writing this book, none of my goals were to tell you to change a particular part of your life. That is—completely—up to you. However, one of my goals is to provide you with all the information necessary for you to become (re)aware of your potential and actual levels of happiness, pleasure, and contentment. Well, guess what? I have just reached that goal. Now, I have but one last goal to obtain in the writing of this book. That is the goal of providing you with all the information necessary to change your potential and actual levels of happiness, pleasure, and contentment for specific parts of your life. If you are ready to do just that, then turn the page to **Chapter Six**.

Chapter Six

Being Content and Living Longer

So this is how it ends...

In this last chapter, I will show you an additional way to calculate SEA scores for your various parts of life. This way does not involve quizzes or tests; it involves introspection. After showing you this way, I'll show you how to change the various parts of a SEA score—allowing you to transform some of the environmental part of the SEA score into the action part, or transforming some of the selfish part of the SEA score into the environmental part, or transforming some of the action part of the SEA score into the selfish part, etc. I'll end this chapter—and really this book—by applying Being Theory to something entirely different from positive emotions. This something is your longevity. Being Theory addresses not only our emotions, but also our longevity. I know, I know, you still don't believe me... Well, read on and see it for yourself.

Another way to calculate your SEA scores: Defining a life part

I introduced the concept of introspection at the beginning of the previous chapter. This chapter we won't be talking about introspection—we'll be *doing* it. Eight immediate and introspective steps allow for an analysis of happiness, pleasure, and contentment for a particular part of your life. For a similar immediate, but not introspective, analysis of your life relative to positive emotions, please see Nobel Prize winner in Economics Daniel Kahneman's moment-based approach (Kahneman & Tversky, 2000).

If you would be so kind, while following these steps, use one of the copies of the **Worksheet** from **Appendix Two** in the back of this book.

Step 1. To begin, select a part of your life that you would like to further analyze. This can be any of the parts of life you selected in **Chapter Five**, or some new part of life. To refresh your memory, the eleven parts of life are: learning, playing, possessions, family, home, friendships, partner, money, work, health, and self.

To help explain the eight steps to you, I'll provide an example after I describe what is required within a particular step. For this first step, I will do the Work part of life as an example.

What part of life are you going to analyze?

Step 2. List all of the things that you do that are associated with the part of life you selected in **Step 1**. To complete this step, you may want to virtually walk through a typical day that involves this part of life. Sometimes, you may need to walk through more than one typical day (maybe a weekday and a weekend day) to get a full description of the part of life. Be as detailed as you can in your descriptions of the things you do for this part of life.

For the example, I will make up a hypothetical professor. Let's virtually walk through the things this hypothetical professor does at work. We'll mark each item as W (weekdays only), WE (weekends only), or WWE (weekdays and weekends)—you may want to do the same.

- Grade online courses, WWE.
- Post on online courses, WWE.
- Read posts on online courses, WWE.
- Meet with students individually, W.
- Meet with colleagues, W.
- Meet with administrators, W.
- Meet with book vendors, W.
- Read research articles, WWE.
- Write research articles, WWE.
- Write emails, WWE.
- Read emails, WWE.
- Design research studies, WWE.
- Collect data for research studies, W.
- Analyze data from research studies, WWE.
- Help students, WWE.
- Help colleagues, W.
- Teach on-campus courses, W.
- Prepare courses, WWE.
- Grade papers, WWE.
- Read student papers, WWE.
- Grade quizzes, WWE.
- Think, WWE.
- Laugh, WWE.
- Write letters of recommendation, WWE.
- Schedule courses/hiring, W.
- Write grading rubrics, W.
- Write teaching rubrics, W.
- Deal with professor-student conflicts, W.
- Counsel students, W.
- Prepare departmental statistics, W.
- Learn, WWE.
- Compromise, WWE.
- Eat, WWE.

Please note at least three things about this list. The first thing I want you to note is the length of the list. The list is long and comprehensive—make sure you are as comprehensive as possible in your description of the things that you do associated with your part of life. You will be doing a series of analyses on this list, so please make sure your list is complete, thorough, and true. You may want to start it one day. Sleep on it. Then complete it the following day or two. Know that you are most likely to omit something that you do—you are very unlikely (unless you're a habitual liar) to put something on your list that you do not do. Therefore, you cannot put too many items that describe what you do associated with your part of life—but you can put too few.

The second thing I want you to note is that the list has some items that are certainly going to be on other parts of life's lists, too. For example, eating, laughing, and learning are going to be a part of other aspects of life. Each list is certainly not going to be completely unique from every other list. As I mentioned before, the parts of life are not completely independent of one another. Instead, the gestalt (there's that word again—are you going to look it up?!) of the lists will be different.

The third thing I want you to note is that some of the items on the list are not necessarily separate from other items on the list. For example, I have thinking and learning listed—well, I hope thinking and learning are always going on throughout the other items on the list. However, there are times in which this hypothetical professor is just thinking—and doing nothing else, or just learning and doing nothing else—and that is why these items can be combined as well as separate from the other items on the list.

Step 3. Calculate the amount of time you spend, on average, in a typical day, week, or month on each of the items that you listed as being associated with the part of life you selected in **Step 1**. Then, write down the amount of time spent adjacent to each of the listed items you developed in **Step 2**.

Since some of the things within the list the hypothetical professor does not do every day, I'll do the time estimates (in hours) relative to a week (168 hours), on average:

- Grade online courses, WWE (10 hours).
- Post on online courses, WWE (2 hours).
- Read posts on online courses, WWE (2 hours).
- Meet with students individually, W (4 hours).
- Meet with colleagues, W (5 hours).
- Meet with administrators, W (1 hour).
- Meet with book vendors, W (½ hour).
- Read research articles, WWE (5 hours).
- Write research articles, WWE (5 hours).

- Write emails, WWE (3 hours).
- Read emails, WWE (1 hour).
- Design research studies, WWE (2 hours).
- Collect data for research studies, W (2 hours).
- Analyze data from research studies, WWE (2 hours).
- Help students, WWE (1 hour).
- Help colleagues, W (1 hour).
- Teach on-campus courses, W (6 hours).
- Prepare courses, WWE (2 hours).
- Grade papers, WWE (2 hours).
- Read student papers, WWE (2 hours).
- Grade quizzes, WWE (1 hour).
- Think, WWE (3 hours).
- Laugh, WWE (½ hour).
- Write letters of recommendation, WWE (½ hour).
- Schedule courses/hiring, W (½ hour).
- Write grading rubrics, W (½ hour).
- Write teaching rubrics, W (½ hour).
- Deal with professor-student conflicts, W (¼ hour).
- Counsel students, W (½ hour).
- Prepare departmental statistics, W (¼ hour).
- Learn, WWE (1 hour).
- Compromise, WWE (½ hour).
- Eat, WWE (2 hours).

Something to keep in mind when you are estimating your times, because I did the above estimated times on average, per week—all the times will not necessarily be correct for any given week. For example, I said only ½ hour for scheduling courses and hiring. But in reality, when schedules are being prepared during the semester, this hypothetical professor may spend upwards of 10 hours per week preparing schedules and (re)hiring adjunct professors. But on other weeks—in the middle of the semester for example, this hypothetical professor may not spend any time at all on scheduling/hiring. Thus, on average it works out to about ½ hour per week throughout the semester. Please make sure your estimates of time are as accurate as possible—you will be doing a series of analyses on these times.

Step 4. Pose each of the following three question-pairs to the items you listed in Step 2. Then, take the question-pair that most accurately reflects *the reason you do the item* that you listed in Step 2, and write down the question-pair's label adjacent (within parentheses before the question-pair) to the list you developed in Step 3. Upon completing this step, you should have the label selfish, environmental, or action next to the times of every one of the items you listed in Step 3.

Question-pair one (selfish): Do I primarily do this because I *want* to? And, am I mostly *in control* of doing this?

Question-pair two (environmental): Do I primarily do this because I *have* to? And, is some person, place, or thing—*other* than me—mostly in control of doing this?

Question-pair three (action): Do I primarily do this just *for the sake of experiencing it*? And, is there nobody, not I, nor any other person, place, or thing in control of this?

- Grade online courses (10 hours); environmental.
- Post comments on online courses (2 hours); 50% selfish, 50% environmental.
- Read posts on online courses (2 hours); 40% selfish, 40% environmental, 20% action.
- Meet with students individually (4 hours); selfish.
- Meet with colleagues (5 hours); 50% selfish, 50% action.
- Meet with administrators (1 hour); 50% selfish, 50% environmental.
- Meet with book vendors (½ hour); selfish.
- Read research articles (5 hours); 50% selfish, 50% action.
- Write research articles (5 hours); 50% selfish, 40% environmental, 10% action.
- Write emails (3 hours); 50% selfish, 50% environmental.
- Read emails (1 hour); action.
- Design research studies (2 hours); action.
- Collect data for research studies (2 hours); environmental.
- Analyze data from research studies (2 hours); 50% action, 50% environmental.
- Help students (1 hour); action.
- Help colleagues (1 hour); action.
- Teach on-campus courses (6 hours); 50% selfish, 50% action.
- Prepare courses (2 hours); 50% selfish, 50% environmental.
- Grade papers (2 hours); environmental.
- Read student papers (2 hours); 50% selfish, 50% action.
- Grade quizzes (1 hour); environmental.
- Think (3 hours); action.
- Laugh (½ hour); action.
- Write letters of recommendation (½ hour); environmental.
- Schedule courses/hiring (½ hour); 50% selfish, 50% environmental.
- Write grading rubrics (½ hour); environmental.
- Write teaching rubrics (½ hour); selfish.
- Deal with professor-student conflicts (¼ hour); environmental.
- Counsel students (½ hour); action.
- Prepare departmental statistics (¼ hour); environmental.
- Learn (1 hour); selfish.
- Compromise (½ hour); selfish.
- Eat (2 hours); environmental.

Some of the items in your list may fit more than one of the observer-perspective question-pairs, or parts of the SEA score. For instance, you may think that an item in your list is classified as being environmental today, but selfish tomorrow. Before splitting the item into two or three parts of the SEA score, make every effort to see if it in fact does fit into one part of the SEA score, but if it in fact does *not*, then put a percentage of what two or three parts of the SEA score with which the item is associated (see **Worksheet**).

Step 5. Using the list you developed in **Step 4**, add up the amount of time you experience your part of life from a(n):

1. Selfish Perspective Total time = ________.
2. Environmental Perspective Total time = ________.
3. Action Perspective Total time = ________.

The hypothetical professor's numbers are as follows:

1. Selfish Perspective Total time = 23.05 hours per week.
2. Environmental Perspective Total time = 25.55 hours per week.
3. Action Perspective Total time = 19.9 hours per week.

Step 6. Using the list you developed in **Step 3**, add up the total amount of time you spend on your part of life (per day, week, or month):

The total amount of time (per day, week, or month) I spend on my part of life is ________.

The total amount of time the hypothetical professor spends per week on his/her work part of life is: 68.5 hours.

Step 7. Divide each of the observer-perspective times calculated in **Step 5** by the total amount of time you spend on the part of life calculated in **Step 6.** The result is your SEA score for this part of life:

1. Percentage of time experiencing the Selfish Perspective = ____
   S = **Step 5.1** divided by **Step 6.**

2. Percentage of time experiencing the Environmental Perspective = ____
   E = **Step 5.2** divided by **Step 6.**

3. Percentage of time experiencing the Action Perspective = ____
   A = **Step 5.3** divided by **Step 6.**

The hypothetical professor's percentages are as follows:

1. Percentage of time the hypothetical professor is experiencing work from a Selfish Perspective = 34
2. Percentage of time the hypothetical professor is experiencing work from an Environmental Perspective = 37
3. Percentage of time the hypothetical professor is experiencing work from an Action Perspective = 29

Step 8. To calculate your SEA score for another part of life, simply go back to **Step 1** and run through each of the eight steps again.

A FOREVER-CHANGING SEA

Changing your SEA-weighting score. Before I show you how you can change your SEA scores, I probably should at least mention how you can change your SEA-weighting score. Changing a SEA-weighting score is much more intuitive and obvious than changing a SEA score. Your SEA-weighting score is composed of the ingredients of the Happiness and You recipe, with the addition of three items: sleeping, exercising, and helping behavior. Sleeping, exercising, and helping behaviors automatically affect (positively or negatively) the Happiness and You ingredients. Unhealthy amounts of sleep (less than 7 or more than 10 hours per night), exercise (less than 3 hours per week), and helping (none per week) lay the foundation for negative emotions. Thus, the first thing you should do to change your SEA-weighting score is confirm or change your sleeping patterns to be between 7 and 10 hours (every) night, confirm or change your aerobic and anaerobic exercising to more than 3 hours per (every) week, and change your helping/volunteering behavior to at least 1 hour per week. The remaining changes to your SEA-weighting score should occur relative to the importance of the ingredients that compose it. An ingredient's importance is defined by the number of points of the SEA-weighting score it will affect. So, for example, being married or not affects between –2 and +2 points of the SEA-weighting score, whereas friendships—a more important ingredient—affects between –3 and +3 points of the SEA-weighting score, and employment—an even more important ingredient—affects between –2 and +4 points of the SEA-weighting score (see **Appendix Three**). The following list has empathy and the nine ingredients of the Happiness and You recipe in order of importance, with the first item in the list being the most important (social situations) and the last item being the least important (money). You'll want to confirm or change your SEA-weighting score by focusing on the first item in the list, then the second, then the third item...

The list

1. Social situations (increase your opportunities for social interaction).
2. Friends (increase the number of friends and the quality of the ones that you do have).
3. Employment (make sure that you are employed, and if you are, then make sure you are employed in something that is more about what you want to do and less about money or something you have to do).
4. Empathy (increase your empathy—make this a habit; make sure you care for not only those who are close to you, but others who are not).
5. Health (increase your knowledge about your diet, sleep, and exercise).
6. Marriage (if you are not married, then you may want to be, but only if you know marriage will be born out of commitment and caring—if it is not, then make it).
7. Religion/faith (be involved in a religion/faith that believes in something greater and more positive than yourself, but be careful not to be involved in judgment).
8. Extraversion (you don't have to be the "star of the party," but make yourself motivated to get into social situations—when the opportunity arises for a social situation, do not pass it up).
9. Optimism (be more hopeful—especially when life is objectively negative, recognize life is for the good before it is for the bad).
10. Money (make and use your money for the action-observer perspective and for helping).

Changing your SEA score. Although the hypothetical professor's SEA score for work 34:37:29 is within the average range according to **Table 3**, he/she wouldn't mind making some changes to it. The hypothetical professor would like to make some changes to his/her work SEA score in regard to the S and E part of it. The S is a bit too low and the E is a bit too high. What do you think? Can the hypothetical professor change his/her SEA score—and *love* his/her work—even more? Let's take a look at what we would need to do in order to change a SEA score.

There are three different techniques you can use to change a SEA score. The easiest technique to change a SEA score is to add or subtract time to the items on the list that define the life part. Every part of life is composed of lists that have selfish, environmental, and action items on them. With this fact in mind, it is easy to change your SEA score by adding time to or subtracting time from selfish, environmental, and action items. Using this technique, the hypothetical professor can decrease the environmental part of his/her work SEA score by decreasing the amount of time he/she spends on the environmental items on his/her list (e.g., grading quizzes, grading papers, collecting data for research studies, etc.).

Additionally, the hypothetical professor could use this technique to increase the selfish part of his/her work SEA score by increasing the amount of time he/she spends on the selfish items on his/her list (e.g., meeting with students, meeting with book vendors, composing teaching rubrics, etc.).

Another technique requires you to change your definition of the life part. Simply add to or subtract from the list of items that define the life part. Using this technique, the hypothetical professor can decrease the environmental part of his/her work SEA score by deleting environmental items on his/her list (e.g., grading quizzes, grading papers, collecting data for research studies, etc.). Once deleted, the hypothetical professor's definition of work changes; it no longer is defined by grading quizzes, grading papers, and collecting data for research studies (the hypothetical professor's Dean may have something to say about this!), and his/her work SEA score changes too, with a substantial decrease in the environmental part, and thereby a substantial increase in the selfish and action parts. Also, the hypothetical professor could use this technique to add selfish items to his/her list that defines work. The more selfish items he/she adds (e.g., going out to lunch with friends, gossiping, etc.), the higher the selfish part of the hypothetical professor's work SEA score will become, and relatively speaking, the lower the environmental part will become.

CALVIN AND HOBBES © 2010 Watterson. Dist. By UNIVERSAL PRESS SYNDICATE. Reprinted with permission.

The last technique to change a SEA score is to transform one form of energy into another—change a selfish perspective into an action perspective, or an environmental perspective into a selfish perspective, or an action perspective into an environmental perspective... This is the most difficult way to change a SEA score. Remember, *you* are the one defining whether an experience is selfish, environmental, or action. By that same token, you are the one who has the power to redefine an experience as being selfish, environmental, or action. One item the hypothetical professor does not have on his/her list to define work, but he/she probably should have, is his/her commute. I would imagine this is an item that is on most people's lists to define work. Most commutes, in big cities with traffic (redundant), are most likely labeled environmental—you have to drive to and from work. But wait. Can you redefine this seemingly entrenched environmental item to be a selfish or action item? Sure you can—I have absolute faith in you! As an example, I have a colleague who hated her commute. It was definitely an environmental, have-to, part of her day. I asked her why she defined it this way, and she told me about the traffic she's constantly in—and she hates traffic. I told her, traffic *can* be a wonderful thing! After she got done laughing at me, I told her how: traffic equals time—your time to do anything that you want to. Do you want to people watch? Talk on the phone to a long-lost friend—or otherwise? Pay a bill over the Internet? Shave? Be a racecar driver? Clip your nails? As I was saying this, a grin came over her face. And this time, it wasn't a grin that would be preceding laughing at me; it was a grin of insightfulness and recognition. She then asked, "can I listen to books on CD?" Of course you can! She went on, "I haven't had much time lately to keep up with reading the books on the best-seller list; maybe I can start "reading" some of them by listening to them in the car..." My colleague, now looks forward—repeat: she looks forward—to traffic. It *is* all a matter of perspective.

I'M SO HAPPY, I WANT TO LIVE!

So what do you think? Are you happier? Will you be happier? Are you truly happy? I hope so. I hope you're so happy, that you want to live an even longer life! I'm going to end this book by showing you one way that may help you achieve this want.

One of the primary reasons people (scientists and non-scientists alike) are so interested in Einstein's theories of time and space is that his theories bring on the possibility of time travel (however, see Hawking, 1988; Hawking & Penrose, 1996, for the problems with this possibility). Being Theory does not allow for time travel, but it does lend itself to slowing the aging process, in spite of time passing. I'm sounding like an infomercial at this point, aren't I? Bear with me—I speak the truth. (There's that damn truth again!) Your physical age is equal to the amount of time that has passed since you were born—your answer to the question: how old are you? Your potential for accidents, disease, and exposure to violence, as well as your diet, exercise, sleeping behavior, gender, stress levels, and genetics determine how long you're going to live (for a wonderful expansion of and details about this "longevity list," see www.realage.com). My addition to this list is the action part of your SEA scores. As we saw in **Chapter Four**, for every life experience that is action-specific rather than selfish or environmental, your perception of time slows. Psychophysical time is slower than physical time during action experiences. People underestimate the amount of time that has passed during action-specific experiences. This leaves us with a question: When psychophysical time slows, does aging slow as well? In other words, what has more of an impact on your longevity—time by way of physics (i.e., measured by an atomic clock) or time by way of psychophysics (measured by you)?

These questions may not be as infomercial-like or far-fetched as you might first think, especially when we examine the relationship between aging and happiness. Research on individuals living significantly longer than average life spans has found these individuals to be happier than the general population (e.g., Danner, Snowdon, & Friesen, 2001). For instance, Dorly Deeg and Robert van Zonneveld (1989) analyzed the elderly and found happiness and other positive emotions account for up to 8.1% of the variance associated with aging. They found the life expectancy for the typical 70-year-old man to be about 10 years; this life expectancy increases to 12 years if this man is relatively happy. Deborah Danner and her colleagues analyzed autobiographies of 180 Catholic nuns written in the early part of the 20th century upon entering the convent. They were about 22 years of age. Danner reviewed the autobiographies for words and sentences associated with positive (happiness, love, hope, amusement, etc.) and negative (sadness, anxiety, shame, anger, etc.) emotions, and then placed the nuns into two groups: a high positive emotion group, which had autobiographies composed mostly of positive emotions and few negative emotions, and a low positive emotion group, which had autobiographies composed mostly of negative emotions and few positive emotions. Danner then calculated mortality rates for the two groups; 76% of the members within the high positive emotion group were alive at age 80, while only 46% of the members in the low positive emotion group were alive at this age. Danner concluded that perceiving your life through a lens of positive emotions as opposed to one of negative emotions adds about 9.4 years to your life. It *is* a matter of perspective.

Other factors positively associated with longevity and happiness include optimism, reduced stress levels, extraversion, spirituality, friendships, marriage, subjective health, exercise, and a decreased probability of depression. Additionally, scientists have long known that a significant decrease in daily caloric intake (30–40% less than what is normal for the species) can increase the lifespan of an animal by two or three times (Sinclair, 2005). This is an especially interesting finding when we examine food intake and eating behavior relative to SEA scores. Eating is most apt to be associated with the environmental part of SEA scores because eating is outside of our control—regardless of our wants or wishes, the nervous system demands to be fed, else we die. Thus, we may suppose that people who spend more time having SEA scores with excessive environmental parts are likely to eat more because they will more often find themselves aware of their eating needs. Further, these individuals will not live as long because they are less likely to meet the decreased caloric-intake standard that is associated with longevity. A recent scientific study has demonstrated just how destructive the environmental part of SEA scores can be to our longevity (Bellis, Hennell, Lushey, Hughes, Tocque, & Ashton, 2007). This study measured the survival rates of 1,064 of the most popular rock and pop stars from North America and Europe with an average birth year of 1957. The researchers found the average age of death for the North American rock stars to be 41.8 years, and for the European rock stars to be only 35.2 years. Compare these ages to the average American's age at death—for men, 73.2 years, and for women, 79.7 years. The top four causes of death for the rock stars were, in order: (1) drug/alcohol overdose, (2) cancer, (3) accidents, (4) cardiovascular disease—for the general population, the top four causes of death are, in order: (1) cardiovascular disease, (2) cancer, (3) stroke, (4) lower respiratory diseases.

This supposition of the environmental part of the SEA scores decreasing our longevity becomes even stronger when the focus is on the relationship between the environmental and action parts of SEA scores, because the experiences associated with the action part of SEA scores are most likely to require *no* eating and yield *no* awareness of a person's intrinsic eating needs. In the hopes of developing a drug that may mimic the effects of a significant caloric decrease in diet, geneticists are mapping the genes that are affected by (or affect) a reduction in food intake (Sinclair & Guarente, 2006). Being Theory shows that you do not need drugs to live longer; you need action experiences.

People who are happier than the general population spend about 29% of their time on a day-to-day basis having action-based experiences and about 24% of their time having environmental-based experiences; whereas people who are unhappier than the general population spend about 23% of their time on a day-to-day basis having action-based experiences and about 32% of their time having environmental-based experiences (Lucas, 2004; Lucas, Kaylor, & Magaloni, 2004). Psychophysically, we saw in **Chapter Four** that action-based experiences negate time, environmental-based experiences append time, and selfish-based experiences do not affect time. Thus, we can calculate the psychophysical age of a person relative to his/her physical age by the equation: psychophysical age, PsyA = (physical age, PhA – [percentage of your life time in action experiences, A × PhA] + [percentage of your life spent in environmental experiences, E × PhA]), or simply,

$$\text{PsyA} = (\text{PhA} - [\text{A} \times \text{PhA}] + [\text{E} \times \text{PhA}]).$$

Figure 26 shows the dramatic effect positive emotions have on an 80-year-old person's psychophysical age. The happy 80-year-old person's psychophysical age is 76 years (80 – [.29 × 80] + [.24 × 80]); and the unhappy 80-year-old person's psychophysical age is 88 years (80 – [.22 × 80] + [.32 × 80]). Time travel

Figure 26. Predicting how psychophysically old a happy 80-year-old person and an unhappy 80-year-old person are relative to his/her environmental and action life experiences.

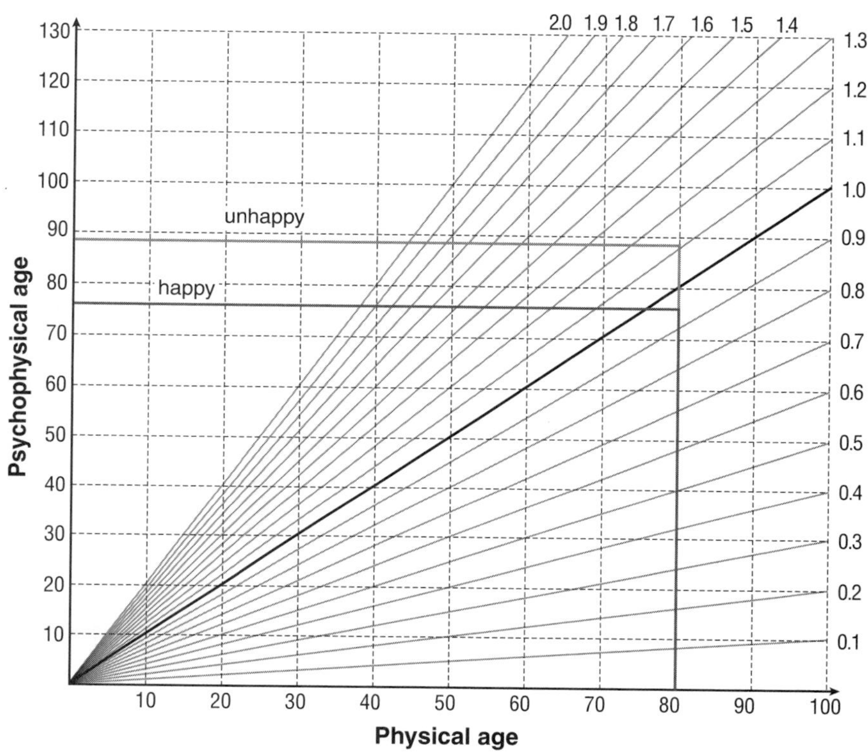

does not seem readily possible in the physical or psychophysical worlds; however, slowing down the aging process appears not only possible, but also probable, within the psychophysical world.

So how psychophysically old are you? In order to find this out, you'll need to calculate your overall SEA score by following these six steps.

Step 1: Calculate your SEA scores for all eleven parts of life, see **Another Way to Calculate Your SEA Scores: Defining a Part of Life.**

Step 2: Figure out what percentage of your life is composed of each of these parts—what percentage of your life is spent with friends, at work, at home, at leisure, etc.

Step 3: Multiply the percentages you calculated in Step 2 by their corresponding SEA scores. For example, if the hypothetical professor found him/herself at work 30% of his/her life, then he/she would multiply .3 (30%) by his/her work SEA score 34:37:29, resulting in 10.2:11.1:8.7.

Step 4: Add the eleven selfish numbers you calculated in Step 3 together. This is the selfish part of your overall SEA score. Add the eleven environmental numbers you calculated in Step 3 together. This is the environmental part of your overall SEA score. Add the eleven action numbers you calculated in Step 3 together. This is the action part of your overall SEA score.

Now, you may simply plug in your physical age (PhA), the action (A), and environmental (E) parts of your overall SEA score into the PsyA equation:

$$PsyA = (PhA - [A \times PhA] + [E \times PhA])$$

Not really the end

Two hundred pages or so ago, I made some promises to you. By far the most important promise I made was to show you how to be happy—to be *truly* happy. Almost as important, I wanted to show you how to define, distinguish, and maintain happiness, pleasure, and contentment so that you can use and gain these specific positive emotions over your lifetime.

Well? How did I do? Did I come through on my promises? Let's make this an environmental-specific experience—what *grade* did I earn? Why don't you do this. Email my grade and your comments to me at drdon@beingtheory.com; I look forward to hearing from you.

If you gave me a passing grade, you now know your positive and your negative emotions are controlled by a combination of SEA-weighting scores and SEA scores. You know SEA-weighting scores are mostly composed of the matter within your life, and SEA scores are composed of psychophysical time and perspective. You also know that different parts of your life—and the things that compose these parts—do not necessarily cause emotions. Instead, these things are likely a *result* of your emotions. Lastly, you know a significant factor associated with aging and health is your action-observer perspective.

Let me end by thanking you for being a part of it all. It has been an adventure for me—a wonderful adventure of writing, reading, and learning with you. Which reminds me—you can stop forgetting now. Before I bid you adieu, I must tell you that we may be "seeing" one another again—for I see myself writing a book specifically addressing each of the eleven parts of life.

What do you think? Maybe you and I will be together on another adventure soon? I hope. Until then, be happy—truly happy.

Appendix One
References

Abdel-Khalek, A. M. (2006). Measuring happiness with a single-item scale. *Social Behavior and Personality, 34,* 139–150.

Adler, M. J. (1984). *A vision of the future: Twelve ideas for a better life and a better society.* New York: Macmillan Publishing Company.

Allie, C. (1975). *Time Travel,* as cited within http://www.brianbosak.com/ on August 9, 2008.

American Psychiatric Association (2000). *Diagnostic and statistical manual of mental disorders, fourth edition, text revision.* Washington, D.C.: American Psychiatric Association.

Ancira, J., & Lucas, D. R. (2007). *Distinguishing among Pleasure, Happiness, and Contentment.* Paper presented at the annual meeting of the Southwestern Psychological Association, Fort Worth, Texas.

Andrews, F. M., & Withey, S. B. (1976). *Social indicators of well-being: Americans' perceptions of life quality.* New York: Plenum.

Argyle, M. (2001). *The psychology of happiness.* New York: Routledge.

Beamer, W., Bermant, G., & Clegg, M. (1969). Copulatory behavior of the ram, *Ovis aries.* II. Factors affecting copulatory satiety. *Animal Behavior, 17,* 706–711.

Begley, S. (2007). *Train your mind change your brain.* New York: Ballantine Books.

Bellis, M. A., Hennell, T., Lushey, C., Hughes, K., Tocque, K., & Ashton, J. R. (2007). Elvis to Eminem: Quantifying the price of fame through early mortality of Europeans and North American rock and pop stars. *Journal of Epidemiological Community Health, 61,* 896–901.

Ben-Shahar, T. (2007). *Happier: Learn the secrets to daily joy and lasting fulfillment.* New York: McGraw-Hill.

Bentham, J. (1843). *The works of Jeremy Bentham,* published under the Superintendence of his Executor, John Bowring (Edinburgh).

Bermant, G. (1976). Sexual behavior: Hard times with the Coolidge Effect. In M. H. Siegel & H. P. Zeigler (Eds.), *Psychological research: The inside story* (pp. 76–103). New York: Harper & Row.

Berns, G. (2005). *Satisfaction: The science of finding true fulfillment.* New York: Henry Holt and Co.

Blanchflower, D. G., & Oswald, A. J. (2004). Money, sex, and happiness: An empirical study. *The Scandinavian Journal of Economics, 106,* 393–415.

Blanchflower, D. G., & Oswald, A. J. (2008). Is well-being U-shaped over the life cycle? *Social Science & Medicine, 66,* 1733–1749.

Bolt, M. (2004). *Pursuing human strengths.* New York: Worth.

Bradburn, N. (1969). *The structure of psychological well-being.* Chicago: Aldine.

Brewster, A. L., Nelson, J. P., Hymel, K., Colby, D. R., Lucas, D. R., McCanne, T. R., & Milner, J. S. (1998). Victim, perpetrator, family, and incident characteristics of 32 infant-maltreatment death cases in the United States Air Force. *Child Abuse and Neglect, 22,* 91–101.

Brewster, A. L., Nelson, J. P., McCanne, T. R., Lucas, D. R., & Milner, J. S. (1998). Gender differences in physiological reactivity to infant cries and smiles in a military sample. *Child Abuse and Neglect, 22,* 775–788.

Brickman, P., & Campbell, D. T. (1971). Hedonic relativism and planning the good society. In M. H. Appley (Ed.). *Adaptation level theory: A symposium* (pp. 287–302). New York: Academic Press.

Brickman, P., Coates, D., & Janoff-Bulman, R. (1978). Lottery winners and accident victims: Is happiness relative? *Journal of Personality and Social Psychology, 36,* 917–927.

Brinton, L. A., Lubin, J. H., Cay Burich, M., Colton, T., & Hoover, R. N. (2001). Mortality among augmentation mammoplasty patients. *Epidemiology, 12,* 321–326.

Brinton, L. A., Lubin, J. H., Cay Burich, M., Colton, T., & Hoover, R. N. (2006). Mortality among augmentation mammoplasty patients: An update. *Epidemiology, 17,* 162–169.

Brody, S., & Krüger, T. H. C. (2006). The post-orgasmic prolactin increase following intercourse is greater than following masturbation and suggests greater satiety. *Biological Psychology, 71,* 312–315.

Buck, R. (1980). Nonverbal behavior and the theory of emotion: The facial feedback hypothesis. *Journal of Personality and Social Psychology, 38,* 811–24.

Byrne, R. (2006). *The secret.* New York: Atria Books.

Camacho, T. C., Roberts, R. E., Lazarus, N. B., Kaplan, G. A., & Cohen, R. D. (1991). Physical activity and depression: Evidence from the Alameda County study. *American Journal of Epidemiology, 134,* 220–231.

Campbell, A., Converse, P. E., & Rodgers, W. L. (1975). *The quality of American Life: Perceptions, Evaluations, and Satisfactions.* New York: Russell-Sage Foundation.

Campbell, N. A., & Reece, J. B. (2005). *Biology.* San Francisco: Pearson.

Carr, A. (2004). *Positive psychology: The science of happiness and human strengths.* New York: Brunner-Routledge.

Carroll, J. B., Davies, P., & Richman, B. (1971). *Word frequency book.* New York: American Heritage.

Cash, T. F., Duel, L. A., & Perkins, L. L. (2002). Women's psychosocial outcomes of breast augmentation with silicone gel-filled implants: A 2-year prospective study. *Plastic & Reconstructive Surgery, 109,* 2112–2121.

Clark, M.S., & Mills, J. (1993). The difference between communal and exchange relationships: What it is and is not. *Personality and Social Psychology Bulletin, 19,* 684–691.

Cobb, C. M., Glickman, M., & Cheslog, C. (2001). *Redefining Progress for People, Nature and the Economy* (www.RedefiningProgress.org).

Cohen, B. L., & Lee, I-S. (1979). A catalog of risks. *Health Physics, 36,* 707–722.

Comer, R. J. (2004). *Abnormal psychology.* New York: Worth.

Compton, W. C. (2004). *An introduction to positive psychology.* New York: Thomson-Wadsworth.

Covey, S. R. (1990). *The seven habits of highly affective people: Restoring the character ethic.* New York: Simon & Schuster.

Crawford, J. R., & Henry, J. D. (2004). The positive and negative affect schedule (PANAS): Construct validity, measurement properties, and normative data in a large non-clinical sample. *British Journal of Clinical Psychology, 43,* 245–265.

Csikszentmihalyi, M. (1990). *Flow.* New York: Harper & Row.

Csikszentmihalyi, M. (2000). Happiness, flow, and economic equality. *American Psychologist, 55,* 1163–1164.

Csikszentmihalyi, M. (1999). If we are so rich, why aren't we happy? *American Psychologist, 54,* 821–827.

Csikszentmihalyi, M., & LeFevre, J. (1989). Optimal experience in work and leisure. *Journal of Personality and Social Psychology, 56,* 815–822.

Dalai Lama, & Cutler, H. C. (1998). *The art of happiness: A handbook for living.* New York: Riverhead Books.

Danner, D. D., Snowdon, D. A., & Friesen, W. V. (2001). Positive emotions in early life and longevity: Findings from the nun study. *Journal of Personality and Social Psychology, 80,* 804–813.

Davis, M. H. (1980). A multidimensional approach to individual differences in empathy. *JSAS: Catalog of Selected Documents in Psychology, 10,* 85–104.

Decety, J., Michalska, K. J., Akitsuki, Y., & Lahey, B. B. (2008). Atypical empathic responses in adolescents with aggressive conduct disorder: A functional MRI investigation. *Biological Psychology,* doi:10.1016/j.biopsycho.2008.09.004

Deeg, D. J. H., & van Zonneveld, R. J. (1989). *Does Happiness Lengthen Life?* In Ruut Veenhoven (Ed.) How Harmful Is Happiness? Consequences of enjoying life or not. Universitaire Pers Rotterdam, The Netherlands.

Derogatis, L. R., & Melisaratos, N. (1983). The Brief Symptom Inventory: An introductory report. *Psychological Medicine, 13,* 595–605.

Diener, E., & Biswas-Diener, R. (2008). *Happiness: Unlocking the mysteries of psychological wealth.* Malden: Blackwell.

Diener, E., & Diener, C. (1996). Most people are happy. *Psychological Science, 7,* 181–185.

Diener, E., Emmons, R., Larson, R., & Griffin, S. (1985). The satisfaction with life scale. *Journal of Personality and Social Psychology, 49,* 71–75.

Einstein, A. (1905). On the electrodynamics of moving bodies (special relativity). *Annalen der Physik, 17,* 891–921.

Ekman, P., Davidson, R. J., & Friesen, W. V. (1990). The Duchenne smile: Emotional expression and brain physiology: II. *Journal of Personality and Social Psychology, 58,* 342–353.

Ekman, P., & Oster, H. (1979). Facial expressions of emotion, *Annual Review of Psychology, 30,* 527–554.

Emmons, R. A., & McCullough, M. E. (2003). Counting blessings versus burdens: An experimental investigation of gratitude and subjective well-being in daily life. *Journal of Personality and Social Psychology, 84,* 377–389.

Evans, A. M., Guerra, S. L., Romero, S. A., & Lucas, D. R. (2008). *Mistaking contentment for happiness.* Paper presented at the annual meeting of the Southwestern Psychological Association, Kansas City, Missouri.

Festinger, L. (1954). A theory of social comparison processes. *Human Relations, 7,* 117–40.

finfacts.ie, http://www.finfacts.ie/biz10/globalworldincomepercapita.htm, cited on July 10, 2007.

Field, (1998). Massage therapy effects. *American Psychologist, 53,* 1270–1281.

Frankl, V. E. (1959). *Man's search for meaning.* New York: Beacon Press.

Frey, B. S., Benesch, C., & Stutzer, A. (2007). Does watching TV make us happy? *Journal of Economic Psychology, 28*, 283–313.

Gibson, J. J. (1979). *The ecological approach to visual perception*. Boston: Houghton Mifflin.

Gilbert, D. (2006). *Stumbling on happiness.* New York: Knopf.

Givens, D. (2005). *Love signals: A practical field guide to the body language of courtship.* New York: St. Martin's Press.

Goldenberg, J. L., McCoy, S. K., Greenberg, J., Pyszczynski, T., & Solomon, S. (2000). The body as a source of self-esteem: The effect of mortality salience on identification with one's body, interest in sex, and appearance monitoring. *Journal of Personality and Social Psychology, 79,* 118–130.

Gonzalez, A., & Zimbardo, P. G. (1985). Time in perspective: A *Psychology Today* survey report. *Psychology Today, 19,* 21–26.

Hacker, D. (2006). *The Bedford handbook.* Boston: Bedford/St. Martins.

Haegeman, L., & Gueron, J. (1999). *English grammar: A generative perspective.* Oxford: Blackwell.

Haidt, R. (2006). *The happiness hypothesis: Finding modern truth in ancient wisdom.* New York: Basic Books.

Harlow, H. (1959). Love in monkeys. *Scientific American, 200,* 68–74.

Harlow, H. F., Harlow, M. K., & Suomi, S. J. (1971). From thought to therapy: Lessons from a private laboratory. *American Scientist, 59,* 538–549.

Harris, J. D. (1941). Forward conditioning, backward conditioning, and pseudoconditioning, and adaptation to the conditioned stimulus. *Journal of Experimental Psychology, 28,* 491–502.

Harrison, L., Ohvet, L., Cunningham, K., Bodin, M. B., & Hicks, C. (1996). Effects of Gentle Human Touch on Preterm Infants: Pilot Study Results. *Neonatal Network, 15,* 35–42.

Hawking, S. (1988). *A brief history of time.* New York: Bantam.

Hawking, S., & Penrose, R. (1996). *The nature of space and time.* Princeton, NJ: Princeton University Press.

Haybron, D. (2007). Life satisfaction, ethical reflection, and the science of happiness. *Journal of Happiness Studies, 8,* 99–138.

Hills, P., & Argyle, M. (2002). The Oxford Happiness Questionnaire: a compact scale for the measurement of psychological well-being. *Personality and Individual Differences, 33,* 1073–1082.

Holmes, T. H., Rahe, R. H. (1967). The Social Readjustment Rating Scale. *Journal of Psychosomatic Research, 11,* 213–218.

Howe, M. L., & Courage, M. L. (1993). On resolving the enigma of infantile amnesia. *Psychological Bulletin, 113,* 305–326.

http://sports.espn.go.com/mlb/news/story?id=1777832 retrieved on August 3, 2006.

Hyde, J. S., & Linn, M. C. (1988). Gender differences in verbal ability: A meta-analysis. *Psychological Bulletin, 104,* 53–69.

Inglehart, R. (1997). *Culture shift in advanced industrial society.* Princeton, NJ: Princeton University Press: Harper & Row.

James, W. (1890). *Principles of psychology.* New York: Holt.

John, O. P., & Srivastava, S. (1999). The Big-Five trait taxonomy: History, measurement, and theoretical perspectives. In L. A. Pervin & O. P. John (Eds.), *Handbook of personality: Theory and research* (Vol. 2, pp. 102–138). New York: Guilford Press.

Johnson, C. (2003). *Eating chocolate naked.* Naperville: Sourcebooks.

Jung, R. (1978). *Systems of decision.* In Richard Jung's, *Experience and Action: Selected Items in System Theory. Vol. 4 of the Series: Complexity.* http://www.richardjung.cz/R03.pdf.

Kahneman, D. & Tversky, A. (2000). (Eds.), *Choices, values and frames.* New York: Cambridge University Press and the Russell Sage Foundation.

Kant, I. (1929). *Critique of pure reason.* (translated by Norman Kemp Smith). New York: St. Martin's Press.

Kawakami, K., Takai-Kawakami, K., Tomonaga, M., Suzuki, J., Kusaka, T., & Okai, T. (2006). Origins of smile and laughter: A preliminary study. *Early Human Development, 82*, 61–66.

Kessler, R. C. (2002). Epidemiology of depression. In I. H. Gotlib & C. L. Hammen (Eds.), *Handbook of depression* (pp. 23–42). New York: Guilford.

King, L. A. (2001). The health benefits of writing about life goals. *Personality and Social Psychology Bulletin, 27,* 798–807.

Klein, S. (2005). *The science of happiness: How our brains make us happy—and what we can do to get happier.* Marlowe & Company.

Kunda, Z. (1987). Motivation and inference: Self-serving generation and evaluation of evidence. *Personality & Social Psychology Bulletin, 53,* 636–647.

Lane, R. D., Reiman, E. M., Bradley, M. M., Lang, P. J., Ahern, G. L., Davidson, R. J., & Schwartz, G. E. (1997). Neuroanatomical correlates of pleasant and unpleasant emotion. *Neuropsychologia, 35,* 1437–1444.

Layard, R. (2005). *Happiness: Lessons from a new science.* New York: The Penguin Press.

Lester, G. L., & Gorzalka, B. B. (1988). Effect of novel and familiar mating partners on the duration of sexual receptivity in the female hamster. *Behavioral Neural Biology,* 49, 398–405.

Levin, R. J., & Wagner, G. (1985). Orgasm in women in the laboratory: Quantitative studies on duration, intensity, latency, and vaginal blood flow. *Archives of Sexual Behavior, 14,* 439–449.

Lucas, D. R. (2004). *Happiness in activity.* Paper presented at the annual meeting of the American Psychological Association, Honolulu, Hawaii.

Lucas, D. R., & Ancira, J. (2007). *I'm happy—you're not!* Paper presented at the annual meeting of the Southwestern Psychological Association, Fort Worth, Texas.

Lucas, D. R., Evans, A. M., Huegel, A., Barba-Escobedo, P. A., & Sanchez, A. (2009). *Validating the SEA-Weighting Instrument: A New Measure of Happiness.* Paper presented at the annual meeting of the Southwestern Psychological Association, San Antonio, Texas.

Lucas, D. R., & Kaylor, C. (2005). *The Being Within Life Situations Instrument (BWLSI).*

Lucas, D. R., Kaylor, C., Burgess, A., & Nigh, C. (2007). *An initial validation and reliability test of the Being Within Life Situations Instrument (BWLSI).*

Lucas, D. R., Kaylor, C., & Magaloni, I. R. (2004). *Happiness in people, places, things, and activity.* Paper presented at the annual meeting of the Southwestern Psychological Association, San Antonio, Texas.

Lucas, D. R., Lloyd, J. A., & Magaloni, I. R. (2005). *In spite of content, activity begets happiness.* Paper presented at the annual meeting of the Southwestern Psychological Association, Memphis, Tennessee.

Lucas, D. R., Wezner, K. C., Milner, J. S., McCanne, T. R., Harris, I. N., Monroe-Posey, & Nelson, J. P. (2002). Victim, perpetrator, family, and incident characteristics of infant and child homicide in the United States Air Force. *Child Abuse and Neglect, 26,* 167–186.

Lykken, D. (1999). *Happiness.* New York: Golden Books.

Lykken, D. T., & Tellegen, A. (1996). Happiness is a stochastic phenomenon. *Psychological Science, 7,* 186–189.

Lyubomirsky, S. (2008). *The how of happiness: A scientific approach to getting the life you want.* New York: Penguin.

Lyubomirsky, S. (2001). Why are some people happier than others? *American Psychologist, 56,* 239–249.

Lyubomirsky, S., King, L., & Diener, E. (2005). The benefits of frequent positive affect: Does happiness lead to success? *Psychological Bulletin, 131,* 803–855

Lyubomirsky, S., & Lepper, H. (1999). A measure of subjective happiness: Preliminary reliability and construct validation. *Social Indicators Research, 46,* 137–155.

Martini, F. H. (2006). *Fundamentals of anatomy & physiology.* San Francisco: Pearson.

McMahon, D. M. (2006). *Happiness: A History.* New York: Atlantic Monthly Press.

Meston, C. M., & Frohlich, P. F. (2003). Love at first fright: Partner salience mediates roller-coaster induced excitation transfer. *Archives of Sexual Behavior, 32,* 537–544.

Moody, P. M., Memon, A., Sugathan, T. N., El-Gerges, N. S., & Al-Bustan, M. (1999). Factors associated with the initiation of smoking by Kuwaiti males. *Journal of Substance Abuse, 10,* 375–384.

Myer, D. (2008). *Why we hate us: American discontent in the new millennium.* New York: Crown Publishing Group.

Myers, D. G. (2000). The funds, friends, and faith of happy people. *American Psychologist, 55,* 56–67.

Myers, D. G. (2004). *Psychology.* New York: Worth.

Myers, D. G. (1992). *The pursuit of happiness: Discovering the pathway to fulfillment, well-being, and enduring personal joy.* New York: Avon.

Nettle, D. (2005). *Happiness: The science behind your smile.* Oxford University Press.

Nisbett, R. E., & Wilson, T. D. (1977). The halo effect: Evidence for the unconscious alteration of judgments. *Journal of Personality and Social Psychology, 35,* 450–456.

Pavlov, I. P. (1927). *Conditioned reflexes: An investigation of the physiological activity of the cerebral cortex. Translated and Edited by G. V. Anrep.* London: Oxford University Press.

Pelletier, M., Bouthillier, A., Levesque, J., Carrier, S., Breault, C., Paquette, V., Mensour, B., Leroux, J. M., Beaudoin, G., Bourgouin, P., & Beauregard, M. (2003). Separate neural circuits for primary emotions? Brain activity during self-induced sadness and happiness in professional actors. *Neuroreport, 14,* 1111–1116.

Pennebaker, J. W. (2006). Writing about emotional experiences as a therapeutic process. *Psychological Science, 8,* 162–166.

Peterson, C., & Seligman, M. E. P. (2004). *Character strengths and virtues.* New York: Oxford.

Powers, W. T. (1973). *Behavior: The control of perception.* Chicago: Aldine Publishing.

Powers, W. T. (1989). An outline of control. In G. Williams, *Living control systems* (pp. 253–293). Gravel Switch, KY: The Control Systems Group.

Qin Guan of the Song Dynasty (960–1279). *Fairy of the Magpie Bridge,* translated by Kylie Hsu, as cited on http://app1.chinadaily.com.cn/star/2002/0815/cu18-1.html on June 3, 2007.

Raleigh, W. (1970). *The complete works of George Savile.* Augustus M. Kelley Publishers.

Ricard, M. (2007). *Happiness: A guide to developing life's most important skill.* Little, Brown, & Company.

Rotter, J. B. (1966). Generalized expectancies for internal versus external control of reinforcement. *Psychological Monographs, 80,* (1, Whole No. 609).

Sax, L. J., Lindholm, J. A., Astin, A. W., Korn, W. S., & Mahoney, K. M. (2001). *The American Freshman: National Norms for Fall 2001.* Los Angeles: Higher Education Research Institute, UCLA.

Scheier, M. F., Carver, C. S., & Bridges, M. W. (2004). Distinguishing optimism from neuroticism (and trait anxiety, self-mastery, and self-esteem): a reevaluation of the Life Orientation Test. *Journal of Personality and Social Psychology, 67,* 1063–1078.

Seligman, M. E. P. (2002). *Authentic happiness.* New York: Free Press.

Seligman, M. E. P. (1999). The President's Address (Annual Report). *American Psychologist, 54,* 559–562.

Seligman, M. E. P., Rashid, T., & Parks, A. C. (2006). Positive psychotherapy. *American Psychologist, 61,* 774–788.

Seligman, M. E. P., Steen, T. A., Park, N., & Peterson, C. (2005). Positive psychology progress: Empirical validation of interventions. *American Psychologist, 60,* 410–421.

Sheldon, K. M., & Lyubomirsky, S. (2006). How to increase and sustain positive emotion: The effects of expressing gratitude and visualizing best possible selves. *The Journal of Positive Psychology, 1,* 73–82.

Sidgwick, H. (1874/1907). *The methods of ethics.* London: MacMillan.

Sinclair, D. A. (2005). Toward a unified theory of caloric restriction and longevity regulation. *Mechanisms of Ageing and Development, 125,* 987–1002.

Sinclair, D. A., & Guarente, L. (2006). Unlocking the secrets of longevity genes. *Scientific American, 294,* 48–57.

Skinner, B. F. (1974). *About behaviorism.* New York: Random House.

Smith, T. W. (2007). *Job satisfaction in America.* Chicago: National Opinion Research Center (NORC).

Snyder, C. R., & Lopez, S. J. (2006). *Positive psychology: The scientific and practical explorations of human strengths.* New York: Sage Publications.

Spitz, R. A. (1945). Hospitalism: An inquiry into the genesis of psychiatric conditions in early childhood. *Psychoanalytic Study of the Child, 1,* 53–74.

Spitz, R. A. (1946). Hospitalism—A Follow-Up Report on Investigation Described in Volume I, 1945. *Psychoanalytic Study of the Child, 2,* 113–117.

Stern, J. M. (1986). Licking, touching, and suckling: Contact stimulation and maternal psychobiology in rats and women. *Annals of the New York Academy of Sciences, 474,* 95–107.

Stutzer, A., & Frey, B. S. (2006). Does marriage make people happy, or do happy people get married? *Journal of Socio-Economics, 35*, 326–347.

Tapia, M., & Marsh, G. E., II (2004). The relationship of math anxiety and gender. *Academic Exchange Quarterly, 8*, 130–134.

Thoits, P. A., & Hewitt, L. N. (2001). Volunteer work and well-being. *Journal of Health and Social Behavior, 42,* 115–131.

Tomarken, A. J., Davidson, R. J., Wheeler, R. E., & Doss, R. C. (1992). Individual differences in anterior brain asymmetry and fundamental dimensions of emotion. *Journal of Personality and Social Psychology, 62,* 676–687.

Tulving, E. (1983). *Elements of episodic memory,* Oxford: University Press.

Turner, M. S. (1990). *Dark matter in the Universe.* Technical report presented at 90 Nobel symposium: The Birth and Early Evolution of our Universe. Ostersund, Sweden.

Uvnas-Moberg, K. (1998). Oxytocin may mediate the benefits of positive social interaction and emotions. *Psychoneuroendocrinology, 23*, 819–835.

Veenhoven, R. (2000). The four qualities of life: Ordering concepts and measures of the good life. *Journal of Happiness Studies, 1,* 1–39.

Veenhoven, R. (2006). *Happiness in hardship,* in Bruni, L., & Porta (Eds.) Economics and happiness: Framing the analysis. Oxford University Press, pp. 248–266.

Waite, L. J., & Gallagher, M. (2000). *The case for marriage: Why married people are happier, healthier, and better off financially*. New York: Doubleday.

Watson, J. (1928). *The ways of behaviorism*. New York: Harper & Brothers Pub.

Watson, D., Clark, L. A., & Tellegen, A. (1988). Development and validation of brief measures of positive and negative affect: The PANAS scales. *Journal of Personality and Social Psychology, 54*, 1063–1070.

Watterson, B. (1989). *Yukon ho!* Kansas City: Andrews and McMeel.

Webster's Ninth New Collegiate Dictionary (1985). Springfield, Massachusetts: Merriam-Webster.

White, N. P. (2006). *A brief history of happiness.* Malden, Massachusetts: Blackwell Publishing.

Wilson, E. (2008). *Against happiness: In praise of melancholy.* New York: Sara Crichton Books.

Wuthnow, R. (1998). *Poor Richard's principle: Recovering the American dream through the moral dimension of work, business, and money.* Princeton University Press.

Zajonc, R. B. (1965). Social facilitation. *Science, 149,* 269–274.

Zeanah, C. H., & Fox, N. A. (2004). Temperament and attachment disorders. *Journal of Clinical Child and Adolescent Psychology, 33,* 32–41.

Zillman, D. (1971). Excitation transfer in communication-mediated aggressive behavior. *Journal of Experimental Social Psychology, 7,* 419–434.

Appendix Two
Worksheets

Worksheet

Date: ______________________________

Life part: ______________________________

This part of life is defined by the following list:

Item	Time/units	Circle	Item	Time/units	Circle
__________	(time/units)	(S E A) circle	__________	(time/units)	(S E A) circle
__________	(time/units)	(S E A) circle	__________	(time/units)	(S E A) circle
__________	(time/units)	(S E A) circle	__________	(time/units)	(S E A) circle
__________	(time/units)	(S E A) circle	__________	(time/units)	(S E A) circle
__________	(time/units)	(S E A) circle	__________	(time/units)	(S E A) circle
__________	(time/units)	(S E A) circle	__________	(time/units)	(S E A) circle
__________	(time/units)	(S E A) circle	__________	(time/units)	(S E A) circle
__________	(time/units)	(S E A) circle	__________	(time/units)	(S E A) circle
__________	(time/units)	(S E A) circle	__________	(time/units)	(S E A) circle
__________	(time/units)	(S E A) circle	__________	(time/units)	(S E A) circle
__________	(time/units)	(S E A) circle	__________	(time/units)	(S E A) circle
__________	(time/units)	(S E A) circle	__________	(time/units)	(S E A) circle
__________	(time/units)	(S E A) circle	__________	(time/units)	(S E A) circle
__________	(time/units)	(S E A) circle	__________	(time/units)	(S E A) circle
__________	(time/units)	(S E A) circle	__________	(time/units)	(S E A) circle

SEA score for this part of life

Selfish: (time/units) divided by (total time for this part of life/units) = S

Environmental: (time/units) divided by (total time for this part of life/units) = E

Action: (time/units) divided by (total time for this part of life/units) = A

Worksheet

Date: ______________________________

Life part: ______________________________

This part of life is defined by the following list:

________	(time/units)	(S E A) circle	________	(time/units)	(S E A) circle
________	(time/units)	(S E A) circle	________	(time/units)	(S E A) circle
________	(time/units)	(S E A) circle	________	(time/units)	(S E A) circle
________	(time/units)	(S E A) circle	________	(time/units)	(S E A) circle
________	(time/units)	(S E A) circle	________	(time/units)	(S E A) circle
________	(time/units)	(S E A) circle	________	(time/units)	(S E A) circle
________	(time/units)	(S E A) circle	________	(time/units)	(S E A) circle
________	(time/units)	(S E A) circle	________	(time/units)	(S E A) circle
________	(time/units)	(S E A) circle	________	(time/units)	(S E A) circle
________	(time/units)	(S E A) circle	________	(time/units)	(S E A) circle
________	(time/units)	(S E A) circle	________	(time/units)	(S E A) circle
________	(time/units)	(S E A) circle	________	(time/units)	(S E A) circle
________	(time/units)	(S E A) circle	________	(time/units)	(S E A) circle
________	(time/units)	(S E A) circle	________	(time/units)	(S E A) circle
________	(time/units)	(S E A) circle	________	(time/units)	(S E A) circle
________	(time/units)	(S E A) circle	________	(time/units)	(S E A) circle
________	(time/units)	(S E A) circle	________	(time/units)	(S E A) circle
________	(time/units)	(S E A) circle	________	(time/units)	(S E A) circle

SEA score for this part of life

Selfish: (time/units) divided by (total time for this part of life/units) = S

Environmental: (time/units) divided by (total time for this part of life/units) = E

Action: (time/units) divided by (total time for this part of life/units) = A

Worksheet

Date: ______________________________

Life part: ______________________________

This part of life is defined by the following list:

Item	time/units	circle	Item	time/units	circle
________	( )	(S E A)	________	( )	(S E A)
________	( )	(S E A)	________	( )	(S E A)
________	( )	(S E A)	________	( )	(S E A)
________	( )	(S E A)	________	( )	(S E A)
________	( )	(S E A)	________	( )	(S E A)
________	( )	(S E A)	________	( )	(S E A)
________	( )	(S E A)	________	( )	(S E A)
________	( )	(S E A)	________	( )	(S E A)
________	( )	(S E A)	________	( )	(S E A)
________	( )	(S E A)	________	( )	(S E A)
________	( )	(S E A)	________	( )	(S E A)
________	( )	(S E A)	________	( )	(S E A)
________	( )	(S E A)	________	( )	(S E A)
________	( )	(S E A)	________	( )	(S E A)
________	( )	(S E A)	________	( )	(S E A)
________	( )	(S E A)	________	( )	(S E A)
________	( )	(S E A)	________	( )	(S E A)
________	( )	(S E A)	________	( )	(S E A)

SEA score for this part of life

Selfish: (time/units) divided by (total time for this part of life/units) = S

Environmental: (time/units) divided by (total time for this part of life/units) = E

Action: (time/units) divided by (total time for this part of life/units) = A

Worksheet

Date: ______________________________

Life part: ______________________________

This part of life is defined by the following list:

	time/units	circle		time/units	circle
______________	( )	(S E A)	______________	( )	(S E A)
______________	( )	(S E A)	______________	( )	(S E A)
______________	( )	(S E A)	______________	( )	(S E A)
______________	( )	(S E A)	______________	( )	(S E A)
______________	( )	(S E A)	______________	( )	(S E A)
______________	( )	(S E A)	______________	( )	(S E A)
______________	( )	(S E A)	______________	( )	(S E A)
______________	( )	(S E A)	______________	( )	(S E A)
______________	( )	(S E A)	______________	( )	(S E A)
______________	( )	(S E A)	______________	( )	(S E A)
______________	( )	(S E A)	______________	( )	(S E A)
______________	( )	(S E A)	______________	( )	(S E A)
______________	( )	(S E A)	______________	( )	(S E A)
______________	( )	(S E A)	______________	( )	(S E A)
______________	( )	(S E A)	______________	( )	(S E A)
______________	( )	(S E A)	______________	( )	(S E A)
______________	( )	(S E A)	______________	( )	(S E A)
______________	( )	(S E A)	______________	( )	(S E A)

SEA score for this part of life

Selfish: (time/units) divided by (total time for this part of life/units) = S

Environmental: (time/units) divided by (total time for this part of life/units) = E

Action: (time/units) divided by (total time for this part of life/units) = A

WORKSHEET

Date: ______________________________

Life part: ______________________________

This part of life is defined by the following list:

	time/units	circle		time/units	circle
________	( )	(S E A)	________	( )	(S E A)
________	( )	(S E A)	________	( )	(S E A)
________	( )	(S E A)	________	( )	(S E A)
________	( )	(S E A)	________	( )	(S E A)
________	( )	(S E A)	________	( )	(S E A)
________	( )	(S E A)	________	( )	(S E A)
________	( )	(S E A)	________	( )	(S E A)
________	( )	(S E A)	________	( )	(S E A)
________	( )	(S E A)	________	( )	(S E A)
________	( )	(S E A)	________	( )	(S E A)
________	( )	(S E A)	________	( )	(S E A)
________	( )	(S E A)	________	( )	(S E A)
________	( )	(S E A)	________	( )	(S E A)
________	( )	(S E A)	________	( )	(S E A)
________	( )	(S E A)	________	( )	(S E A)
________	( )	(S E A)	________	( )	(S E A)
________	( )	(S E A)	________	( )	(S E A)
________	( )	(S E A)	________	( )	(S E A)

SEA score for this part of life

Selfish: (time/units) divided by (total time for this part of life/units) = S

Environmental: (time/units) divided by (total time for this part of life/units) = E

Action: (time/units) divided by (total time for this part of life/units) = A

Worksheet

Date: ____

Life part: ____

This part of life is defined by the following list:

	time/units	circle		time/units	circle
__________	( )	(S E A)	__________	( )	(S E A)
__________	( )	(S E A)	__________	( )	(S E A)
__________	( )	(S E A)	__________	( )	(S E A)
__________	( )	(S E A)	__________	( )	(S E A)
__________	( )	(S E A)	__________	( )	(S E A)
__________	( )	(S E A)	__________	( )	(S E A)
__________	( )	(S E A)	__________	( )	(S E A)
__________	( )	(S E A)	__________	( )	(S E A)
__________	( )	(S E A)	__________	( )	(S E A)
__________	( )	(S E A)	__________	( )	(S E A)
__________	( )	(S E A)	__________	( )	(S E A)
__________	( )	(S E A)	__________	( )	(S E A)
__________	( )	(S E A)	__________	( )	(S E A)
__________	( )	(S E A)	__________	( )	(S E A)
__________	( )	(S E A)	__________	( )	(S E A)
__________	( )	(S E A)	__________	( )	(S E A)
__________	( )	(S E A)	__________	( )	(S E A)
__________	( )	(S E A)	__________	( )	(S E A)

SEA score for this part of life

Selfish:	(time/units)	divided by	(total time for this part of life/units) =	S
Environmental:	(time/units)	divided by	(total time for this part of life/units) =	E
Action:	(time/units)	divided by	(total time for this part of life/units) =	A

WORKSHEET

Date: ____________________

Life part: ____________________

This part of life is defined by the following list:

	time/units	circle		time/units	circle
________	( )	(S E A)	________	( )	(S E A)
________	( )	(S E A)	________	( )	(S E A)
________	( )	(S E A)	________	( )	(S E A)
________	( )	(S E A)	________	( )	(S E A)
________	( )	(S E A)	________	( )	(S E A)
________	( )	(S E A)	________	( )	(S E A)
________	( )	(S E A)	________	( )	(S E A)
________	( )	(S E A)	________	( )	(S E A)
________	( )	(S E A)	________	( )	(S E A)
________	( )	(S E A)	________	( )	(S E A)
________	( )	(S E A)	________	( )	(S E A)
________	( )	(S E A)	________	( )	(S E A)
________	( )	(S E A)	________	( )	(S E A)
________	( )	(S E A)	________	( )	(S E A)
________	( )	(S E A)	________	( )	(S E A)
________	( )	(S E A)	________	( )	(S E A)
________	( )	(S E A)	________	( )	(S E A)
________	( )	(S E A)	________	( )	(S E A)

SEA score for this part of life

Selfish: (time/units) divided by (total time for this part of life/units) = S

Environmental: (time/units) divided by (total time for this part of life/units) = E

Action: (time/units) divided by (total time for this part of life/units) = A

WORKSHEET

Date: ____

Life part: ____

This part of life is defined by the following list:

	time/units	circle		time/units	circle
____________	( )	(S E A)	____________	( )	(S E A)
____________	( )	(S E A)	____________	( )	(S E A)
____________	( )	(S E A)	____________	( )	(S E A)
____________	( )	(S E A)	____________	( )	(S E A)
____________	( )	(S E A)	____________	( )	(S E A)
____________	( )	(S E A)	____________	( )	(S E A)
____________	( )	(S E A)	____________	( )	(S E A)
____________	( )	(S E A)	____________	( )	(S E A)
____________	( )	(S E A)	____________	( )	(S E A)
____________	( )	(S E A)	____________	( )	(S E A)
____________	( )	(S E A)	____________	( )	(S E A)
____________	( )	(S E A)	____________	( )	(S E A)
____________	( )	(S E A)	____________	( )	(S E A)
____________	( )	(S E A)	____________	( )	(S E A)
____________	( )	(S E A)	____________	( )	(S E A)
____________	( )	(S E A)	____________	( )	(S E A)
____________	( )	(S E A)	____________	( )	(S E A)
____________	( )	(S E A)	____________	( )	(S E A)

SEA score for this part of life

Selfish: (time/units) divided by (total time for this part of life/units) = S

Environmental: (time/units) divided by (total time for this part of life/units) = E

Action: (time/units) divided by (total time for this part of life/units) = A

WORKSHEET

Date: ______________________________

Life part: ______________________________

This part of life is defined by the following list:

________ (time/units) (S E A) circle	________ (time/units) (S E A) circle
________ (time/units) (S E A) circle	________ (time/units) (S E A) circle
________ (time/units) (S E A) circle	________ (time/units) (S E A) circle
________ (time/units) (S E A) circle	________ (time/units) (S E A) circle
________ (time/units) (S E A) circle	________ (time/units) (S E A) circle
________ (time/units) (S E A) circle	________ (time/units) (S E A) circle
________ (time/units) (S E A) circle	________ (time/units) (S E A) circle
________ (time/units) (S E A) circle	________ (time/units) (S E A) circle
________ (time/units) (S E A) circle	________ (time/units) (S E A) circle
________ (time/units) (S E A) circle	________ (time/units) (S E A) circle
________ (time/units) (S E A) circle	________ (time/units) (S E A) circle
________ (time/units) (S E A) circle	________ (time/units) (S E A) circle
________ (time/units) (S E A) circle	________ (time/units) (S E A) circle
________ (time/units) (S E A) circle	________ (time/units) (S E A) circle
________ (time/units) (S E A) circle	________ (time/units) (S E A) circle
________ (time/units) (S E A) circle	________ (time/units) (S E A) circle
________ (time/units) (S E A) circle	________ (time/units) (S E A) circle
________ (time/units) (S E A) circle	________ (time/units) (S E A) circle

SEA score for this part of life

Selfish: (time/units) divided by (total time for this part of life/units) = S

Environmental: (time/units) divided by (total time for this part of life/units) = E

Action: (time/units) divided by (total time for this part of life/units) = A

Worksheet

Date: ______________________________

Life part: ______________________________

This part of life is defined by the following list:

________ (time/units) (S E A) circle	________ (time/units) (S E A) circle
________ (time/units) (S E A) circle	________ (time/units) (S E A) circle
________ (time/units) (S E A) circle	________ (time/units) (S E A) circle
________ (time/units) (S E A) circle	________ (time/units) (S E A) circle
________ (time/units) (S E A) circle	________ (time/units) (S E A) circle
________ (time/units) (S E A) circle	________ (time/units) (S E A) circle
________ (time/units) (S E A) circle	________ (time/units) (S E A) circle
________ (time/units) (S E A) circle	________ (time/units) (S E A) circle
________ (time/units) (S E A) circle	________ (time/units) (S E A) circle
________ (time/units) (S E A) circle	________ (time/units) (S E A) circle
________ (time/units) (S E A) circle	________ (time/units) (S E A) circle
________ (time/units) (S E A) circle	________ (time/units) (S E A) circle
________ (time/units) (S E A) circle	________ (time/units) (S E A) circle
________ (time/units) (S E A) circle	________ (time/units) (S E A) circle
________ (time/units) (S E A) circle	________ (time/units) (S E A) circle
________ (time/units) (S E A) circle	________ (time/units) (S E A) circle
________ (time/units) (S E A) circle	________ (time/units) (S E A) circle
________ (time/units) (S E A) circle	________ (time/units) (S E A) circle

SEA score for this part of life

Selfish: (time/units) divided by (total time for this part of life/units) = S

Environmental: (time/units) divided by (total time for this part of life/units) = E

Action: (time/units) divided by (total time for this part of life/units) = A

Worksheet

Date: ____________________

Life part: ____________________

This part of life is defined by the following list:

Item	Time/units	Circle	Item	Time/units	Circle
________	( )	(S E A)	________	( )	(S E A)
________	( )	(S E A)	________	( )	(S E A)
________	( )	(S E A)	________	( )	(S E A)
________	( )	(S E A)	________	( )	(S E A)
________	( )	(S E A)	________	( )	(S E A)
________	( )	(S E A)	________	( )	(S E A)
________	( )	(S E A)	________	( )	(S E A)
________	( )	(S E A)	________	( )	(S E A)
________	( )	(S E A)	________	( )	(S E A)
________	( )	(S E A)	________	( )	(S E A)
________	( )	(S E A)	________	( )	(S E A)
________	( )	(S E A)	________	( )	(S E A)
________	( )	(S E A)	________	( )	(S E A)
________	( )	(S E A)	________	( )	(S E A)
________	( )	(S E A)	________	( )	(S E A)
________	( )	(S E A)	________	( )	(S E A)
________	( )	(S E A)	________	( )	(S E A)
________	( )	(S E A)	________	( )	(S E A)

SEA score for this part of life

Selfish: (time/units) divided by (total time for this part of life/units) = S

Environmental: (time/units) divided by (total time for this part of life/units) = E

Action: (time/units) divided by (total time for this part of life/units) = A

Worksheet

Date: ____________________

Life part: ____________________

This part of life is defined by the following list:

Item	time/units	circle	Item	time/units	circle
________	( )	(S E A)	________	( )	(S E A)
________	( )	(S E A)	________	( )	(S E A)
________	( )	(S E A)	________	( )	(S E A)
________	( )	(S E A)	________	( )	(S E A)
________	( )	(S E A)	________	( )	(S E A)
________	( )	(S E A)	________	( )	(S E A)
________	( )	(S E A)	________	( )	(S E A)
________	( )	(S E A)	________	( )	(S E A)
________	( )	(S E A)	________	( )	(S E A)
________	( )	(S E A)	________	( )	(S E A)
________	( )	(S E A)	________	( )	(S E A)
________	( )	(S E A)	________	( )	(S E A)
________	( )	(S E A)	________	( )	(S E A)
________	( )	(S E A)	________	( )	(S E A)
________	( )	(S E A)	________	( )	(S E A)
________	( )	(S E A)	________	( )	(S E A)
________	( )	(S E A)	________	( )	(S E A)
________	( )	(S E A)	________	( )	(S E A)

SEA score for this part of life

Selfish: (time/units) divided by (total time for this part of life/units) = S

Environmental: (time/units) divided by (total time for this part of life/units) = E

Action: (time/units) divided by (total time for this part of life/units) = A

Appendix Three
Scoring the SEA-weighting Instrument

Scoring instructions: Begin by using the SEA-scoring sheet (on the following page) to mark how many points each of your responses was worth. Every response you made was worth between negative 2 (–2) and positive three (+3) points.

- Total up your points.
- Your total points (that is, your score) should range between –22 to +32.
- Subtract 5 from your score.
- Your score now should be somewhere on the continuum of –27 to +27

This score, called your SEA-weighting score, we will be using throughout the rest of the book. This is a basis for your happiness, pleasure, and contentment—but it doesn't tell you how to get or keep these positive emotions. The remaining part of the book—specifically, our introduction to Being Theory, will address these two issues.

SEA-weighting scores can only be used in context with SEA scores!

Once you have a SEA score, you will be developing these in **Chapters Four** through **Six**, you may interpret your SEA-weighting score as telling you:

- The lower your test score (i.e., scores less than 0), the more likely Selfish percentages should be interpreted as predicting SADNESS; Environmental percentages should be interpreted as predicting PAIN; and Action percentages should be interpreted as predicting DEPRESSION.
- The higher your test score (i.e., scores greater than 0), the more likely Selfish percentages should be interpreted as predicting HAPPINESS; Environmental percentages should be interpreted as predicting PLEASURE; and Action percentages should be interpreted as predicting CONTENTMENT.

Descriptive statistics for the SEA-weighting Instrument were gained from a study by Lucas, Evans, Huegel, Barba-Escobedo, & Sanchez (2009). Based upon a sample of 317 participants that ranged in age from 18 to 52 (average = 22.2),

Lucas, et al. found the average SEA-weighting Instrument Score to be +3.3 with a standard deviation of 5.3. The minimum score within this sample was –14 and the maximum score was +16. The mode was +1 and the median was +3. The 10th percentile was –3, the 25th percentile was 0, the 75th percentile was +7, and the 90th percentile was +10. There were no significant differences in scores between men and women.

1. On average, how many hours of sleep do you get per night?

Less than 4	**–2 points**
4 to 6	–1
7 to 10	+2
11 to 12	–1
More than 12	–2

2. On average, how many hours of exercise do you do per week?

0	**–2 points**
1 to 3	0
4 to 7	+1
8 to 13	+2
More than 13	+3

3a. What is your overall score (add your score for items 1 through 4) on the Empathy scale?

a. Less than 5	**–2 points**
b. Between 5 and 8	–1
c. Between 9 and 12	+1
d. Greater than 12	+2

3b. Do you have at least one good friend? Yes (+2) or No (–2)
If question 3b is "No," skip to question 4a.

3c. If question 3b is "Yes," how many good friends do you have?

1 to 2	**+1 points**
3 to 5	+2
More than 5	–1

4a. During your waking hours on weekdays, what percentage of your time, on average, is spent with other people?

0 to 25%	**–1 points**
26% to 50%	+2
51% to 75%	+1
More than 75%	–1

4b. During your waking hours on weekends, what percentage of your time, on average, is spent with other people?

0 to 25%	**–1 points**
26% to 50%	+2
51% to 75%	+1
More than 75%	–1

5. Are you happily married? Yes (+2) or No (–2)

6a. Are you employed? Yes (+2) or No (–2)
If question 6a is "No," skip to question 7a.

6b. If question 6a is "Yes," does your employment require you to work outside of your home? Yes (+1) or No (–1)

6c. If question 6a is "Yes," do you enjoy being employed? Yes (+1) or No (–1)

7a. How many people, including yourself, live at your household?
For all answers = **0**

7b. How much money (after taxes) does your household earn per year? (Make sure the household is not substantially greater than 4 people.)

a. Less than $20,650	**–2 points**
b. Between $20,650 and $100,000	**0**
c. More than $100,000	+1

8. What is your score on the Extraversion scale?

a. Less than 17	**–1 points**
b. Between 17 and 24	**0**
c. Between 25 and 32	+1
d. Greater than 32	+2

9. What is your score on the Optimism scale?
   a. Less than 13 — **–1 points**
   b. Between 13 and 17 — **0**
   c. Greater than 17 — +2

10a. Do you have faith in something greater than human existence, knowledge, and power? Yes (**+1**) or No (**–1**)

10b. What percentage of your time is devoted to helping others; for example, volunteerism?
   a. Less than 10% — **0 points**
   b. Between 10% and 30% — +1
   c. Greater than 30% — +2

10c. Do you attend church, synagogue, or mosque on at least a weekly basis? Yes (**+1**) or No (**0**)

11. Using the following scale, how do you rate your general physical health?
   a. Very unhealthy — **–2 points**
   b. A little unhealthy — –1
   c. Neutral — **0**
   d. A little healthy — +1
   e. Very healthy — +2

Appendix Four
Quiz Answers

Answers from quiz on page 60: 1b, 2b, 3c, 4c, 5a

Answers from quiz on pages 107 and 108: 1b, 2c, 3a, 4c, 5b

Answers from quiz on pages 124 and 125: 1c, 2a, 3b, 4c, 5b, 6b

Answers from quiz on page 140: 1a, 2b, 3c, 4a, 5b, 6c

Index